UK Specification for Ground Investigation

Site Investigation in Construction series

Prepared under the guidance of the **Site Investigation Steering Group**, the series aims to provide guidance to help improve the quality of site investigation and obtain better value for money for the construction industry and its clients.

The second edition of the series, published by ICE Publishing, updates the documents published by Thomas Telford Limited in 1993 and includes:

Effective Site Investigation
ISBN 978-0-7277-3505-8

UK Specification for Ground Investigation
ISBN 978-0-7277-3506-5

Guidance for Safe Investigation of Potentially Contaminated Land
ISBN 978-0-7277-3507-2

To read more about these books as well as the importance of the ground in construction and the consequences of inadequate site investigation go to:

www.icevirtuallibrary.com/siteinvestigation

The Site Investigation Steering Group is a national collaboration between professional and governmental bodies, trade sector organisations, and Infracos formed to provide advice on site investigation to clients and their construction professionals and to set out good practice.

UK Specification for Ground Investigation
Second edition

Site Investigation Steering Group

Prepared by

Soil Mechanics (Environmental Scientifics Group) and the Association of Geotechnical and Geoenvironmental Specialists

on behalf of Site Investigation Steering Group

Published by ICE Publishing, 40 Marsh Wall, London E14 9TP.

Full details of ICE Publishing sales representatives and distributors can be found at:
www.icevirtuallibrary.com/info/printbooksales

First published 2012
Reprinted 2012

www.icevirtuallibrary.com

A catalogue record for this book is available from the British Library

ISBN 978-0-7277-3506-5

Cover images courtesy of iStockphoto.com: excavator © Adivin 2008; drill bit ©
Peter Ingvorsen 2005; wind turbine farm © Rafa Irusta 2006

ICE Publishing is a division of Thomas Telford Ltd, a wholly-owned subsidiary of the
Institution of Civil Engineers (ICE).

Associate Commissioning Editor: Jennifer Barratt
Production Editor: Imran Mirza
Market Development Executive: Catherine de Gatacre

Typeset by Academic + Technical, Bristol
Printed and bound in Great Britain by CPI Group (UK) Ltd, Croydon, CR0 4YY

Contents

Notes for guidance
Notes on Specification clauses are presented alongside Specification clauses
Notes on preparation of the Schedules are presented alongside or immediately preceding Schedules

ANNEXES

Notes for guidance
Notes on the Bill of Quantities are presented immediately prior to relevant bill
(Notes on the preamble are presented alongside preamble items)

Acknowledgements

This document is part of the *Site Investigation in Construction* series. The documents have been prepared under the guidance of the Site Investigation Steering Group, a body with a wide membership, sponsored by the Ground Forum and the Institution of Civil Engineers, with the aim of providing guidance for the effective investigation of UK construction sites.

The first edition of the *Site Investigation in Construction* series was published in 1993 by Thomas Telford Limited. Since then the documents have become the industry standard, but there have been many advances and regulatory changes affecting ground investigation, particularly in respect of contaminated ground, dealing with waste materials and different investigatory techniques.

The second edition is based on the first edition but represents a major revision and extension of the series with the aim of bringing together the whole site investigation industry and is intended for general application to all ground investigation work. Input has been provided by key client organisations such as the Highways Agency, Network Rail, British Waterways and National House-Building Council.

SITE INVESTIGATION STEERING GROUP MEMBERSHIP
The following organisations, associations and professional bodies are all represented on the Site Investigation Steering Group chaired by Professor Chris Clayton.

Association of Geotechnical and Geoenvironmental Specialists
British Drilling Association
British Geotechnical Association
British Geological Survey
British Tunnelling Society
British Waterways
Chartered Institution of Water and Environmental Management
Construction Industry Research and Information Association (CIRIA)
County Surveyors Society
Engineering Group of the Geological Society
Environment Agency
Federation of Piling Specialists
Ground Forum
Highways Agency
Institute of Field Archaeologists
Institute of Materials, Minerals and Mining
Institution of Civil Engineers
International Geosynthetics Society (UK Chapter)
National House-Building Council (NHBC)
Network Rail
Pipe Jacking Association
Specialist in Land Condition

Thanks are extended to the individuals who comprised the Site Investigation Steering Group for giving their time, experience and expertise in helping to progress the revision of the series. Particular thanks are given to employers who have supported individual's membership of the steering group.

Prof Chris Clayton	University of Southampton (Chairman)
Mr Derek Smith	Coffey Geotechnics Ltd (Secretary)
Mr Martin Ball	Formerly British Waterways
Mrs Madeleine Bardsley	Enviros
Mr Terry Clark	Geotechnics Ltd
Mr Jim Cook	Buro Happold
Mr Andrew Dukes	Highways Agency
Mr Eifion Evans	Network Rail
Mr Keith Gabriel	Gabriel GeoConsulting Ltd
Mr Dick Gosling	Environmental Scientics Group
Mr Bob Handley	Aarsleff Piling Ltd
Mr John Harris	Thames Water
Mr Peter Hinton	Institute for Archaeologists

Mr Peter Hobbs   British Geological Survey
Mr Hugh Mallett   Buro Happold
Mr Keith Montague   CIRIA
Mr Paul Nowak   Atkins Ltd
Mr Neil Parry   Geotechnical Engineering Ltd
Mr David Shohet   National House Building Council
Mr Ian Stanley   Carillion Trenchless Solutions
Mr Brian Stringer   British Drilling Association
Mr Mike Summersgill   CIWEM
Mr Steve Wade   Skanska Ltd
Mr John Wilson   CECA
Mr Graham Woodrow   Institute of Materials, Minerals and Mining

UK Specification for Ground Investigation

This document, part of the updated *Site Investigation in Construction* series, was written by Soil Mechanics, a trading division of the Environmental Scientifics Group (ESG), in association with and under contract to the Association of Geotechnical and Geoenvironmental Specialists (AGS).

The AGS, ESG and the Highways Agency are thanked for their technical and financial contribution to the writing of this Specification which was carried out under the guidance of the AGS Steering Group, comprising:

AGS Steering Group

Mr Mike Groves (Chair)   Halcrow *formerly of* White Young Green
Mr Raphael Lung   Highways Agency
Mr Terry Clark   Geotechnics Limited
Mr Nick Burt   Halcrow
Dr Madeleine Bardsley   SKM Enviros
Miss Victoria Ferguson   Alcontrol

Soil Mechanics (Environmental Scientifics Group)

Dr Mike Atkinson   Chief Author
Mr Peter Whittlestone   Project Manager
Mr Julian Lovell   Project Manager

The authors acknowledge the technical contributions made by many other members of ESG staff and other colleagues of AGS Steering Group members during the drafting of the document.

Input has been obtained from key client organisations and the UK Specification for Ground Investigation has been endorsed by both the Highways Agency and Network Rail.

Foreword and essential reading

Site Investigation Steering Group: This Specification, the *UK Specification for Ground Investigation*, is one of the suite of three documents that comprise the Site Investigation in Construction documentation. This Specification should be read in conjunction with *Effective Site Investigation* and *Guidance for Safe Investigation of Potentially Contaminated Land*.

Specification: This Specification retains the essentials of the original format, including associated Schedules and Notes for Guidance. The Specification has been written to be contract and measurement neutral so it may be used with any form of Conditions of Contract and Method of Measurement. The NEC3 Engineering and Construction Contract (2005) provides one such suitable form of conditions. The Specification clauses meet current practice and standards at the time of publication.

Schedules: All the relevant Schedules must be completed for each investigation in order to fully detail both the information provided to the contractor and work which is to be undertaken. If necessary, the Schedules (and the Bill of Quantities) can be extended to provide for increased levels of technical complexity to meet the needs of an individual project, e.g. where a site contains or may contain archaeological remains, scheduled monument(s) or is of an environmentally sensitive nature (SSSI, AONB, etc.). Where a Schedule is not relevant then the words 'Not required' should be inserted alongside the Schedule title; where none of the sub-items are required they can then be omitted for brevity. Those Schedules which are not required for the particular investigation should also be listed in Schedule S1.5.

Bill of Quantities: A Bill of Quantities, together with a Preamble which defines payment details, is provided in an Annex. The Bill of Quantities is drafted to be compatible with the Specification and Conditions of Contract, such as NEC3 Engineering and Construction Contract (2005) (Option B or Option D). It is provided so that the majority of ground investigations can make use of it as the standard form in the Contract: the Bill items correspond to those of the Specification. However, some procurers may opt to use the Specification on its own with alternative forms of Contract and to use a formal method of measurement and item coverage (with an appropriate Bill of Quantities). The contract documentation must make it clear whether the Bill of Quantities in the Annex is to be adopted for the particular investigation.

Notes for Guidance: Notes for Guidance, which do not form part of the contract, are provided for the Specification, Schedules and Bill of Quantities.

Ground Practitioners: The involvement of one or more ground practitioners of suitable experience, relevant to the work required, is essential in the planning, procurement and supervision of ground investigation work.

Desk Study: A properly designed and executed desk study is essential for all ground investigations. The results of the study need to be provided to the contractor undertaking the investigation.

CDM (Construction Design & Management Regulations 2007): CDM defines construction work as the carrying out of any building, civil engineering or engineering construction work and includes, amongst others, 'the preparation for an intended structure, including ... exploration, investigation ... and excavation'. This clearly includes both the intrusive and non-intrusive parts of the ground investigation.

Pre-construction Information: Under CDM, Pre-construction Information that includes details of any safety hazards must be provided at tender stage. Such details would include underground services, site categorisation (see *Guidance for Safe Investigation of Potentially Contaminated Land*, etc.).

Feedback: Feedback is important and it is recognised that the Specification and accompanying documentation will benefit from updating in the future. Users are invited to submit recommendations for revision by email (see page 307).

Introduction

Use of the *UK Specification for Ground Investigation*

The *UK Specification for Ground Investigation* is intended for general use in ground investigation, for contracts of any size. The emphasis is on encouraging carefully designed and safely executed good-quality work.

The Specification is independent of the Conditions of Contract, although the NEC3 Engineering and Construction Contract (2005) Conditions of Contract, will often be the most convenient and appropriate to apply. It has been assumed that the Employer will appoint an Engineer, or equivalent person e.g. Project Manager, as defined in the Conditions of Contract. If an independent Engineer/Project Manager is not appointed, the Employer should nominate an appropriate individual to act as the Engineer/Project Manager who may, for instance, be employed by the Contractor. It has further been assumed that technical direction of the investigation will be the responsibility of the Investigation Supervisor, an experienced ground practitioner, who may be the Engineer/Project Manager or someone appointed to assist and advise the Engineer. Where the roles of Engineer/Project Manager and Investigation Supervisor are combined and fulfilled by a member of the Contractor's staff, the investigation will become a 'Design and Investigate' form.

Depending upon the complexity of the investigation, other specialists may need to be involved in the work in order that the full range of disciplines (e.g. geotechnics, contamination, waste assessment, geophysics, archaeology, ecology and safety) relevant to the specific investigation are adequately covered. Appropriately qualified and experienced ground practitioners may be from the staff of the Engineer, may be independent specialist consultants or may be employees of the Contractor. This involvement of ground practitioners is considered to be essential to the success of any ground investigation.

The Specification relies heavily on compliance with good practice as set out in BS 5930, *Code of Practice for site investigations* (partly superseded by BS EN 1997). BS 5930 is continuing to undergo amendment at the time of publication of this document. The reproduction of parts of BS 5930 in the Specification, although in some ways preferable to cross-references, has been rejected in favour of keeping the Specification as brief as possible. Particular reference should also be made to the CIRIA *Site investigation manual*, SP25 and to BS 1377, *Methods of test for soils for civil engineering purposes* (also partly superseded by BS EN 1997). Attention is drawn to the increasing use of previously developed and contaminated land which will require specific and detailed investigation, particularly with respect to previous history. There are several important publications in connection with investigating contaminated land which are extensively referenced in the Specification, e.g. the CLR reports and BS 10175, *Investigation of potentially contaminated sites – Code of Practice*. Special consideration must also be given to the hazards and risks to which all staff on site and the public may be exposed (see the companion publication *Guidance for Safe Investigation of Potentially Contaminated Land* and CIRIA C681, *Unexploded ordnance, A guide for the construction industry*).

CDM pre-construction information should include a properly designed and executed desk study for all ground investigations, especially where previous industrial or commercial use of the land has taken place. The importance of making the results of the desk study available to all parties cannot be over-emphasised if a safe and effective investigation is to be designed and undertaken. If a desk study has not been carried out prior to an intrusive investigation, it is strongly recommended that this essential preliminary study is included in the scope of the investigation works.

If inappropriate or incomplete pricing is to be avoided, with the consequent risk of subsequent claims and disruption to the investigation, the information provided and the investigation requirements need to be fully detailed in the Schedules. For example, if aquifer protection measures are required, then the method of protection to be adopted (e.g. multiple casing sizes with seals between them) needs to be stated together with the expected number of casing size reductions, the lengths of and materials to be used for seals and whether allowance for standing time is required. A similar approach of providing full details needs to be taken by the investigation procurer to many other items e.g. traffic management, additional Personal Protective Equipment over and above statutory minimum requirements, access limitations, etc. This Specification is general in nature and may require to be modified for a specific investigation. In recognition of this need for flexibility, the Schedules provide for additions and/or modifications to the published Specification.

It is also recognised that many investigations now require combinations of methods to a much greater extent than was previously the case, e.g. field and laboratory testing and sampling both during the intrusive phase of work and subsequently from installed instruments. Furthermore, sampling for geotechnical purposes and for contamination or waste assessments demands different techniques, transport and storage conditions and, in respect of contamination and waste consideration aspects, laboratory testing needs to be carried out within much shorter timescales. The second edition reflects this situation with an increased number of sub-divisions.

Successful ground investigation work will only be accomplished when the quality and appropriateness of the work, rather than the lowest cost, are recognised as the first priority. Attention must therefore be given to initial desk studies, careful planning, the employment of properly equipped contractors utilising trained and qualified operatives and the supervision of the field and laboratory work by experienced personnel. The following Notes for Guidance are intended to assist with the Contract documentation, but experienced ground practitioners should be involved for an appreciation of the technical aspects of the work.

Ground practitioners and other personnel provided by the Contractor
If the Bill of Quantities and associated Preamble (provided in Annex 1) is incorporated into the contract documentation, then ground practitioners and other personnel provided by the Contractor for professional attendance will be paid for on a time and expenses basis either under Bill Item A7 or using the rates tendered in Appendix A. The Contractor's management and superintendence of the investigation should be included in the rates. The provision of advice and assistance to the Engineer or Investigation Supervisor would be paid for on a time and expenses basis, as would the cost of preparing any desk study, Ground Investigation Report and Geotechnical Design Report.

Contract documentation
Information and requirements specific to the particular contract are to be inserted in the Schedules which are cross-referenced to the clause numbers in the Specification and accompanying Notes for Guidance. Any amendments or additions to the Specification should be identified within the appropriate Schedule. It is intended that the *UK Specification for Ground Investigation* be simply referenced in any contract documentation, with the Schedules included as necessary.

Documentation for a particular contract should comprise:

Instructions for Tendering (separate document)
Letter or Form of Agreement (and Appendix)
Conditions of Contract (reference to published Document)
Amendments and additions to Conditions of Contract
Pre-construction Information

Specification for Ground Investigation (reference to published Document)

Schedules
Schedule 1: Information
Schedule 2: Exploratory holes
Schedule 3: Investigation Supervisor's facilities
Schedule 4: Specification amendments
Schedule 5: Specification additions

If required, the Contract may also include the Bill of Quantities for ground investigation contained in Annex 1, comprising:

Preamble (reference to published document)
Preamble amendments
Works Items
Summary of Bill of Quantities
Appendix A: Rates for ground practitioners and other personnel
Appendix B: Long-term sample storage

It should be noted that a formal Method of Measurement and Item Coverage are not required for use with the Annex 1 Bill, as the Specification, together with the Preamble to the Bill of Quantities, adequately defines the Bill items for payment. Additional items may be included in the Specification and Bill with the minimum of documentation. Alternatively, a formal Method of Measurement and Item Coverage (together with an appropriate Bill of Quantities) may be included with the Contract documentation. This is likely to result in duplication of statements and increase the complexity of the documentation, however, particularly when additional items are included.

UK Specification for Ground Investigation
ISBN: 978-0-7277-3506-5

ICE Publishing: All rights reserved
doi: 10.1680/uksgi.35065.001

Specification and Notes for Guidance

1 Information

Notes for Guidance

1.1 General

Information and requirements specific to a particular ground investigation are to be fully detailed in the Schedules which form part of the Specification.

Not all the Schedules will necessarily be applicable to any particular investigation; those not required shall be identified in Schedule S1.5 'Scope of Investigation' as 'Not required'.

Full details of the information and requirements specific to the particular contract are to be inserted in the Schedules: vague outline descriptions will not suffice.

Work over water or over unstable ground including mineshafts, for example, is not extensively dealt with in the Specification. This is work of a specialist nature and will require additional Specification, and Bill of Quantity documentation.

Schedules S4 and S5 are provided for Specification amendments and additions respectively, while additional Bill of Quantity items should be included in the space provided at the end of each Bill.

2   Definitions

Notes for Guidance

2.1   General

These definitions are for the purposes of this ground investigation Specification.

Terms which are defined in most Conditions of Contract are not repeated in this Specification.

2.2   Investigation supervisor

The term 'Investigation Supervisor' means the named individual having responsibility to see that the technical objectives and quality of the investigation are met within the programme and cost constraints. The Investigation Supervisor shall act in a professional and independent manner in order to achieve the technical objectives. The Investigation Supervisor shall be appointed or agreed by the Employer and shall have a level of competency and experience appropriate to the size, nature and complexity of the investigation.

The name, contact details, powers delegated under the Contract and other relevant information shall be set out and fully defined in Schedule S1.2.

The Investigation Supervisor may be appointed from any of the parties involved in the ground investigation process, but more usually from the Employer's, Consultant's or Contractor's staff, or may be appointed from an independent organisation.

In some cases the designer of the proposed investigation works may be directly appointed as Investigation Supervisor by the Contractor but must remain independent from the Contractor's influence.

The Investigation Supervisor may be part time or full time and may require the assistance of one or more specialists, dependent upon the nature, size and complexity of the investigation.

2.3   Ground practitioners and other personnel

Ground practitioners include, but are not necessarily limited to, geotechnical engineers, geologists, engineering geologists, geoenvironmental engineers, environmental scientists, geochemists and geophysicists. They shall be competent to undertake the work required and the key element of this is having relevant experience. Categories of personnel who may be required by the Contract are as follows

(a) Technician
(b) Graduate ground engineer
(c) Experienced ground engineer
(d) Registered Ground Engineering Professional
(e) Registered Ground Engineering Specialist
(f) Registered Ground Engineering Adviser

Other personnel include, but are not necessarily limited to, drilling supervisor, highway traffic safety officer, marine supervisor, ecologist, archaeologist and railway trained staff.

The definitions for Categories d, e and f are those set out by the Institution of Civil Engineers (ICE 3009, 2010) although equivalent European qualifications would be equally acceptable.

An experienced ground engineer would typically be one with at least 3 years of relevant experience since graduation with an appropriate degree, or alternatively with at least 5 years of experience if not a graduate.

In recognition of training requirements, a graduate ground engineer or experienced ground engineer working under the close supervision of a Registered category of person would be acceptable for certain activities by agreement with the Investigation Supervisor.

2.4   Hazardous ground

The term 'hazardous ground' shall be deemed to include, but not be limited to, soil, rock or groundwater which is known to have or is suspected of having hazardous properties, unstable ground and that containing or suspected of containing unexploded ordnance.

The term 'hazardous ground' is not synonymous with 'hazardous waste', which is subject to statutory definition.

The 14 categories of hazardous properties are defined in the Hazardous Waste (England and Wales) Regulations 2005 and The List of Waste Regulations, although within the United Kingdom there are regional versions of these documents.

2.5   Land affected by contamination

The term 'land affected by contamination' shall be deemed to include any soils, rocks and/or groundwater which are known to be or are suspected of being contaminated or to contain ground gas.

The term is not necessarily synonymous with Statutory Contaminated Land as defined by Part IIA of the Environmental Protection Act 1990.

2.6   Topsoil

The word 'topsoil' shall mean the top layer of material that contains humus and can support vegetation.

2.7   Soil

The word 'soil' shall include any natural or artificial material not classified herein as topsoil, hard stratum or hard material.

2.8   Hard material, hard stratum and obstruction

The terms 'hard material' and 'hard stratum' are used in preference to 'rock' as they are more general and more easily defined.

If a maximum period is to be set for boring, pitting or trenching through a hard stratum, hard material or an obstruction before alternative measures are adopted, this should be specified in Schedule S1.8.14.

2.8.1

The terms 'hard stratum', 'hard material' and 'obstruction' shall mean natural or artificial material, including rock, which cannot be penetrated except by the use of hard boring techniques (chisel/shell with additional weights, etc.) during cable percussion boring, rotary drilling, blasting or powered breaking tools.

2.8.2

The terms 'hard stratum' and 'obstruction' shall apply to percussive boring, only where it is shown that condition (1) and either condition (2) or condition (3) below are fulfilled, provided that the boring rig involved is in good working order and is fully manned. The progress rate observations and driving tests shall be repeated at hourly and 0.50 m depth intervals, respectively.

2.8.3

Condition (1): Boring with normal appropriate tools cannot proceed at a rate greater than 0.50 m/hour. The stated rate shall be applicable to the boring operation alone and exclude sampling/in situ testing and standing time.

2.8.4

Condition (2): 100 mm diameter undisturbed sample tubes cannot be driven more than 300 mm with 50 blows of the driving hammer.

See also NG 7.6.5 regarding the use of sinker bars appropriate to the ground conditions and that should therefore be taken into account when addressing blow count.

2.8.5

Condition (3): A Standard Penetration Test (SPT) shows a resistance in excess of 35 blows/75 mm.

2.8.6

The term 'hard material' shall apply only to machine excavation of trial pits and trenches and observation pits and trenches where it is shown that conditions (4) or (5) below are fulfilled.

2.8.7

Condition (4): Natural or artificial material, including rock, is encountered in masses exceeding 0.20 cubic metres which cannot be penetrated except by the use of powered breaking tools.

2.8.8

Condition (5): Existing pavements, footways, paved areas (but excluding unbound materials) and foundations in masses exceeding 0.20 cubic metres which cannot be penetrated except by the use of powered breaking tools.

2.8.9

The term 'hard material' shall apply only to hand excavation of inspection pits and observation pits and trenches where it is shown that conditions (6) or (7) below are fulfilled.

2.8.10

Condition (6): Natural or artificial material, including rock, is encountered in masses exceeding 50 kg which cannot be penetrated except by the use of powered breaking tools.

2.8.11

Condition (7): Existing pavements, footways, paved areas (including unbound fill materials) and foundations in masses exceeding 50 kg which cannot be penetrated except by the use of powered breaking tools.

2.9   Fill

The term 'fill' shall mean any deposits which have been formed by persons under a designed and controlled scheme of placement and compaction in order to achieve a specified quality of ground.

2.10   Made ground

The term 'made ground' shall mean deposits which have been formed by persons, as distinct from geological processes, but without the design and control required for fill.

2.11   Exploratory hole

The term 'exploratory hole' shall mean any hole formed for the purpose of ground investigation.

2.12   Surface water bodies

The term 'surface water bodies' shall include rivers, streams, canals, ditches (or any other surface watercourse), lakes and ponds.

2.13 Percussion boring

The term 'percussion boring' shall mean the formation of exploratory holes using percussive boring methods, including dynamic (window and windowless) sampling.

2.14 Rotary drilling

The term 'rotary drilling' shall mean the formation of exploratory holes by rotary drilling techniques and auger methods.

2.15 Resonance drilling

The term 'resonance drilling' also known as sonic drilling shall mean the formation of exploratory holes using high-frequency mechanical vibration of the casing and sampling tools to advance the hole, with optional rotation.

2.16 Inspection pit

The term 'inspection pit' shall mean a hand-excavated hole using appropriate tools to locate and avoid existing buried services at exploratory hole positions.

See also 6.1 and NG 6.1.

2.17 Trial pits and trenches

The terms 'trial pit' and 'trial trench' shall mean excavations to enable visual examination of the ground conditions and any required sampling from outside the pit or trench without personnel entering into the excavation.

See also 6.2 and NG 6.2.

2.18 Observation pits and trenches

'Observation pits' and 'trenches' shall mean excavations to enable personnel to enter safely and carry out in situ examination of the ground conditions, sampling and testing as required.

See also 6.3 and NG 6.3.

2.19 Sample

The term 'sample' shall mean soil, water or ground gas collected from a specified sampling point, irrespective of the number and type of containers required to collect that sample.

Individual samples may require more than one container or type of container. For example, a large bulk sample may need to be collected in two separate bulk bags to comply with manual handling guidelines. Similarly, a sample for contamination testing may require material to be collected in plastic tubs and various glass jars.

2.20 Hygiene facility

The term 'hygiene facility' shall mean designated washing or showering facilities for personnel and other specific cleansing facilities as specified in Schedule S1.8.16.

The welfare facilities are now specified in Schedule 2 of CDM (2007) and apply regardless of whether an investigation is notifiable or not.

2.21 Sampling well

The term 'sampling well' shall mean standpipes or piezometers from which samples of groundwater, ground gas or vapour can be taken for analysis.

2.22   Daily record

The term 'daily record' shall mean the record for each exploratory hole and all other specified measurements, observations and test results deriving from works separate from exploratory holes.

The daily record was formerly known as the 'driller's log'. The definition is now extended to include all required measurements, observations and test results obtained during the site operations.

In practice, a daily record sheet designed for recording the information required for exploratory holes may not be suitable for recording information from some in situ testing, sampling and monitoring, particularly where these activities are independent of exploratory holes. In such cases, separate purpose-designed record sheets may be necessary.

2.23   Electronic information

The term 'electronic information' shall mean the electronic equivalent of paper records, reports or photographs and the data derived from fieldwork, monitoring and laboratory tests in digital format.

See also Clauses 16.5, 16.6.3, NG 16.5 and NG 16.6.3.

3   General requirements

Notes for Guidance

3.1   Work not required

Any clauses of this Specification which relate to work or materials not required in the Schedules shall be deemed not to apply.

3.2   British Standards and equivalent

The work shall be carried out in accordance with the relevant British Standards or equivalent European Standards, in particular BS EN 1997-2, BS EN ISO 22475-1, BS EN ISO 22475-2, BS EN ISO 22475-3, BS 1377, BS 5930 and BS 10175, or other recognised standards or Codes of Practice, current on the date of invitation to tender.

Any reference in the Contract to a Standard published by the British Standards Institution, or to the Specification of another body, shall be construed equally as reference to an equivalent one.

Sections of BS 5930 and BS 1377 will be progressively replaced by BS EN publications under BS EN 1997-2.

It is implicit that to carry out the investigation to the relevant Standards all plant and equipment should be in good condition and manufactured to British or equivalent European Standards where they exist. All relevant certificates should be in date and available for inspection.

3.3   Quality management

When specified in Schedule S1.8.1, all work shall be carried out in accordance with a quality management system(s) established in accordance with BS EN ISO 9001, BS EN ISO 14001 and BS OHSAS 18001. Records to demonstrate compliance shall be made available to the Investigation Supervisor on request.

Where Accreditation to BS EN ISO 9001, BS EN ISO 14001 and BS OHSAS 18001 is required, this should be stated in Schedule S1.8.1.

Requirements for particular laboratory tests to be carried out by a laboratory accredited by the United Kingdom Accreditation Service (UKAS) to BS EN ISO/IEC 17025 (or an equivalent in a Member State of the European Community) should be given in Schedules S1.19.4 and S1.20.2. All such tests must comply with UKAS requirements.

The Association of Geotechnical and Geoenvironmental Specialists provides information on quality management in geotechnical engineering (AGS, 1991).

3.4   Investigation Supervisor's facilities

When required, accommodation and equipment shall be supplied and maintained for the sole use of the Investigation Supervisor in accordance with Schedule S3. All accommodation, furnishings, services, equipment and vehicles shall be ready for occupation and use by the Investigation Supervisor on the date for commencement of the Site Operations, and shall be removed at the end of the Site Operations unless otherwise directed by the Investigation Supervisor.

The requirements for the Investigation Supervisor's office and facilities required should be listed in Schedule S3. This should include any motor vehicles for the use of the Investigation Supervisor and detail the vehicle insurance requirements/limitations.

3.5   Management, Superintendence and Professional Attendance

The Contractor shall provide the necessary Contract Management and Superintendence of the works and Professional Attendance compatible with the scope and nature of those works and to the requirements, if any, detailed in Schedule S1.8.2.

3.5.1 Contract Management and Superintendence

The Contractor's Contract Management and Superintending staff shall be responsible for the works being carried out in accordance with the Contract, Specification and Schedules.

Contract Management and Superintendence includes the support services of accountancy, IT, quantity surveying, legal, quality control, auditing, commercial and marketing.

3.5.2 Professional Attendance

Professional Attendance shall be provided by the Contractor in the form of the provision of technical staff as necessary to fulfil the technical, logistical and quality requirements of the works.

The level of Professional Attendance shall be compatible with the scope and nature of the works and with the requirements, if any, detailed in Schedule S1.8.2, and shall also take into consideration whether full-time or part-time supervision is required.

The number and experience of technical staff required will vary depending upon the scope and nature of the works being undertaken. If the Professional Attendance supplied by the Contractor is to be specified at the time of tender, the requirements should be defined in detail in Schedule S1.8.2.

The on-site services provided by the technical staff comprise the technical supervision of site activities, site liaison, logistics, logging, in situ testing and sampling, photography and the preparation of daily records and preliminary logs (except where any of the above activities are carried out by site operatives and boring/drilling operatives). Any additions to or deletions from this list should be detailed in Schedule S1.8.2.

3.6 Ground practitioners and other personnel

The Contractor may be required to provide the services of ground practitioners and/or other personnel.

The need for the services of ground practitioners and/or other personnel to be supplied by the Contractor may be known at the time of tender, in which case the services should be requested at that time. Otherwise, the initiative lies with the Investigation Supervisor to request them as required.

3.6.1 Ground practitioners

The Contractor may be required to provide the services of ground practitioners as defined in Schedule S1.8.3, or as requested by the Investigation Supervisor during the course of the works, for advice, assistance and/or the preparation of the Ground Investigation Report and/or the Geotechnical Design Report as defined in Schedules S1.21.8 and S1.21.9. The Contractor shall submit adequate records of time and expenses to the Investigation Supervisor. If required by the Investigation Supervisor, details of the qualifications and experience of the personnel shall be supplied.

Schedule S1.21.8 should detail the elements of the Ground Investigation Report which are to be compiled by the Contractor. See also Clause 16.8.

Schedule S1.21.9 should state whether the Contractor is to contribute to the Geotechnical Design Report and, if so, detail the elements which are required. See also Clause 16.9.

3.6.2 Other personnel

The Contractor may be required to provide the services of other personnel as defined in Schedule S1.8.3 to advise the Investigation Supervisor or assist in the running of the investigation. The Contractor shall submit adequate records of time and expenses to the Investigation Supervisor. If required by the Investigation Supervisor, details of the qualifications and experience of the personnel shall be supplied.

Other personnel could include a drilling supervisor, highway traffic safety officer, marine supervisor, ecologist, archaeologist or railway trained staff.

See also Clause 3.12.

3.7 Information on existing site conditions

Safety aspects are paramount and all relevant known information about the site should be listed in the S1 series of Schedules and made available to the Contractor. CDM places a legal duty on the client to provide information on safety and health hazards (including all known services information) in the pre-construction information. See also NG 3.7.1 and NG 3.7.2.

3.7.1 Hazardous ground and land affected by contamination

The presence and nature of areas of hazardous ground or land affected by contamination shall be detailed in Schedules S1.8.4 and S1.8.6, including classification of the site in accordance with the Guidance for Safe Investigation of Potentially Contaminated Land (SISG, 2011).

As described in the definitions of hazardous ground and land affected by contamination (Clauses 2.4 and 2.5), Schedule S1.8.4 and S1.8.6 should include both areas that are known or suspected of being hazardous or contaminated.

Land affected by contamination may also be hazardous and, in such cases, this should be noted in Schedule S1.8.4.

Other hazards could include, e.g., ground at risk of landslips or collapse from underground voids or unexploded ordnance.

Sampling and/or testing for explosives, pathogens, asbestos and high-activity radioactive material requires the use of specialist contractors and/or specialist advisors with appropriate experience and knowledge, whose advice should be sought where the site-specific desk study indicates that such materials could be present.

See also NG 7.1.

3.7.2 Services

The client or client's agent shall supply all available service drawings and documentation with the pre-construction information, as required by CDM (2007). The positions of all known mains, services, drains, sewers, tunnels and pipelines owned by statutory undertakers, public authorities and private individuals, shown on the Drawing(s) detailed in Schedule S1.7, are based on information extracted from the records of the various bodies and shall be regarded as approximate only.

Any additional information not shown on the Contract Drawing(s) shall be detailed in Schedule S1.8.5.

Reference shall also be made to Clauses 3.8.3 and 6.1.

The service drawings and documentation should be provided by the client/client's agent. Nevertheless, responsibility for confirming the locations and protecting services on site rests with the Contractor regardless of any information provided to assist in their location.

The presence of overhead services should be checked.

Services to individual properties are likely to exist but there may be insufficient information to enable their details to be included on the Drawing(s).

Reference to statutory distances from any known services, or the required safe distances if these exceed statutory requirements, should be included in Schedule S1.8.5 unless included in the Special Requirements of the Conditions of Contract.

The Contractor can be allocated the task of assembling all the known information on services, but sufficient time before commencement of site works must be allowed for this within the programme of the works.

Drawings supplied to the Contractor should preferably be in an appropriate CAD format. However, to minimise transcription errors it is recommended that the original service drawings (or copies thereof) provided by the statutory authorities are also provided to the Contractor.

3.7.3 Mineral extractions

The positions of any known mine workings, mineral extractions, quarries, shafts or similar works within the area and at a depth likely to affect the proposed investigation shall be shown on the Drawing(s) detailed in Schedule S1.7.

See also NG 5.5.

The presence and nature of known or suspected mine workings, mineral extractions, etc. shall be detailed in Schedule S1.8.6.

3.7.4 Protected species

The presence and nature of protected species of flora and/or fauna which may affect or be affected by the investigation shall be detailed in Schedule S1.8.7.

The heading of protected species should be taken to encompass not only legally protected species and habitats but also the bird nesting and lambing seasons and the limitations that these may impose on investigations.

When the areas of protected species can be defined, those areas should be shown on the Drawing(s) detailed in Schedule S1.7.

3.7.5 Archaeology

The presence and nature of any known archaeological remains shall be detailed in Schedule S1.8.8

When the areas of archaeological remains can be defined those areas should be shown on the Drawing(s) detailed in Schedule S1.7.

It should be noted that work within Scheduled Monuments requires Schedule Monument Consent and may be subject to restrictions set by the local planning authority.

3.8 General safety requirements

3.8.1 Safety legislation

The investigation shall comply with all relevant safety legislation.

Relevant safety legislation includes but is not limited to:

The Construction (Design and Management) Regulations (2007);
The Management of Health and Safety at Work and Fire Precautions (Workplace) Regulations 1999 and 2003 amendment;
Control of Pollution Act, 1974 and Amendment Schedule 23, 1989;
Personal Protective Equipment at Work Regulations 1992 (as amended);
Safe Use of Lifting Equipment – Lifting Operations and Lifting Equipment Regulations (LOLER) 1998;
Safe Use of Work Equipment – Provision and Use of Work Equipment Regulations (PUWER) 1998;
Manual Handling Operations Regulations 1992 (as amended).

Investigations which are notifiable under CDM Regulations will require a CDM Coordinator and Principal Contractor to be appointed by the Client. Non-notifiable projects require a named person or body to be appointed by the Client and who will be responsible for safety. However, whether notifiable or not, CDM regulations apply to all investigations.

Account should also be taken of the information contained in the *Guidance for Safe Investigation of Potentially Contaminated Land* (SISG, 2012).

3.8.2 Risk assessment and method statements

Prior to the start of site operations the Contractor shall provide to the Investigation Supervisor risk assessments and method statements covering all aspects of the work to be carried out. In addition, a construction phase health and safety plan shall be prepared in accordance with CDM and submitted to the CDM Coordinator.

All these documents shall be reviewed and, if necessary, amended whenever there are changes and/or additions to the originally planned work or when evidence of further hazardous or contaminated ground is encountered during the works.

Pre-construction information (in accordance with CDM), including desk study information, must be provided to the Contractor to enable preparation of method statements and risk assessments.

The Contractor's risk assessment and method statement should address, among other things:

(a) provisions for dealing with ground gas
(b) measures when unexploded ordnance may be present
(c) the proposals for restoration of exploratory holes so that they do not become a hazard to the public or the environment; backfilling with arisings may not be acceptable
(d) provision for the collection and safe disposal of contaminated soil and liquid arisings from exploratory holes
(e) procedures to be adopted to protect the environment (e.g. not to place contaminated soil onto unprotected ground and aquifer protection)
(f) very restricted addition of water (Clause 4.2) because of the danger of spreading contamination
(g) procedures to be adopted where geotechnical testing is required on samples suspected or known to be contaminated.

Guidance on assessing and mitigating the risks from unexploded ordnance is given in Report No. C681 Unexploded Ordnance (UXO) – A Construction Industry Guide (CIRIA, 2009).

There may be a need to agree the approach to be adopted with the appropriate statutory agency prior to the works commencing.

3.8.3   Indirect detection of buried services

Unless specifically identified in Schedule S1.11.1 as not being required, the position of any services at or near the proposed exploratory hole location shall be pinpointed as accurately as possible by means of a locating device, the principle type being a Cable Avoidance Tool (CAT) and generator operated by a suitably trained person.

With inspection pits CAT scanning shall be carried out prior to commencement, at frequent intervals during and on completion of the pit.

For trial pit/trench and observation pit/trench locations, CAT scanning shall be carried out prior to the start of excavation and, without personnel entry into the excavation, at frequent depth intervals during excavation until it's unsafe to do so due to the depth of the excavation.

Details of the CAT scanning, its findings and any consequent actions taken shall be included in the daily records.

Reference shall also be made to Clauses 3.7.2 and 6.1.

Notwithstanding that the designer of an investigation should, as far as possible, site proposed exploratory holes in order to be well clear of all known and suspected services, all exploratory holes should be risk assessed prior to commencement.

The use of a 'Permit to Dig' system is recommended but the service drawings should always be available on site and consulted for all proposed exploratory holes.

The use of locating devices should wherever possible prove the positive presence of services shown on the drawings rather than purely their absence.

Although CAT scanning will be the principle means of detection, consideration should also be given to the use of sondes, ground-probing radar (GPR) and other geophysical methods.

Schedule S1.11.1 should be used to identify any exploratory hole locations where CAT scanning is not required. Overwater investigations are one example where CAT scanning is not practical. Subject to the risk assessment, exporatory holes located where there is a significant thickness of backfill may be a further case where the exclusion of CAT scanning could be appropriate.

Further guidance on avoiding the dangers from underground services is given in the HSE publication HSG 47 (2000).

See also NG 3.7.2 and NG 6.1.

3.8.4   Welfare facilities

Welfare facilities shall be provided, appropriate to the scale and nature of the investigation.

The welfare facilities provided for all investigations must meet the minimum requirements set out in Schedule 2 of CDM (2007).

Where a site is extensive, e.g. for a long length of highway, consideration should be given to satellite welfare facilities local to any remote location.

Where an investigation is on a construction site or within an existing development, welfare facilities may be available through a main Contractor or the employer. Such instances should be identified in Schedule S1.3.

3.8.5   Personal protective equipment

All site staff shall be provided with and use the Personal Protective Equipment (PPE) appropriate to the work involved and the classification of the site, according to the companion document Guidance for Safe Investigation of Potentially Contaminated Land (SISG, 2011).

The need for PPE, over and above statutory requirements, should be identified in Schedule S1.8.4 and/or S1.8.6 as appropriate. If additional PPE is to be provided by the Contractor for sole use of the Investigation Supervisor, this should be identified in Schedule S3.6.

3.9 Notice of entry

In addition to any notices required to be given under the Contract, at least one working day's notice shall be given by the Contractor to the owner and/or occupier of the intended time of entry on to the site.

It is normally the responsibility of the Client or Client's representative to arrange and agree preliminary access details with the owner/occupier.

3.10 Access routes

Only the agreed access routes (as defined on the Drawings included in Schedule S1.7) to, from and between exploratory positions shall be used.

Agreed access routes should be defined on the Drawing(s) at the time of tender with due consideration having been given to the site conditions likely to persist at the time of investigation and of the plant expected to be used.

Any access difficulties, including restrictions where passes are required, should be detailed in the description of the site Schedule S1.3.

If the detailed arrangements for entry and access routes, the provision of access route drawings, etc. are delegated to the Investigation Supervisor, this needs to be defined in Schedule S1.2.

3.11 Security of site

Unless otherwise stated in Schedule S1.8.9, all barriers breached or otherwise disturbed during the execution of site operations shall be immediately repaired or replaced to the same standard.

Permanent barriers, such as those forming the boundaries between adjacent fields or different properties, should not be breached unless clearly instructed by the client or the client's representative with the full assurance that agreement has been given by the land/property owner and that the Contractor does not become liable for damages.

Depending on the powers delegated to the Investigation Supervisor, the latter may be authorised to instruct the Contractor to breach permanent barriers.

3.12 Traffic safety and management

Traffic safety and management measures shall be provided as the progress of the site operations requires. Measures shall be taken in accordance with any statutory requirements and any special requirements in Schedule S1.8.10. Where the circumstances of any particular case are not covered by the statutory requirements or described in the Schedules, proposals for dealing with such situations shall be submitted to the Investigation Supervisor for approval.

Work on or adjacent to public highways, motorways, waterways and rail tracks requires the utmost care and attention to traffic safety and management, including the safety of the general public. Any particular constraints and requirements should be given in Schedule S1.8.10. Highway works, for example, must comply with recommendations contained in Chapter 8 of the *Traffic Signs Manual* (DFT, 2006) and any amendments thereto.

If the Contractor is to supply highway traffic safety officers or other personnel (e.g. railway or waterways trained staff) or special traffic measures, the requirements should be included in either Schedule S1.8.3 and/or S1.8.10, as appropriate.

3.13 Working hours

Working hours shall be restricted to those specified (if any) in Schedule S1.8.11.

3.14 Qualifications of site operatives

3.14.1 All site operatives

Site operatives shall hold a National Vocational Qualification (NVQ), or equivalent European Union qualification (where available), appropriate to their status and to the type of work being undertaken.

All site operatives employed on the contract shall also hold a valid and current CSCS card for their occupation as issued by Construction Skills Certification Scheme Ltd or an equivalent body in a State of the European Union. In the case of boring and drilling operatives, this should be a CSCS blue skilled (Land Drilling) card but Clause 3.14.3 also applies.

It is intended that all site works are carried out by appropriately trained and qualified personnel.

Technical Standard CEN ISO/TS 22475-3 requires the competency of operatives to be verified at regular intervals to ensure ongoing competence and for operatives to hold an identification card which provides formal recognition of their competence. The identification card should include a photograph of the qualified operator.

Blue CSCS cards also include Experienced Worker cards.

Trainee operatives in boring and drilling may hold a red CSCS trainee card and must be under the direct supervision on site of a CSCS Land Drilling (Lead Driller) audit card holder. The BDA/Construction Skills Lead Driller Apprenticeship Scheme is available for industry new entrants.

Whether trainee operatives are permitted on a particular contract should be specified in Schedule S1.8.12.

3.14.2 Plant operatives

Operatives using plant covered by the Construction Plant Competence Scheme (CPCS), e.g. excavators, dumpers, etc., employed on the contract shall hold an appropriate card as issued by CPCS or a CSCS card endorsed for that particular plant item.

In the case that the plant is a combination CPCS category/drilling unit, then Clause 3.14.3 also applies.

3.14.3 Boring and drilling operatives

All boring and drilling operatives, including Lead Drillers and Drillers (Drilling Support Operatives), employed on the contract shall hold an NVQ in Land Drilling and hold a valid and current audit card of competence, for example as issued by the British Drilling Association Ltd or an equivalent body in a State of the European Union. This shall be applicable to the work and specific drilling operation on which they are engaged.

They shall also hold a CSCS blue skilled Land Drilling card.

See also Clause 3.14.1.

BS EN ISO 22475-3 requires the competency of operatives to be verified at regular intervals to ensure ongoing competence, e.g. the BDA Audit carried out by the British Drilling Association Ltd.

Entry to the BDA Audit is subject to the operative having obtained an NVQ in Land Drilling and a CSCS Land Drilling card.

The words 'applicable to the work and specific drilling operation' can be further defined. For a Lead Driller in ground investigation, the audit card should carry one or more of the following endorsements:

- Ground Investigation – Cable Percussion
- Ground Investigation – Rotary
- Ground Investigation – Dynamic Sampling

See also NG 3.14.1.

3.15   Care in executing the work

The Condition of the site prior to and subsequent to the work should be agreed by all parties, using photographs if appropriate. Damage resulting from the work should be the subject of an agreed joint record by the Investigation Supervisor and Contractor.

3.15.1   Least damage

All work shall be carried out with the least possible damage to the site and its environs.

3.15.2   Avoidance of further contamination

On land affected by contamination, the formation and back-filling of exploratory holes and the handling and storage of samples and arisings, including groundwater, shall not cause or spread contamination. Contaminated and non-contaminated samples and arisings shall be stored separately.

See also NG 3.8.2.

If special measures such as jet-washing facilities, vegetable-oil-based lubricants, etc. are required, their details should be specified in Schedule S1.8.13.

3.15.3   Aquifer protection measures

Where specified in Schedule S1.8.13, or as directed by the Investigation Supervisor during the course of the fieldwork, aquifer protection measures shall be invoked in forming the exploratory holes.

Aquifer protection will usually be required when explora-tory holes penetrate through an aquiclude into an under-lying aquifer to prevent upward/downward groundwater migration. Aquifer protection is particularly important where the ground overlying the aquiclude is contaminated. Multiple aquifers (possibly including perched water systems) will need the protection measures to be repeated for each aquiclude/aquifer system. The protection measures will normally be formed by:

(a) boring or drilling (both with temporary casing) a suit-able depth into but not penetrating through the aqui-clude;
(b) forming a bentonite plug in the base of the hole then pulling back the temporary casing to just below the top of the bentonite seal;
(c) installing a secondary smaller diameter temporary casing through the seal to the depth required.

When only a single aquiclude/aquifer boundary is pene-trated, the depth to which the secondary temporary casing extends will be governed by the need to prevent collapse of the exploratory hole wall. Where the hole is to penetrate through more than one aquiclude/aquifer boundary the secondary temporary casing must be extended into the lower aquiclude, then steps (b) and (c) above repeated with a tertiary casing.

The detailed design (hole and casing diameters, depths, etc.) will need to be specified to meet site-specific condi-tions.

Further guidance is available in 'Technical Report P5-065/TR' in 'Technical aspects of site investigation' Volume 2 (Environment Agency, 2000).

3.16   Working areas

3.16.1   General

Operations shall be confined to the minimum area of ground required for the safe execution of the Works.

Unless otherwise specified in Schedule S1.8.15, on completion of each exploratory hole all equipment, surplus material and rubbish of every kind shall be cleared away. Surplus material and rubbish shall be removed from the site to a disposal point licensed to accept the waste concerned.

The whole of the site and any ancillary works shall be left in a clean and tidy condition.

On land affected by contamination, all necessary precautions to control and secure the working area shall be taken at all times. Access to and from that area shall be via a single designated point where, if specified in Schedule S1.8.16, a hygiene facility for personnel and a wheel wash facility shall be provided.

On land affected by contamination, arisings from exploratory holes shall be placed on heavy-gauge polythene sheeting and covered in wet or windy weather in order to prevent the spread of contamination (or alternatively placed in covered skips).

3.16.2   Turf and topsoil

Turf and topsoil shall be stripped at the site of each exploratory hole and stockpiled separately for reuse. Turf and topsoil adjacent to the exploratory hole which may be damaged by the operations shall either be removed and stockpiled as above, or otherwise protected from damage. After completion of the hole the topsoil shall be re-spread and the turf relayed.

3.16.3   Paved areas

Paved areas (other than paving slabs and blocks) shall be broken out to the minimum extent necessary for each exploratory hole. After completion of the hole the paved area shall be reinstated.

Highway reinstatement shall be in accordance with the Specifications for the reinstatement of openings in the highways (DFT) (2011).

3.16.4   Paving slabs and blocks

Paving slabs and blocks shall be removed at the site of each exploratory hole and stored separately for reuse. Paving slabs and blocks which are liable to be damaged by the operations shall either be removed and stored as above or otherwise protected from damage. After completion of the hole, the paving slabs and blocks shall be re-layed.

See also Clause 3.26 and NG 3.26

Alternative reinstatement requirements may be stated in Schedule S1.8.15. For example full reinstatement at the exploratory hole locations may not be required if construction works are to follow immediately.

Where unavoidable damage (e.g. rutting of access routes under normal plant passage) is required to be made good by the Contractor, this should be stated in Schedule S1.8.17.

Paved areas comprise all those surfaced with man-made materials, e.g. blacktop, concrete and paving slabs and blocks.

Details of the reinstatement required should be specified in Schedule S1.8.15.

3.17 Claims for damage

Any damage, or claim by owners or occupiers for compensation for damage, shall be reported to the Investigation Supervisor.

3.18 Methods of investigation

The Schedules and/or the Investigation Supervisor may require investigation to be carried out by all or any of the methods described in the Specification.

3.19 Location of exploratory holes

Each exploratory hole shall be set out at the location given to the nearest 1 m or to the accuracy (if any) described in Schedule S1.8.18, using the survey data provided. The as-built position of each hole shall be determined in relation to either a local or National Grid system as specified in Schedule S1.8.18, and to the nearest 1 m or accuracy as specified in Schedule S1.8.18. The as-built position shall be recorded on a plan as referred to in Clause 16.8.1 and all reference points used shall be included in the Factual Report.

The use of National Grid coordinates and Ordnance Datum levels are advisable wherever possible to define the exploratory hole location. These will ensure the data remain of value if location plans are misplaced or ground surface levels are subsequently changed by site operations. Where local grid coordinates and datums are used they should, if possible, be related to National Grid coordinates and Ordnance Datum. Benchmarks and surveying reference points should be shown on the Contract drawings.

If benchmarks and surveying reference points are not available, the Contractor should be informed in Schedule S1.7. However, most Conditions of Contract will require adjustment to instruct the Contractor to provide these data.

3.20 Ground elevation of exploratory holes

During the period of the site operations, the elevation of the ground at each as-built exploratory hole related to Ordnance Datum or other datum as specified in Schedule S1.8.18 shall be established to the nearest 0.05 m.

3.21 Exploratory work

The location and depth of each exploratory hole shall be as described in Schedule S2. The Investigation Supervisor may, after consultation with the Contractor, vary the location and depth of any exploratory hole and the sequence or quantity of sampling or in situ testing depending on the actual ground and groundwater conditions encountered. Accurate and comprehensive records shall be kept of the work actually carried out. When the position of an exploratory hole has been varied, the Contractor shall take all necessary measurements and shall inform the Investigation Supervisor of the revised coordinates and ground elevation or other measurements required to locate the as-built exploratory hole.

The nature of ground investigation requires reasonable flexibility from the Contractor. The Investigation Supervisor and Employer must make provision for possible effects on the Contractor's programme if the number of exploratory holes, their locations, access routes and quantities of sampling and in situ testing are significantly changed.

3.22 Notifiable and invasive weeds

Any known notifiable and/or invasive weeds shall be detailed in Schedule S1.8.4 and the exclusion zones shown on the drawings. If such weeds are encountered during an investigation they shall be left undisturbed and an appropriate exclusion zone established around the infestation. Their presence shall be notified immediately to the Investigation Supervisor who will give instructions on any actions to be taken by the Contractor.

Japanese Knotweed is an invasive weed which has no indigenous naturally occurring controls and it therefore overpowers all other plants. New colonies are easily formed from either small pieces (20 mm long) of its rhizome or above-ground stem fragments, the latter often being transported by water. However, the many publications on Japanese Knotweed suggest a wide range of distances, up to 25 m, over which the rhizomes can extend from the obvious above-ground infestation.

Other invasive or notifiable weeds (Giant Hogweed, Himalayan Balsam, Ragwort, etc.) may allow work to be undertaken closer than 25 m to the infestation and such cases should be identified in Schedule S1.8.4.

3.23   Anomalous conditions

Where anomalous or unexpected features are revealed the Contractor shall inform the Investigation Supervisor immediately.

Any observed feature which is not referred to in the site-specific desk study (e.g. including but not limited to buried archaeology, old foundations, free phase contaminants) should be advised to the Investigation Supervisor.

3.24   Surface water control

Surface water or other water shall be prevented from entering the exploratory hole from ground surface level, except as permitted in Clause 4.2.

3.25   Photographs

Photographs may be requested for any purpose including rock cores, pits and trenches as detailed. Other applications may be to record before and after conditions along access routes or at exploratory hole locations.

3.25.1

Where specified in Schedule S1.8.19, colour photographs shall be taken and supplied by the Contractor. Each photograph shall clearly show all necessary details and contain a graduated scale which shall be the same in every photograph of a particular type. A standard colour chart and monochrome step wedge shall also be included in each photograph.

3.25.2

Photographs shall be digital and the image shall be a minimum of 5 million pixels in resolution (minimum 2560 pixels by 1920 pixels).

3.25.3

A JPG format file of each photograph shall be submitted to the Investigation Supervisor for his approval and retention within 3 working days of the photography. In the event that the photographs are of a quality unacceptable to the Investigation Supervisor, they shall be retaken at no extra cost.

Photographs should be submitted in the shortest possible timescale to facilitate approval and to avoid both delay in the operations and the possible need to have to repeat operations where unacceptable photographs have been obtained.

3.25.4

On acceptance of the quality of the photographs, a complete set of prints (size 150 mm × 100 mm) of all the photographs shall be presented with the Ground Investigation Report (as applicable). Unless otherwise specified in Schedule S1.8.19, only a single copy of each photograph will be required.

If interim hard copies of the photographs are required instead of, or in addition to, the JPG files this should be detailed in Schedule S1.8.19.

3.25.5

Particular requirements for photographs of cores and pits and trenches are given in Clauses 5.8 and 6.12.

3.26   Disposal of Arisings

The off-site disposal of all types of arisings shall be subject to the relevant waste transport and disposal regulations.

Disposal of arisings is likely to have to await the results of laboratory testing to enable the waste to be characterised and Waste Acceptance Criteria determined.

4 Percussion boring

Notes for Guidance

4.1 Method and diameter

The method of advancement and the diameter of a borehole shall be such that the boring can be completed (without undue ground disturbance or ground loss) and logged to the scheduled depth, samples of the specified diameter can be obtained, in situ testing carried out and instrumentation installed as described in the Schedule S2.

Any general restrictions to be imposed on the Contractor on percussion boring methods should be included in Schedule S1.9.1.

Any particular requirement for the use of nested casings with intervening seals to avoid cross-contamination between different soil horizons should be detailed in Schedule S1.8.13.

4.2 Addition of water to the borehole

4.2.1

Water shall not generally be used to assist advancement of the borehole through clay strata except as detailed in Clause 4.2.2 below or where approved by the Investigation Supervisor.

Subject to agreement by the Investigation Supervisor, small amounts of water may be splashed onto the boring tools to aid the removal of spoil from the tools.

4.2.2

Where the borehole penetrates below the water table in laminated clay strata and disturbance of the soils is likely, a positive head of water shall be maintained in the borehole and the Investigation Supervisor shall immediately be informed of the details.

Strata comprising principally clay but with laminations or thin bands of granular material (generally sand) are particularly prone to disturbance due to water head imbalance. In such cases, it is often beneficial to maintain the hole full of water.

4.2.3

Where the borehole penetrates through granular strata above the standing groundwater level, water may be added to the borehole to assist boring.

4.2.4

Where the borehole penetrates through granular strata below the standing groundwater level, a positive hydraulic head shall be maintained in the borehole.

In addition to maintaining a positive head in the borehole, the use of undersize boring tools will also assist in minimising disturbance at and below the base of the hole.

4.3 Hard stratum or obstruction in percussion boring

Where a hard stratum or obstruction is encountered, the Contractor shall employ hard boring techniques for a period of up to 1 hour or as specified in Schedule S1.8.14. Should this not penetrate through the hard stratum or obstruction the Contractor shall inform the Investigation Supervisor, who may instruct the use of one or more of the following:

See also Clause 2.8.

(a) continuation of appropriate techniques (e.g. chisel/shell with additional weights, see also Clause 2.8.1);
(b) rotary or other approved drilling until the stratum is proved for a sufficient depth (should the hard stratum prove to be a thin layer and further boring be required beneath, the Contractor shall break it out sufficiently to enable boring, in situ testing and sampling to proceed);

(c) abandonment of the borehole and a further borehole started nearby to obtain the required samples and/or in situ tests.

The progress rate observations and driving tests necessary under Clause 2.8.2 to demonstrate that a 'hard stratum' or 'obstruction' has been encountered shall be included on the daily record.

4.4   Artesian water

Where artesian water is encountered the Contractor shall cease progressing the hole, immediately inform the Investigation Supervisor and attempt to contain the artesian head by extending the casing above the existing ground level by as much as is practical.

Puncturing the aquiclude above a stratum containing an artesian head of water can lead to many severe problems if inappropriate or no action is taken. The most important first requirement is to stem the water egress from the hole as quickly as possible.

The achievable height of casing extension above ground level is likely to be site specific; for example, if the rig is being operated from staging, greater extension heights can be achieved. If extending the casing fails to stem the egress of groundwater, an alternative is for the Contractor to cap the borehole and fit a by-pass and pressure gauge to measure the pressure head of the artesian water.

4.5   Backfilling

Successful backfilling of boreholes, particularly when grout is used, requires conditions of little or no groundwater flow into or out of the borehole.

Backfilling with arisings generally settles with time and needs to be topped up after a suitable time delay. Backfilling with grout usually also requires to be topped up once the initially placed grout has set. Any settlement developing after backfilling will be a hazard and, in such cases, measures will need to be taken to preclude both personnel (including members of the public) and livestock entry to the borehole location until permanent reinstatement of the ground surface can be effected.

4.5.1   No artesian head

Except on land affected by contamination or as required in Schedule S1.9.2, the Contractor shall backfill boreholes on completion of the boring with arisings in such a manner as to minimise subsequent depression at the ground surface due to settlement of the backfill. On land affected by contamination, or where specified in Schedule S1.9.2, backfill shall comprise either bentonite pellets or cement/bentonite grout as specified in Clause 5.7 or otherwise required by the Investigation Supervisor.

In selecting grout materials, consideration needs to be given to any environmental protection measures required by the site-specific conditions. There may be a need to seek Environment Agency sanction for particular conditions.

4.5.2   Artesian head less than 1 m above ground level

On completion of the boring, the exploratory hole shall be sealed using bentonite pellets or a grout mix injected through a tremie pipe. The method to be used shall be approved by the Investigation Supervisor. If it is not possible to extract the casing it shall be left in the hole permanently.

If casings are left in the ground permanently, the details should be included in the Factual Report and the Health and Safety file.

4.5.3 Artesian head more than 1 m above ground level

On completion of the boring the exploratory hole shall be grouted up as specified in Clause 4.5.2, except that grouting operations shall be carried out by appropriate methods approved by the Investigation Supervisor.

Grouting carried out through the by-pass or a 'stuffing box' may be appropriate.

4.6 Dynamic (window and windowless) sampling

Dynamic (window or windowless) sampling shall be carried out at the locations specified in Schedule S2, or as directed by the Investigation Supervisor.

Guidance on safety in respect of dynamic sampling equipment is given in the BDA publication BDA Guidance for the safe operation of dynamic sampling rigs and equipment, 2007.

Access constraints and the resulting need to use hand-held equipment should be identified in Schedule S1.3.

The type of dynamic sampling required should be identified in Schedule S1.9.3.

The small tracked rigs typically used for dynamic sampling are also capable of undertaking a conventional geotechnical sampling sequence of standard penetration tests (SPTs) and driven U100 samples but to much lesser depths than conventional cable tool boring rigs.

4.6.1 Window sampling

Window sampling shall be carried out using hollow steel tubes incorporating a longitudinal access slot and a cutting shoe in order to recover a nominally continuous soil sample for examination/sub-sampling at the time of sinking the hole.

4.6.2 Windowless sampling

Windowless sampling shall be carried out using hollow steel tubes incorporating a removable liner and cutting shoe in order to recover a nominally continuous soil sample for retention.

4.6.3 Sample tube diameters

The range of sampling tube diameters brought to site and used at the start of the hole shall be compatible with achieving the scheduled depths and quality of sample in the expected ground conditions.

Where necessitated by the ground conditions, the sampling tube diameter may be sequentially reduced with increasing hole depth in order to maximise the depth of investigation.

4.6.4 Combined sampling and probing

Where dynamic sampling is combined with dynamic probing, the distance between the probing and sampling locations shall be between 0.5 and 1.0 m.

Probing should be carried out prior to sampling: it has the potential to give advance warning of obstructions and results in a smaller lateral extent of ground disturbance than if sampling is carried out before probing.

4.6.5 Backfilling

Dynamic sampling holes shall be backfilled with cement/bentonite grout, bentonite pellets or as directed by the Investigation Supervisor.

4.6.6 Packing and labelling of windowless samples

Where windowless samples have been taken to obtain chemical test samples, the liner tubes should be split, logged and sub-sampled for chemical testing at the earliest possible opportunity.

All other windowless samples shall immediately have the top and bottom of the liner tube marked in indelible ink and the ends of liners shall be capped and sealed using adhesive tape. Liners shall be cut to the length of the enclosed sample.

4.6.7 Storage of windowless samples

Samples in their liner tubes shall be kept horizontal and moved and handled with care at all times. They shall be stored in a suitably cool environment and protected to ensure that their temperature does not fall below 2°C. They shall also be protected from direct heat and sunlight. At the end of each day's work, tube samples shall be stored secure from interference and protected from the weather.

4.6.8 Retention and disposal of windowless samples

Samples shall be kept for a period of 28 days after submission of the approved final report or as described in Schedule S1.12.2. After this time, the Investigation Supervisor's permission should be sought for their disposal. The Contractor shall dispose of all samples, other than those delivered to the address in Schedule S1.12.1, in accordance with the relevant waste transport and disposal regulations.

Consideration will need to be given to health and safety, possible contamination of the surrounding area and cross-contamination in determining the arrangements for chemical test sub-sampling.

Samples need to be stacked carefully to avoid deformation of the plastic liner tubes.

See also NG 7.5.

5 Rotary drilling

Notes for Guidance

5.1 Augering

Augering shall be carried out as specified in Schedule S1.10.1, or as instructed by the Investigation Supervisor.

5.1.1 Hand augering

Hand auger boring may be required in suitable self-supporting strata.

5.1.2 Continuous flight augering

Where continuous flight auger boring is required, it shall be carried out under the full-time supervision of an experienced ground engineer meeting the requirements of Clause 2.3 item (c) who shall produce, as augering proceeds, a record of the material and groundwater encountered.

A disadvantage with continuous flight augering can be the difficulty in identifying the depths of changes in strata, unless frequent sampling is carried out through a hollow stem auger.

5.1.3 Hollow stem flight augering

Where hollow stem flight augering is required the equipment used shall be such as to bore and recover samples as specified in the Contract. Sampling shall be carried out through the hollow stem.

A potential limitation of hollow stem flight augering is that of basal failure of the hole below the standing groundwater table.

5.2 Rotary drilling: general

Rotary drilling may be required in soil or rock for the recovery of samples, cores, in situ testing or for 'open hole' drilling, in other words, for the advancement of a hole without core recovery.

Any general restrictions to be imposed on the Contractor on rotary drilling methods and hole diameter should be included in Schedule S1.10.2.

5.3 Drilling fluid (flushing medium)

5.3.1

The drilling fluid shall normally be clean water, air or air mist. However, with the agreement of the Investigation Supervisor, non-toxic drilling muds, additives or foam may be used.

Consideration must be given to environmental constraints in selecting a particular drilling fluid. Any preference or limitation should be detailed in Schedule S1.10.3.

Note should also be taken of the Coal Authority guidance for drilling into coal measures, i.e. air and air mist flushing may not be allowed. See also NG 5.5.2.

5.3.2

Drilling fluid returns must be collected or appropriately controlled. Any particular requirements shall be specified in Schedule S1.10.3.

Off-site disposal of drilling fluids will require the use of a suitably licensed contractor and may require prior laboratory testing.

5.3.3

On land affected by contamination, all necessary precautions shall be taken to contain the drilling fluid returns to prevent surface contamination.

5.4 Rotary drilling with core recovery

5.4.1 Types of equipment

Unless otherwise stated in Schedule S1.10.4, rotary core drilling shall be carried out by a double or triple tube coring system using either conventional or wireline techniques. The triple tube system may be effected by the use of a double tube barrel with an approved semi-rigid liner.

Unless otherwise indicated in Schedule S1.10.4, the Contractor may elect not to use core liner in certain materials where the Specification is met without it.

5.4.2 Core recovery

Rotary core drilling shall produce cores of not less than the diameter specified in Schedule S1.10.4 throughout the core length, and 100% core recovery in any single run should normally be obtained where the condition of the ground permits. Core recovery less than 90% in any drill run will not normally be acceptable unless the Investigation Supervisor is satisfied that more than 90% recovery is impracticable under the prevailing conditions. If more than 90% recovery can be achieved in the opinion of the Investigation Supervisor, the Contractor shall take measures to improve the core recovery after consultation with the Investigation Supervisor.

It is recognised that the expertise to select the appropriate equipment to maximise core recovery of the highest quality generally rests with the Contractor, although particular methods and core diameters may be specified in Schedule S1.10.4. Those methods may include limiting core run length, type of bit, drilling fluid, equipment diameter, rate of rotation and bit pressure.

The specified core recoveries should be achievable in most strata but there will occasionally be difficult ground conditions where high recoveries cannot be obtained.

5.4.3 Drill runs

The first drill run in each hole shall not exceed 1.5 m in length. Subsequent drill runs shall not normally exceed 3 m in length and the core barrel shall be removed from the drillhole as often as is required to obtain the best possible core recovery. The run length shall be immediately reduced by 50% where 90% core recovery has not been attained, and then further reduced by 50% until a minimum run length of 0.5 m is achieved or the recovery exceeds 90%.

The core run should also be terminated where there is any suspicion that forward penetration is not being suitably achieved.

The Investigation Supervisor may specify in situ testing between drill runs.

The length of the first drill run should be restricted so that the risk of losing information in what is likely to be the most weathered material is minimised.

If in situ testing such as a SPT is specified between drill runs, it will inevitably lead to degradation and a likely reduction in core recovery in the succeeding drill run.

5.4.4 Removal of cores and labelling of liners

(a) All operations entailed in recovering the cores from the ground after completion of drilling shall be carried out in a manner such as to minimise disturbance to the cores.

(b) Core barrels shall be held horizontally while the core or innermost liner containing the core is removed without vibration and in a manner to prevent disturbance to the core. The core should be rigidly supported at all times while it is being extruded and during subsequent handling, and the liner containing the core must not be allowed to flex.

(c) Immediately after removing the liner, the top and bottom shall be marked in indelible ink. The ends of liners shall be capped and sealed using adhesive tape. Liners shall be cut to the length of the enclosed core.

(d) Where the length of core recovered from any single core run is such that it cannot be accommodated in one channel of the core box, the liner shall be cut to coincide, if possible, with existing fractures. The liner either side of the cut shall be marked 'cut' and the ends capped as above.

(e) Each section of liner shall be marked with the contract title, exploratory hole reference number, date and the depths of the top and bottom of the drill run.

(f) Core obtained without a liner and that from within the core catcher but not inside the liner shall be wrapped in two layers of plastic cling film and labelled to indicate the depth and exploratory hole reference number.

5.4.5 Core boxes, packing, labelling and storing

Core boxes shall be soundly constructed and fitted with stout carrying handles, fastenings and hinged lids. The total weight of the cores and box together shall be limited to an appropriate value.

Where reasonably practicable, manual handling should be avoided. Where this is not possible, careful consideration should be given to all activities involving manual handling of the core boxes. This should follow the broad structure as set out in Schedule 1 of the Manual Handling Operations Regulations, 1992 (as amended) in order to deduce an appropriate maximum weight for the job-specific circumstances.

The stability of stacks of core boxes also needs to be considered.

Cores shall be rigidly and securely packed at the site of drilling and during all subsequent handling and storage the cores shall remain packed unless required for examination or testing. Cores shall be placed in the box, in their liners where used, with the shallowest core to the top left-hand corner, the top being considered adjacent to the hinged section. Cores from the core catcher shall also be placed in the core boxes at the correct relative depth.

Depths shall be indicated on the core box by durable markers at the beginning and end of each drill run. Rigid core spacers shall be used to indicate missing lengths. The Contract title, exploratory hole reference number and the depth range of core contained in each box shall be clearly indicated in indelible ink inside, on top and on the right-hand end of the box. Core boxes from each hole shall be sequentially numbered from '1 of X' to 'X of X'.

Core boxes containing core shall be kept horizontal and moved and handled with care at all times. Cores shall be stored in a cool environment and protected to ensure that their temperature does not fall below 2°C. They shall also be protected from direct heat and sunlight. At the end of each day's work, core boxes shall be stored secure from interference and protected from the weather.

See also NG 7.5.

5.4.6 Preparation of cores for examination

Cores shall be prepared for examination by the removal of sealing materials and splitting of liners in such a way as to avoid damage to the cores or cause injury to the person splitting the liners. Plastic liners shall be cut lengthwise such that at least half the core circumference is exposed.

Prior to examination or sub-sampling of the core, the Contractor shall photograph the cores as specified in Clause 5.8. The time between commencement of preparation and the examination of the prepared and photographed cores shall be minimised to prevent loss of moisture from the core samples.

The cores shall be examined and described in accordance with BS EN ISO 14688-1, BS EN ISO 14689-1 and BS 5930 by or under the supervision of an experienced ground engineer meeting the requirements of Clause 2.3 item (c).

Where specified in Schedule S1.10.5, the Contractor's site compound shall include all necessary facilities for core logging to be carried out on site. Otherwise cores will be logged at the Contractor's office facility which shall also include all necessary facilities for core logging.

Access for inspection of the cores by the Investigation Supervisor with not less than 48 hours notice shall be provided by the Contractor for the duration of the Contract.

Further guidance on logging cores is given by Valentine and Norbury (2011).

See also NG 5.4.7.

5.4.7 Retention of core sub-samples

Where specified in Schedule S1.10.6, the Contractor shall obtain core sub-samples for possible laboratory testing. The Contractor shall cut the liner and cap and seal the core sub-samples in such a way as to prevent loss of moisture and sample disturbance. They shall be clearly labelled so that the location, depth and origin of the sub-samples can be readily identified. Cores in their liners remaining after the specified sub-samples have been removed shall be end-capped and resealed and replaced in the original core box location. Rigid spacers shall be placed in the spaces in the cores boxes previously occupied by the core sub-samples to prevent movement of adjacent cores, and these shall be labelled identically to the core sub-samples that they replace. The core sub-samples shall be retained in separate core boxes clearly marked to indicate the origin of the cores contained within.

Where the need to retain core sub-samples can be identified prior to the start of the investigation, this should be stated in Schedule S1.10.6.

Detailed logging of core requires parts of it to be broken. This is likely to conflict with any requirement to retain core samples for laboratory strength or modulus testing. It is therefore recommended that logging and the selection of core samples for laboratory testing are carried out concurrently.

Where core sub-samples are required for laboratory testing, the Contractor needs to be informed of this requirement prior to logging the core.

5.4.8 Protection and transportation of cores

The Contractor shall protect all cores and transport them, including loading and unloading:

(a) to the Contractor's premises;
(b) to the address given in Schedule S1.10.7 for a number of selected cores.

5.4.9 Retention and disposal of cores

The Contractor shall retain cores for a period of 28 days after submission of the approved final report. After this time, the Investigation Supervisor's written permission should be sought for their disposal. The Contractor shall dispose of all cores, other than those delivered to the address in Schedule S1.10.7, in accordance with the relevant waste transport and disposal regulations.

It is assumed that long-term storage of rock cores is not generally required as photographic records will suffice.

If long-term storage of cores is required, this should be stipulated in Schedule S1.10.7.

5.5 Non-core rotary drilling

5.5.1

Where instructed by the Investigation Supervisor, rotary open hole or rotary percussive drilling may be used to advance a hole. The hole diameter shall be as stated in Schedule S1.10.8.

Use of specialist drill strings or drilling methods may be required. Where this is the case, the relevant details should be included in Schedule S1.10.8.

5.5.2

When used for the purpose of locating mineral seams, mineworkings, adits, shafts, other cavities or anomalous conditions, drilling shall be under the full-time supervision of an experienced ground engineer meeting the requirements of Clause 2.3 item (c). As drilling proceeds, a systematic record shall be made of the drilling methods, rate of penetration, loss of drilling fluid, drilling fluid colour, the material penetrated, excessive vibration during drilling and any cavities or broken ground encountered.

Where exploratory holes are likely to penetrate coal measures, an application must be made to the Coal Authority for permission to carry out the investigation. Documentation and guidance on its use is available on the Coal Authority website (www.coal.gov.uk). Approximately 4 weeks should be allowed for written permission to be granted after submission of the application.

Investigation of mining features, for example, old shafts, shallow mine workings, etc., should be specifically identified in Schedule S1.10.9 as the work involves the risk of sudden and unpredictable subsidence which can be triggered by the drilling process. The latter may also cause or release toxic or explosive gases which have collected in partially backfilled shafts and old workings.

The investigation planning needs to be based on the results of an exhaustive desk study and take account of considerations such as the likely need for steel grillages to support the drilling rig and tethered full-body harnesses for the operatives and supervisory staff. Additional Specification items will be required.

Such investigation should only be undertaken by personnel knowledgeable in mining methods and conversant with the risks involved.

5.6 Resonance (sonic) drilling

Resonance drilling, more widely known as sonic drilling, may be required in soil or rock for the recovery of samples, cores, in situ testing or for 'open hole' drilling, in other words, for the advancement of a hole without core recovery.

Sonic drilling is a system that uses high-frequency mechanical vibration to advance casing and/or sampling equipment through soil and some bedrock formations. Rotation can be added to assist penetration. It generally requires minimal use of a flushing medium which, in other cases, could contaminate or erode the sample and the immediate environs of the borehole. Borehole diameters generally fall within the range 80–200 mm.

5.6.1

Sonic drilling for 'open hole' drilling, i.e. for the advancement of a hole without core recovery, shall be as specified in Schedule S1.10.10.

Schedule S1.10.10 should specify the required diameter(s), depth(s) and type of drilling bit ('crowd in' displaces the bit face material into the core barrel; 'crowd out' displaces the bit face material into the borehole wall; or 'neutral' allows bit face material to seek the path of least resistance).

5.6.2

Sonic drilling with discrete sampling or continuous coring shall be as specified in Schedule S1.10.11. The sonic drilling shall comply with the requirements of Clauses 5.4.2–5.4.9 inclusive.

Schedule S1.10.11 should specify the information required plus the type(s) and depth(s) of samples and whether semi-rigid sample liners are required.

5.7 Backfilling

5.7.1

Except where otherwise specified in Schedule S1.10.12, the Contractor shall backfill rotary drillholes with a cement/bentonite grout. The grout shall consist of equal portions by weight of CEM1 cement and bentonite mixed by machine or a hand-operated mixer to a uniform colour and consistency before placing, with a moisture content not greater than 250% (i.e. 1:1:5 cement:bentonite:water). Additives such as expanding agents or accelerators may be required, as directed by the Investigation Supervisor. The grout shall be introduced at the bottom of the hole by means of a tremie pipe, which shall be raised as the filling proceeds but kept below the grout surface at all times.

Successful backfilling of boreholes, particularly when grout is used, requires conditions of little or no groundwater flow into or out of the borehole.

Backfill generally settles with time and needs to be topped up after a suitable time delay.

CEM1 (see BS EN 197-1 (2000)) can be difficult to obtain in bagged form; when this is the case the Investigation Supervisor may consider the substitution of CEM2 cement.

5.7.2

Backfilling under artesian water conditions should be carried out as described in Clause 4.5.2 or 4.5.3.

5.7.3

Where voids make normal grouting impracticable, the Contractor shall consult and agree with the Investigation Supervisor a procedure for sealing the drillhole.

5.8 Photographs

In addition to the requirements of Clause 3.25 the Contractor shall, where specified in Schedule S1.10.13 or instructed by the Investigation Supervisor, photograph cores in a fresh condition prior to logging and ensure that the following criteria are fulfilled:

(a) a graduated scale in centimetres is provided
(b) labels and markers are clearly legible in the photograph
(c) a clearly legible reference board identifying the project title, exploratory hole number, date and depth range of drill runs shall be included in each photograph
(d) core boxes are evenly and consistently lit
(e) the length of the core box in each photograph fills the frame
(f) the focal plane of the camera and the plane of the core box are parallel
(g) the camera is placed in the same position with respect to the core box in every photograph.

6   Pitting and trenching

Notes for Guidance

6.1   Inspection pits

Unless otherwise stated in Schedule S1.11.1, inspection pits shall be excavated by hand to an appropriate depth at the locations of all exploratory holes formed by boring, drilling, probing and penetration methods.

Hand-operated specialist power tools (e.g. vacuum excavation tools specifically designed for excavation in close proximity to services) may be used to assist the excavation of inspection pits where it is considered to be safe and necessary.

The positions, depths and dimensions of all services encountered shall be measured and recorded in the daily record with other information as required by Clause 13.2.

Reference shall also be made to Clauses 3.7.2 and 3.8.3.

The use of inspection pits should, wherever possible, prove the positive presence of services rather than their absence.

Where services are suspected, known or found to be in close proximity to the proposed exploratory hole, the Investigation Supervisor should in the first instance relocate the hole to be clear of the services. The revised location should take into account statutory/required safe distances from services. If the location of the exploratory hole cannot be moved it is recommended that, subject to consultation with and the agreement of the relevant utility, further inspection pits are put down to confirm the services and ensure that they will be unaffected by the investigation.

On the basis of safety, a hand-dug inspection pit should always be excavated unless specifically identified in Schedule S1.11.1 as not being required: overwater investigations are one example where neither CAT scanning nor inspection pits are practical. However, the justification for dispensing with CAT scanning and/or inspection pits should be based on a site-specific risk assessment.

The appropriate depth of inspection pits will depend on site-specific circumstances which should be determined by the desk study, but they should generally extend to a minimum depth of 1.2 m below ground level. Although most services will be located between 0.45 and 1.0 m below ground level, some may be at greater depths (e.g. foul sewers and high-voltage electricity cables) and where ground level has been raised after the service was installed. If services are expected at depths greater than 1.2 m, this should be detailed in Schedule S1.11.1 together with the required inspection pit depth(s).

Inspection pits must be of a larger diameter than that of the equipment used to put down the exploratory hole. Inspection pits can be formed at only a slightly larger diameter than most borehole types of exploratory hole using scissor shovels, but they must be of sufficient diameter to allow the ground below the base to be scanned using a CAT.

It will not usually be economically practical to excavate inspection pits over the whole plan area of trial pits/trenches and observation pits/trenches. If these cannot be relocated and the risk assessment does not give surety of safe excavation in the absence of an inspection pit, other methods of investigation may need to be considered. If trial pits/trenches are required they should be excavated under supervision and with care as described in NG 6.2.

Further guidance on avoiding the dangers from underground services is given in HSG 47.

See also Clauses 3.7.2, 3.8.3, 6.4 and NG 6.2.

6.2   Trial pits and trenches

Trial pits and trenches shall be excavated by machine to the required depth to enable visual examination and sampling as required from outside the pit or trench.

Any restrictions on plant or excavation/ground support should be included in Schedule S1.11.2.

As an alternative to providing support to vertically sided excavations, the sides may be battered back to a safe angle.

The stability of all excavations should be risk assessed by a suitably experienced Ground Practitioner, taking into account the type and nature of the strata (including any discontinuities), the groundwater conditions and any slope of the surrounding terrain.

The following method of excavation is recommended, particularly where the risk of below-ground services within or close to the plan area of machine-dug pits/trenches has not been eliminated. A toothless bucket should be used and the excavator operator instructed to dig slowly in thin layers (not more than 100 mm thick). The work should be closely supervised by an appropriately experienced ground engineer.

See also Clauses 2.8 and 6.4.

6.3   Observation pits and trenches

Observation pits and trenches shall be excavated by hand or machine, and shall be adequately supported or battered back to a safe angle to enable personnel to enter safely and permit in situ examination, soil sampling and testing as required.

Risk assessments together with all necessary support design calculations shall be carried out by a suitably qualified and experienced Ground Practitioner for all observation pits and trenches.

Any restrictions on plant or excavation/ground support should be included in Schedule S1.11.2.

The differences between trial pits and trenches and observation pits and trenches (most importantly that of personnel non-entry or entry into the excavation) have been defined in Clauses 2.17 and 2.18.

In all cases, consideration should be given to whether the required information, sampling and/or testing can be carried out so that entry of personnel into the excavation can be avoided.

There may be occasions when observation pits or trenches require to be deepened to examine or sample deeper strata. In such cases, unless the risk assessments, support design and associated calculations are compatible with the proposed greater depth in order to allow continued safe entry of personnel into the deepened excavation, the excavation needs to be reclassified as a pit/trench in order to prohibit further the entry of personnel.

Where observation pits/trenches are to be machine dug, the method of excavation should be that described in NG 6.2.

See also NG 6.2.

See also Clauses 2.8 and 6.4.

6.4   Obstructions and hard material

When an obviously impenetrable obstacle is encountered in any type of pit or trench excavation which prevents excavation to the intended depth, or hard material is encountered which could be part of a buried service, the Contractor shall immediately stop work and inform the Investigation Supervisor, who shall instruct what actions are to be taken.

Subject to the Contractor being satisfied that the obstruction or hard material is not part of a buried service, the Contractor shall attempt to continue the excavation for a period of up to 1 hour, or as specified in Schedule S1.8.14. Should this not penetrate through the hard material the Contractor shall inform the Investigation Supervisor, who may instruct what actions are to be taken.

One example of an impenetrable obstacle would be a reinforced concrete slab.

6.5   Entry of personnel

Unless otherwise specified in Schedule S1.11.3 or permitted by the Investigation Supervisor, observation pits and trenches shall be treated as confined spaces. Only personnel who are appropriately trained for confined-space working shall be permitted to work in observation pit or trench excavations.

If entry of personnel into pits or trenches is essential, then an appropriate risk assessment needs to be carried out and all required safety measures put in place. Appropriate confined-space training will be site specific and depend on the identified risks.

Guidance regarding confined spaces and the factors which affect their safe entry is contained in Health and Safety Executive Guidance INDG 258 (HSE, 2006).

6.6   Excavation

On land affected by contamination, the excavation shall proceed in a series of shallow 'cuts' between 0.2 and 0.3 m thick. Over and above the requirements of Clause 3.16.1, the arisings from distinctly different soil layers shall be stockpiled on separate polythene sheets.

Where the risk of below-ground services within or close to the plan area of machine dug pits/trenches has not been eliminated the method of excavation given in NG 6.2 should be adopted.

6.7   Pit and trench dimensions

Unless otherwise required in Schedule S1.11.4,

(a) trial pits and observation pits shall have a minimum base area of 1.5 m^2
(b) trial trenches and observation trenches shall be a minimum of 0.9 m wide.

6.8   Description

Trial pits, trenches and observation pits shall be examined and described in accordance with BS EN ISO 14688-1, BS EN ISO 14688-2, BS EN ISO 14689-1 and BS 5930 by an experienced ground engineer meeting the requirements of Clause 2.3 item (c) and, if required, photographed.

Logging and sampling of pits and trenches may require experience in both geotechnical and contamination disciplines.

Photographic requirements should be detailed in Schedule S1.11.7.

6.9   Groundwater

Where land affected by contamination is involved, ground-water pumped from pits or trenches may need to be temporarily stored and treated prior to disposal.

6.9.1

The Contractor shall keep pits and trenches free of surface water run-off. Groundwater shall be controlled by pumping from a sump to permit continuous work insofar as the rate of inflow of groundwater can be controlled by use of a 50 mm outlet diameter pump and the excavation remains stable.

6.9.2

On land affected by contamination, any groundwater pumped from a trial pit or trench shall be regarded as contaminated and the Contractor shall agree with the Investigation Supervisor appropriate measures for its collection and disposal.

Where measures for collection and disposal of ground-water pumped from a trial pit or trench can be defined in advance of the investigation, they should be detailed in Schedule S1.11.5.

6.10   Backfilling

Backfilling of the pits and trenches shall be carried out as soon as practicable with material replaced at a similar depth as encountered. The backfill shall be compacted using excavation plant, or as specified in Schedule S1.11.6, in such a manner as to minimise any subsequent depression at the ground surface. In open land, any surplus shall be heaped proud over the pit site.

Backfill generally settles with time and needs to be topped up after a suitable time delay.

In paved areas, reinstatement shall be undertaken in accordance with Clause 3.16.3 or 3.16.4 as appropriate.

6.11   Protection to pits and trenches left open

Where pits and trenches are required to be left open and unattended for any period the Contractor shall, as a minimum, provide fencing together with all necessary lighting and signing.

Where there is any danger that a person or item of mobile plant could fall or drive into a pit or trench, suitable control measures are to be put in place to prevent such an occurrence and to ensure a safe place of work.

Precautions shall be taken to protect the pits and trenches from the adverse effects of weather during this period.

In soils such as stiff overconsolidated clays, there can be advantages in leaving the pit or trench open overnight or possibly up to several days as this allows the excavated surfaces to partially dry, exposing fissures and soil fabric better than immediately after excavation.

Although pits and trenches should not be left open and unattended, if at all possible, if it is essential then an appropriate risk assessment needs to be carried out and all required safety measures put in place.

6.12   Photographs

6.12.1

In addition to the requirement of Clause 3.25, photographs shall clearly show details of the ground conditions in the pit or trench with any support in place and shall contain a graduated scale.

Any additional photographic requirements over and above those of Clauses 3.25 and 6.12 should be detailed in Schedule S1.11.7.

6.12.2

Where detailed in Schedule S1.11.8, appropriate artificial lighting shall be used.

The need for artificial lighting will depend on the ambient light conditions at the time of the works.

6.12.3

A minimum of two photographs will generally be required: one to show the exposed faces in the pit or trench and one of the arisings.

6.13 Daily provision of pitting equipment and crew

When specified in Schedule S1.11.9, pitting equipment and operating crew shall be supplied to work under the direction of the Investigation Supervisor.

Schedule S1.11.9 should include details of the depths of pits to be excavated, any ground support equipment to be provided and whether a suitably qualified and experienced ground engineer meeting the requirements of Clause 2.3 item (c) is required for sampling and/or logging.

7 Sampling and monitoring during intrusive investigation

Notes for Guidance

7.1 General

Sampling may be required for the purposes of geotechnical design, contamination assessment, the characterisation and classification of waste materials or any combination of these.

This section generally addresses only sampling and monitoring during the intrusive phase of an investigation. Sampling from and monitoring of instruments, which often extends beyond the intrusive phase of work, is dealt with in Section 12.

Sampling and testing of surface water bodies is addressed in Clause 12.9.

Samples which are known to have or are suspected of having hazardous properties will require precautions to be taken in sample handling and description, the precautions being specific to the nature of the hazardous properties. Desk study information must be provided to the Contractor to enable the appropriate precautions to be applied.

The level of risk posed by the investigation, handling and sampling of substances such as pathogens, asbestos, explosives and radioactivity will vary depending upon the extent and nature of the substance. The appropriate investigation and sampling procedures should therefore be managed according to the risk. For example, the risks posed by and sampling procedures for the investigation of radioactive substances of a low activity or small amounts of disseminated cement-bound asbestos in made ground should be managed differently from those with higher activity radioactive materials or concentrated bulk accumulations of asbestos.

It is therefore advisable that the project team includes either a contractor and/or specialist advisor with appropriate experience and knowledge where the site-specific desk study indicates that any materials with hazardous properties could be present.

7.2 Recording depths of samples

The depths below ground level at which samples are taken shall be recorded. For open-tube and piston samples, the depth to the top and bottom of the sample and the length of sample obtained shall be given. For bulk and large bulk samples, the limits of the sampled zone shall be recorded.

7.3 Labelling of samples

Samples shall be clearly labelled in accordance with BS 5930 and BS EN ISO 22475-1.

7.4 Description of samples

Samples shall be described in accordance with BS EN ISO 14688-1, BS EN ISO 14688-2, BS EN ISO 14689-1 and BS 5930 by an experienced ground engineer meeting the requirements of Clause 2.3 item (c).

7.5   Storage and protection of samples

Both on site and at the Contractor's premises, samples which are not required for immediate laboratory testing shall be stored so that they are protected from damage and deterioration, from direct heat and sunlight and from frost and precipitation. They shall also be protected to ensure that their temperature remains within the range appropriate to the type and nature of the sample.

Excepting piston samples, tube and core samples shall be stored on their sides in purpose-made racks. Piston samples shall be stored vertically.

Recommended storage temperatures for different types of sample are given in the relevant clauses, for example Clauses 4.6.7 and 5.4.5 for dynamic windowless tube and rotary core samples respectively.

Samples to be tested for chemical aggressiveness to concrete require more controlled temperature conditions than those taken for other geotechnical purposes: see Clause 14.6.

Samples for contamination and waste acceptance criteria testing also require more controlled temperature conditions than those taken for geotechnical purposes: see Clause 7.9.1.

Some guidance on the long-term and short-term storage of samples is given in BS ISO 18512.

7.6   Samples for geotechnical purposes

In the absence of sub-sampling at the time, samples taken for geotechnical purposes are generally unlikely to be suitable for contamination testing; the latter will usually require samples to be taken using different techniques, sample containers and storage conditions. However, samples taken for geotechnical purposes may be contaminated or have hazardous properties and the relevant precautions for handling, transporting, storing and describing contaminated/hazardous samples should be applied.

7.6.1   Transportation of samples

Samples shall be transported to the Contractor's premises. Where required, selected samples shall be delivered to the address given in Schedule S1.12.1.

7.6.2   Retention and disposal of samples

Samples shall be kept for a period of 28 days after submission of the approved final report or as described in Schedule S1.12.2. After this time the Investigation Supervisor's permission shall be sought for their disposal. The Contractor shall dispose of all samples, other than those delivered to the address in Schedule S1.12.1, in accordance with the waste disposal regulations.

It should be noted that most Conditions of Contract also refer to retention and disposal of samples.

Although this clause requires samples to be retained for 28 days after submission of the approved final report, it should be appreciated that samples deteriorate with time; their shelf life can vary from days to months and depends on many factors including the type of sample, the conditions under which it was taken and stored and what the sample contains.

7.6.3   Sampling frequency

Any particular requirements shall be specified in Schedule S1.12.3. In the absence of particular requirements or instructions from the Investigation Supervisor, the requirements for sampling in percussive boreholes, pits and trenches detailed in Clauses 7.6.4 to 7.6.11 shall be observed.

Samples will also need to be taken from the inspection pit preceding the construction of the exploratory hole.

The required frequency of sampling for geotechnical purposes is dependent on both the ground conditions and the type of development proposed. For example, shallow foundations would require close or possibly continuous sampling in the upper levels, whereas piled foundations would require the investigation to extend to at least several pile diameters below the likely pile toe level.

7.6.4 Frequency of sampling in boreholes

(a) The first open-tube sample (generally in clay soils) or SPT (generally in granular soils) shall be taken at 0.5 m below the base of the inspection pit, the next at 1.0 m deeper, thereafter at 1.0 m depth intervals to 5 m depth below ground level then at 1.5 m depth intervals. Where strata changes occur below 5 m depth, the interval between open-tube samples or SPTs shall be reduced back to 1.0 m until 5 m penetration into that stratum has been achieved.

(b) Small disturbed samples shall be taken of the topsoil, at each change in soil type or consistency and midway between successive open-tube samples or SPTs.

(c) Bulk disturbed samples shall be taken of each soil type and where no sample is recovered with an SPT or U100.

(d) Groundwater samples shall be taken whenever groundwater is encountered. Where more than one groundwater level is found, each one shall be sampled separately.

7.6.5 Open-tube and piston samples

Open-tube and piston samples shall be taken using the sampling equipment and procedures as described in BS EN ISO 22475-1 and BS 5930. The nominal diameter shall be 100 mm unless otherwise specified in Schedule S1.12.4.

Before an open-tube or piston sample is taken, the bottom of the hole shall be carefully cleared of loose materials and where a casing is being used the sample shall be taken below the bottom of the casing. Following a break in the work exceeding 1 hour, the borehole shall be advanced by 250 mm before open-tube or piston sampling is resumed.

Where an attempt to take an open-tube or piston sample is unsuccessful, the hole shall be cleaned out for the full depth to which the sampling tube has penetrated and the recovered soil saved as a bulk disturbed sample. A fresh attempt shall then be made from the level of the base of the unsuccessful attempt. Should this second attempt also prove unsuccessful, the Contractor shall agree with the Investigation Supervisor alternative means of sampling.

The samples shall be sealed immediately to preserve their natural moisture content and in such a manner as to prevent the sealant from entering any voids in the sample.

Soil from the cutting shoe of an open tube shall be retained as an additional small disturbed sample.

7.6.6 Standard penetration test samples

When a standard penetration test (SPT) is carried out, the sample from the split barrel sampler shall be retained as a small disturbed sample. Where a sample is not recovered in the split barrel or where a solid cone is used, a bulk disturbed sample shall be taken over the depth range of the test.

Under the requirements of BS EN ISO 22475-1 the U100 sampler, used in the industry for many years, classes as a thick-walled open-tube (OS-TK/W) sampler. As such, it does not produce the class 1 quality of samples which are required for laboratory strength and compressibility testing. This problem can be overcome by the use of thin-walled samplers (OS-T/W) or piston samplers (PS-T/W). The use of thin-walled or piston samplers is recommended where laboratory strength and compressibility testing is to be carried out. The use of UT100 samples, as described by Gosling and Baldwin (2010), can be considered but the possible detrimental effects of the driving mechanism and the number of blows to retrieve the sample should be appreciated.

Where piston sample diameters other than 100 mm are required (e.g. 250 mm), the diameter should be stated in Schedule S1.12.4.

If cutting shoe samples are not to be retained, this should be stated in Schedule S1.12.5. Cutting shoe samples would normally be inspected by the personnel responsible for logging.

Common practice is to use one sinker bar when taking U100 samples in soft and firm clays, but to increase to two sinker bars in stiff overconsolidated clays to maintain the quality of the samples.

7.6.7   Small disturbed samples

1. Except for soil recovered from the cutting shoe of a tube sample or SPT tool, small disturbed samples shall weigh not less than 1.0 kg.
2. All disturbed samples shall be placed immediately in airtight containers, which they should sensibly fill.

Sample containers should be fully filled where possible in order to minimise the space within the container which is occupied by humid air, which promotes sample oxidation and chemical breakdown.

7.6.8   Bulk disturbed samples

Bulk disturbed samples shall weigh between 10 and 25 kg.

To minimise the loss of fines, non-cohesive bulk samples from boreholes need to be collected in a suitable watertight container and the fines allowed to settle before carefully decanting off excess clear water. The remaining solids can then be collected as the bulk sample in a suitable puncture-proof container.

Samples collected in the above manner are likely to be Class 4 or 5 in accordance with BS EN ISO 22475-1.

7.6.9   Large bulk disturbed samples

Large bulk disturbed samples (comprising material collected in two or more containers) shall have a total weight of not less than 30 kg.

Large bulk samples may be required for certain tests such as compaction tests.

To comply with manual handling guidelines, the sample may need to be collected in two or more containers.

Reference should be made to BS1377 to determine the sample size consistent with the maximum particle of the soil.

Large bulk samples will mainly be recovered from trial pits or trenches. Where non-cohesive strata are sufficiently thick to allow large bulk samples to be recovered from boreholes, the sample collection procedure described in NG 7.6.8 needs to be adopted.

7.6.10   Groundwater samples

(a) Where water has been previously added, the hole shall be baled dry or where there is sufficiently rapid groundwater ingress, three times the volume of water within the hole shall be baled out before sampling so that only groundwater is present in the hole. See Clause 12.3.2.
(b) Samples taken for testing in respect of concrete design shall be not less than 0.5 litre.

Groundwater samples taken after water has been added to the borehole may not be representative of in situ conditions, even if the borehole has been baled out prior to taking the sample. Sampling from piezometers which have been purged immediately prior to the sampling operation is recommended. See also Clauses 12.3.1, 12.3.2, NG 12.3.1 and NG 12.3.2.

7.6.11   Sampling in pits and trenches

(a) Small disturbed samples shall be taken of the topsoil at each change in soil type or consistency and between successive bulk disturbed samples.
(b) Bulk disturbed samples shall be taken at 1 m intervals, with at least one large bulk disturbed sample of each soil type and be representative of the zone from which they have been taken.
(c) Groundwater samples shall be taken where there is sufficient ingress to permit samples to be collected. See also 7.6.10 (b).

A series of large bulk samples may be required for earthworks testing, particularly where materials breakdown during compaction testing.

7.6.12 Continuous and semi-continuous sampling

Delft continuous sampling or semi-continuous sampling shall be carried out in accordance with BS 5930. The sampling requirements and sample diameter (nominally 30 or 66 mm) shall be as specified in Schedule S1.12.6, or as instructed by the Investigation Supervisor. Mostap sampling may be required over the full depth penetrated or over discrete depth ranges as instructed by the Investigation Supervisor.

Mostap sampling may need to be instructed on site depending on the conditions encountered in the borehole.

Specialist penetration equipment such as a Cone Penetration Test (CPT) rig will be required to carry out Delft or Mostap sampling.

7.7 Groundwater measurements during exploratory hole construction

Any particular requirements shall be specified in Schedule S1.12.7. In the absence of particular requirements or instructions from the Investigation Supervisor, the measurements detailed in Clauses 7.7.1 to 7.7.3 shall be made.

All the measurements and observations made must be included in the daily record information to be provided under Clause 13.2 item 15.

7.7.1 Encountering groundwater

When groundwater is encountered in exploratory holes, the depth from ground level of the point of entry shall be recorded together with depth of any casing. Exploratory hole operations shall be stopped and the depth from ground level to water level recorded with an approved instrument at 5 minute intervals for a period of 20 minutes. If after 20 minutes the water level is still rising, this shall be recorded together with the depth to water below ground level unless otherwise instructed by the Investigation Supervisor. The exploratory hole operations shall then be continued. If casing is used and this forms a seal against the entry of groundwater, the Contractor shall record the depth of casing at which no further entry or only insignificant infiltration of water occurred. Where applicable, every effort shall be made to seal off each water strike.

7.7.2 Other groundwater level measurements

Water levels shall be measured at the beginning and end of each shift or other rest periods during the work.

7.7.3 Times of measurements

On each occasion when groundwater is recorded, the depth of the exploratory hole, the depth of any casing and the time on a 24 hour clock shall also be recorded.

7.8 Special geotechnical sampling

The Investigation Supervisor may require special sampling. This work will normally require on-site supervision by a suitably experienced ground practitioner and shall be carried out in accordance with BS 5930 or as described in Schedule S1.12.8 of this Specification.

Thin-walled or other special samples should be described in Schedule S1.12.8 with reference to BS 5930 where possible.

7.9 Samples for contamination assessment and Waste Acceptance Criteria testing

Clauses 7.9.4–7.9.6 relate only to soil samples taken during the intrusive phase of the investigation. Groundwater samples generally need to be taken from standpipes or standpipe piezometers and ground gas samples from ground gas standpipes, for which reference should be made to Section 12.

In order to meet with Waste Disposal Regulations, the nature of any contamination and whether materials will be disposed off site will be site specific. The number, type, distribution and weights of samples required, together with the method of sampling, should be specified on a site-by-site basis according to findings from the desk study and the nature of the proposed construction.

Where the nature and extent of contamination is significant and/or complex, it is recommended that an additional schedule is prepared setting out a site-specific overview of the problem together with the investigation objectives and strategy.

7.9.1 Protection of samples

Samples shall be protected to ensure that their temperature is kept within the range $4° \pm 2°C$. Samples shall also be protected from direct heat and sunlight.

Guidance on sample preservation schemes (suitable containers, necessary preservatives and additives, storage conditions and sample shelf lives) for contaminated samples is given in the Department of the Environment CLR reports and BS ISO 18512 (2007).

7.9.2 Transportation and storage of samples

Samples shall be transported in appropriate containers to the Contractor's testing laboratory within 24 hours of the samples being taken and stored correctly until tested. Where required, selected samples shall be delivered to the address given in Schedule S1.12.9.

See also Clause 7.5 and NG 7.5.

All samples shall be subject to a chain of custody documentation.

7.9.3 Retention and disposal of samples

All untested samples and remaining sample portions shall be kept for a period of 28 days after submission of the approved final report or as described in Schedule S1.12.10. After this time, the Investigation Supervisor's permission shall be sought for their disposal. The Contractor shall dispose of all samples in accordance with the Waste Disposal Regulations, other than those delivered to the address in Schedule S1.12.9.

Samples submitted to the chemical testing laboratory for analysis shall be disposed of 28 days after submission unless otherwise instructed.

It should be noted that various Conditions of Contract also refer to retention and disposal of samples.

Although this clause requires samples to be retained for 28 days, it should be appreciated that samples deteriorate with time; their shelf life can vary from days to years and depends on many factors including the type of sample, the conditions under which the samples were taken and stored and what the samples contain. BS ISO 18512 (2007) gives guidance on storage of soil samples.

The costs of storing samples under controlled conditions (particularly temperature) at the testing laboratory can be large and sample shelf lives will generally be shorter than the period between taking the sample and 28 days after final report approval. It is therefore recommended that storage times at the chemical testing laboratory are limited to 28 days from sample receipt.

7.9.4   Frequency of sampling in exploratory holes

Any particular requirements shall be specified in Schedule S1.12.11. In the absence of particular requirements or instructions from the Investigation Supervisor, the following sampling requirements shall be observed.

Disturbed samples should be taken in accordance with BS 10175 and Guidance for Safe Investigation of Potentially Contaminated Land (SISG, 2011) but, in any event, at not more than 1 m depth intervals and at changes in strata type.

Samples will also need to be taken from the inspection pit preceding the construction of the exploratory hole.

Guidance on the design of sampling strategies is given in BS 10175 and CLR4 published by Department of the Environment (1994).

The required frequency of sampling for contamination purposes is dependent on the conceptual site model. The latter is based on a number of factors including the ground conditions and the purpose of the assessment. For example, the assessment of land to be redeveloped for residential housing with gardens is likely to require shallow-level soil sampling and testing for a human health risk assessment.

7.9.5   Sampling method

Samples taken from boreholes and trial pits shall use the procedures identified in BS 10175 (2011) to avoid cross-contamination between samples, spreading of existing contamination and the introduction of external contamination.

Samples for laboratory testing shall be taken using a stainless steel trowel which shall be decontaminated between sampling events and on completion of each exploratory location to avoid cross-contamination between samples.

Samples shall be taken by or under the supervision or direction of an environmental scientist, geoenvironmental engineer or geochemist meeting the requirements of Clause 2.3 item (c) as detailed in Schedule S1.12.12.

The use of lubricants on the boring casing and sample liners needs to be avoided to prevent external contamination being introduced to samples.

Plant and equipment can normally be cleaned by pressure washing or, in ground heavily contaminated with organic chemicals, by steam cleaning. The wash water will likely need to be temporarily stored and treated prior to disposal.

Further guidance on the decontamination of sampling tools and the avoidance of cross-contamination is given in 'Research and development technical report P5-065/TR' in 'Technical aspects of site investigation' Volume 1 (Environment Agency, 2000).

Whether it is more appropriate for samples to be taken by an environmental scientist or by others working under the supervision or general direction of an environmental scientist will necessarily be a site-specific decision taking into account factors such as the scale of the investigation and the nature of the likely contamination.

7.9.6   Sample containers

Disturbed samples may be collected in a variety of plastic and glass containers (including vials), as required for the analysis of the contaminants of concern identified during the desk study.

See also NG 7.9.1.

The size and type of sample and container, method of sampling and time limitations for carrying out specific analyses shall be commensurate with the range of analyses to be carried out or as described in Schedule S1.20.3 for contamination assessment and Schedule S1.20.5 for Waste Acceptance Criteria testing.

7.9.7   Field-based screening

On-site contamination screening of soil and/or water samples using portable test kits may be specified. This is detailed in Clause 10.9.

7.9.8 Headspace testing using flame ionisation detector (FID) or photo ionisation detector (PID)

FID and/or PID testing shall be carried out where specified in S1.12.13, or as instructed by the Investigation Supervisor, to assist in identifying samples to be subjected to laboratory contamination testing for hydrocarbons and volatile organic compounds (SVOC and VOC).

Samples for headspace testing shall not be subjected to direct sunlight and shall be tested on the day of their collection.

Headspace testing shall be carried out as follows.

(a) Half fill a suitable 500 ml container with freshly collected sample and immediately seal the container in order to have approximately equal volumes of sample and air.

(b) In an environment above 0°C, allow a minimum of 20 minutes for headspace development by vigorously shaking the container at the beginning and end of development.

(c) Check the PID/FID is working and calibrate if necessary.

(d) Insert the instrument probe through the seal to about mid-depth of the headspace, taking care to avoid the uptake of water droplets or soil particles.

(e) Record the highest meter response. Erratic meter readings should be discounted.

(f) Record details of the sampling and testing, including comments on results which are inconsistent with visual/olfactory evidence of contamination.

(g) Record details of the ambient weather and temperature during the test.

7.10 Sampling and testing of surface water bodies

Sampling and testing of surface water bodies is dealt with in Clause 12.9.

Where possible the need for FID/PID testing should be identified in Schedule S1.12.13.

Suitable containers for headspace testing are glass jars and plastic freezer bags.

The highest meter readings in the headspace test should occur within a few seconds of probe insertion.

CIRIA Report C665 (2007) provides guidance on headspace testing.

8 Probing and cone penetration testing

Notes for Guidance

8.1 Dynamic probing

The suitability of the various capacity probes (DPL up to DPSH) to differing ground conditions and interpretation of the results is discussed by Butcher, McElmeel and Powell (1995).

8.1.1 Probe capacity

Dynamic probing equipment (light, medium, heavy and super heavy or DPL, DPM15, DPM, DPH and DPSH, respectively) shall comply with the requirements of BS EN ISO 22476-2.

The required capacity of probing equipment should be specified in Schedule S1.13.1.

DPSH-A and DPSH-B differ in respect of the height of the hammer drop (500 mm and 750 mm, respectively). DPSH-B is more commonly used in the UK.

8.1.2 Test procedures

Tests shall be carried out in accordance with BS EN ISO 22476-2.

BS EN ISO 22476-2 recommends that the actual energy (Emeas) delivered to the driving rods is measured and that this is used when the test results are used for quantitative evaluation purposes.

8.2 Static cone penetrometer tests

8.2.1 Test procedures

Cone penetration tests (CPT) using electric friction cones or piezocones shall be carried out in accordance with BS 1377-9 and BS 5930. A suitable means of viewing the raw field data on site shall be provided.

BS EN ISO 22476-1 will in due course supercede BS 1377-9 in respect of cone penetration testing.

The type and size (10,000 or 15,000 mm^2) of electric cone to be used, the pore pressure filter position and whether the cone is to include an inclinometer should be specified in Schedule S1.13.2.

8.2.2 Calibration

Where load, displacement or other measuring equipment is used which necessitates regular calibration, then this shall be carried out in accordance with the manufacturer's instructions and comply with the requirements of BS 1377-9. Evidence of calibrations and copies of calibration charts shall be supplied to the Investigation Supervisor prior to commencing work and when otherwise requested.

8.2.3 Repeat piezocone tests

The Contractor shall repeat tests at no additional charge where the piezocone has become unsaturated during penetration, unless this is clearly attributable to ground conditions.

Where the water table is not close to the ground surface, air entry via the filter element can lead to partial saturation of the piezometric system. This problem can be minimised by the use of water-filled holes which have been pre-bored down to the water table.

8.2.4 Interpretation

Any additional parameters to be reported, over and above those required by BS 1377-9, shall be specified in Schedule S1.13.3.

Schedule S1.13.3 should specify whether additional parameters, such as normalised or derived parameters, for example soil type and c_h, from dissipation tests are required.

8.3 Seismic cone penetrometer tests

8.3.1 Test equipment

The down-hole component of seismic cone penetration equipment shall comprise a piezocone fitted with two sets of geophones separated vertically by 1 m, or as specified in Schedule S1.13.4, each set comprising three geophones mounted in the x, y and z planes. The additional equipment shall comprise a suitable data logger recording system, a surface-mounted shear-wave generator with good ground coupling and a trigger mechanism to initiate data recording. A suitable means of viewing the raw field data on site shall be provided.

Schedule S1.13.4 should specify in detail the equipment required.

8.3.2 Test method

The cone shall be advanced through the soil and temporarily halted at the same depth intervals as the spacing between the geophone sets. At each depth interval a seismic shear wave shall be generated and the travel times to the two sets of geophones recorded by the data logger.

8.3.3 Test locations

Tests shall be carried out at the locations and to the depths specified in Schedule S2, or as directed by the Investigation Supervisor.

8.3.4 Interpretation

The recorded travel times shall be corrected for the horizontal offset between the shear-wave source and the rod string to give corrected vertical travel times, unless otherwise specified in Schedule S1.13.5. The travel time over the prescribed depth range of the two geophone sets is obtained by difference to give the resulting vertical shear-wave velocity V_s. The dynamic shear modulus (G_{max}) shall be calculated using the relationship

$$G_{max} = \gamma_b \cdot V_s^2$$

where γ_b is the soil bulk density.

8.4 Other cones and specialist probes

The use of other cones and specialist probes shall be carried out as described in Schedule S1.13.6.

A range of other cones and probes exists or is being developed to measure electrical conductivity, temperature and to carry out down-hole chemical testing.

Additional Specification items will be required.

8.5 Specialist personnel

Interpretation of all cone penetration tests shall be carried out by specialists experienced in the type(s) of cone being used.

Details of any computer software used in the interpretation of results should be included in the report.

9 Geophysical testing

Notes for Guidance

9.1 General

9.1.1

The objectives of the geophysical survey shall be described in Schedule S1.14.1.

Unless otherwise specified in Schedule S1.14.2, a Ground Specialist geophysicist shall be provided by the Contractor under Clause 3.6 to advise on the types and methods of geophysics to be used.

Any site trials of the selected geophysical methods to be carried out prior to the main survey shall be specified in Schedule S1.14.3.

Types and methods of geophysical surveying shall be specified in Schedule S1.14.4.

Some guidance on the applicability of a range of geophysical methods towards meeting the objectives under a variety of site conditions is given in BS 5930 and CIRIA Report No. C562 (2002). Further guidance is given by Darracott and McCann (1986).

In order to avoid inappropriate methods being specified it is recommended that, if the Investigation Supervisor is not a qualified and experienced geophysicist, such a person is employed to advise the Investigation Supervisor. If the experienced geophysicist is from the Contractor's staff that person should be engaged under Clause 3.6.

It is recommended that Schedule S1.14.4 describes:

(a) whether the works comprise land or overwater surveys
(b) the types of geophysics required (mapping/profiling/borehole geophysics)
(c) the methods to be used:
  (i) land-based mapping (conductivity, magnetic or gravity)
  (ii) land-based profiling (resistivity, seismic or ground probing radar)
  (iii) land-based borehole methods (wireline logging or seismic)
  (iv) overwater mapping (echo sounding, side-scan sonar, magnetic or conductivity)
  (v) overwater profiling (seismic reflection/refraction, resistivity imaging or ground-probing radar).

9.2 Information provided

The survey control, digital mapping, existing ground investigation and geological and topographic data which will be provided to the Contractor shall be specified in Schedule S1.14.5.

Where marine geophysics is to be carried out, the grid reference system should be defined in Schedule S1.14.5.

9.3 Horizontal data density

The number of readings or measurements per unit length (or per unit area) appropriate to the objectives of the survey shall be specified in Schedule S1.14.6.

9.4 Level datum

The level datum to be used for the geophysical survey shall be specified in Schedule S1.14.7.

Where marine geophysics is to be carried out levels may be related to Chart Datum. Its relationship to Ordnance Datum should be stated in Schedule S1.14.7.

9.5 Calibrations and conformance

All instruments shall be calibrated where appropriate and/or conformance to the manufacturer's specification shall be demonstrated on site.

9.6   Site log book

The Contractor shall keep a site log recording:

(a) the timing and scheduling of the survey
(b) instrument serial numbers
(c) site conditions during the survey
(d) any constraints or problems encountered during the survey
(e) any feature likely to influence the data together with details of the plan position, material type, depth and extent of the feature.

Site conditions would include, for example, wind strength and direction, precipitation, sea state (e.g. wave height and direction) and proximity of potential sources of interference.

9.7   Survey report

Unless otherwise specified in Schedule S1.14.8, the Contractor's report shall include:

(a) copy of the site log book
(b) all calibration certificates and serial numbers of the instruments used
(c) for mapping and profiling surveys, one or more chart/plan/section showing the positions of each of the measurement stations and the reduced results of the survey overlain on the Ordnance Survey tile
(d) measurement station descriptions
(e) text outlining the objectives of the survey, a description of the methods used and any limitations affecting the results obtained, the measurement stations/line spacings used, an interpretation of the findings and the likely causes of any anomalies identified in the data
(f) the results of any on-site instrument calibrations or checks of equipment performance
(g) any other information specified in Schedule S1.14.8.

Schedule S1.14.8 should state if interpreted geotechnical parameters are required.

10 In situ testing

Notes for Guidance

10.1 Calibration of measuring instruments

Where load, displacement or other measuring equipment is used this shall be calibrated in accordance with the relevant British Standard and the manufacturer's instructions. Evidence of calibrations and copies of calibration charts shall be supplied to the Investigation Supervisor prior to commencing work and when otherwise requested.

10.2 Testing: general

In situ testing for explosives, pathogens, bulk accumulations of asbestos and high-activity radioactive material requires the use of experienced specialist contractors and/or specialist advisors whose advice should be sought when the site-specific desk study indicates that such materials could be present.

See also NG 3.7.1 and NG 7.1.

10.2.1

For each test the following information shall be included in the daily record, preliminary log and Factual Report or Ground Investigation Report (as applicable):

(a) date of test
(b) project name, exploratory hole number and location
(c) depth and location of test or depths covered by test as appropriate, together with reduced levels on preliminary logs
(d) information on water levels in exploratory hole during testing
(e) original ground level at test site (not required for daily report)
(f) soil type and description as identified from the sample.

10.2.2

All results shall be reported in SI units.

10.3 Tests in accordance with British Standards

The following in situ tests shall be carried out and reported in accordance with the appropriate standards.

1 In situ density (BS 1377) by
   (a) sand replacement, small pouring cylinder method
   (b) sand replacement, large pouring cylinder method
   (c) water replacement method
   (d) core cutter method
   (e) nuclear method.
2 Standard Penetration Test (SPT) (BS EN ISO 22476-3).
3 Plate loading test (BS 1377)
4 Shallow pad maintained load test (BS 1377)
5 California Bearing Ratio (CBR) (BS 1377)
6 Vane shear strength (BS 1377) carried out as
   (a) test at base of borehole
   (b) penetration test from ground level.
7 Apparent resistivity of soil (BS 1377)
8 Redox potential (BS 1377)
9 Constant head permeability test (BS 5930)
10 Variable head permeability test in boreholes and piezometers (BS 5930)
11 Packer permeability test (BS 5930)
   (a) single
   (b) double.

Schedule S1.15.1 should list the tests likely to be required.

BS EN ISO 22476-3 has replaced BS 1377 in respect of the Standard Penetration Test. There will be progressive replacement of both BS 1377 and BS 5930 by BS EN ISO standards.

BS EN ISO 22476-3 states that the energy ratio (E_r) of the SPT equipment used has to be known if the N values are to be used for quantitative evaluation of foundations or comparisons of results. It requires that a calibration certificate of the E_r value immediately below the driving head/anvil shall be available and presents a recommended method for measuring the actual energy. Further guidance is given in Hepton and Gosling (2008).

The nuclear method of in situ density measurement differs from other methods in that it is rapid determination and therefore useful for multiple determinations but does require detailed calibration against the specific soils tested and a licence for use.

See also NG 11.4.5 in connection with permeability tests.

10.4 Hand penetrometer and hand vane for shear strength

10.4.1

Where specified in Schedule S1.15.2 or instructed by the Investigation Supervisor, hand penetrometer and hand vane tests shall be carried out to give a preliminary estimate of undrained shear strength of the soil tested.

It should be noted that the hand vane and hand penetrometer tests are regarded as imprecise tests due to a lack of consistency in procedure for the test. The results may be helpful in formulating a controlled test programme and description of soils. The hand vane should not be confused with the more controlled laboratory vane test described in BS 1377-7.

Some penetrometers directly record unconfined compressive strength in kg/cm^2 ($1 kg/cm^2 = 98 kPa$).

10.4.2

Hand (or pocket) penetrometer equipment shall be of an approved proprietary make with a stainless steel tip with an end area of $31 mm^2$ and an engraved penetration line 6 mm from the tip. The scale shall be suitably graduated. The procedure for the test shall be in accordance with the manufacturer's instructions. Both unconfined compressive strength and estimated shear strength shall be reported for the soil tested.

10.4.3

Hand vane equipment shall be of an approved proprietary make with stainless steel vanes. The scale shall be suitably graduated. The procedure for test shall be in accordance with the principles for the laboratory vane and in situ vane tests (detailed in BS 1377 parts 7 and 9, respectively) and the manufacturer's instructions. Peak shear strength and remoulded shear strength shall be recorded.

Hand vanes are available with a range of vane sizes. Vane diameters vary from about 19 mm to 33 mm and vane heights from about 29 mm to 51 mm. It should be noted that not all vanes have a length-to-diameter ratio of 2:1. It is therefore recommended that shear strength is calculated from the torque M (in Nm) divided by the vane constant K. The torque can be obtained from the recorded dial divisions via the manufacturer's calibration chart of torque versus dial divisions.

10.4.4

The reported shear strength for the hand penetrometer and hand vane shall be the average of a set of three readings in close proximity but avoiding interference between tests. Tests giving inconsistent readings shall be reported and comments on the relevance of the test noted.

10.5   Pressuremeter

Requirements for self-boring pressuremeters and high-pressure dilatometer testing should be detailed in Schedule S1.15.3 in accordance with Schedule A of the publication by Clarke and Smith (1992). Driven and push-in pressuremeter testing is discussed in Clarke *et al.* (2005).

10.5.1   Self-boring pressuremeters and high-pressure dilatometer

Tests shall be carried out in accordance with BS 5930 and as described by Clarke and Smith (1992).

BS EN ISO 22476-4, BS EN ISO 22476-6 and BS EN ISO 22476-8 will in due course supercede BS 5930 in respect of pressuremeter testing and BS EN ISO 22476-5 in respect of dilatometer testing.

The tests required and results to be reported shall be specified in Schedule S1.15.3.

10.5.2   Full displacement driven or push-in pressuremeter

Tests shall be carried out in accordance with BS 5930 and as described by Clarke and Smith (1992) and Clarke *et al.* (2005).

The tests required and results to be reported shall be specified in Schedule S1.15.4.

10.5.3   Menard pressuremeter

The tests required and results to be reported shall be specified in Schedule S1.15.5.

Schedule S1.15.5 should specify, for example, whether tests are to be carried out in pre-drilled pockets or using a driven type of probe, the required probe diameter, calibrations and results to be obtained.

10.6   Soil infiltration test

Tests shall be carried out in accordance with BRE Digest 365 (2007) and as described in Schedule S1.15.6.

Schedule S1.15.6 should specify the infiltration test pit dimensions to be used.

In low permeability soils, the test can continue over several days.

10.7 Special in situ geotechnical testing

Special in situ testing shall be carried out as described in Schedule S1.15.7.

Where testing is required which is not covered by this Specification it should be noted in Schedule S1.15.7 and the Specification provided based on BS EN 1997-2, BS 5930 and BS 1377 where possible.

An example of special in situ testing would be in situ shear testing.

10.8 Interface probe tests

Interface probe tests to determine the presence and thickness of hydrocarbons overlying/underlying groundwater shall be carried out in selected exploratory holes or installations as specified in Schedule S1.15.8, or as instructed by the Investigation Supervisor.

Interface probes may not be able to identify very thin layers of hydrocarbon overlying the groundwater or at its interface with an underlying aquiclude.

10.9 Contamination screening tests

Field-based screening using portable test kits to provide a rapid indicator of grossly contaminated areas shall be carried out as specified in Schedule S1.15.9 or as instructed by the Investigation Supervisor.

Where field-based screening is required, it should be noted in Schedule S1.15.9.

Field-based screening test results can be used to assist in the selection of laboratory analyses that should be carried out and to support visual/olfactory evidence of contamination met with during fieldwork.

10.10 Metal detection

Locating buried metals using metal detectors shall be carried out as specified in Schedule S1.15.10 or as instructed by the Investigation Supervisor.

Where possible the need for identifying the locations of buried metals should be identified in Schedule S1.15.10.

11 Instrumentation

Notes for Guidance

11.1 General

Instrumentation may be required to facilitate sampling and/or monitoring of groundwater, ground gas and ground movements or combinations of these. Instrumentation shall be specified in Schedules S1.16, or as instructed by the Investigation Supervisor.

The extent to which instrumentation can be specified prior to the investigation depends, in part, on the type of investigation to be undertaken; for a preliminary investigation, it may only be possible to give a general indication of the instrumentation likely to be required. On the other hand, if the investigation is supplementary to a previous main investigation it may be possible to fully detail the instrumentation requirements (e.g. their types, locations and depths).

11.2 Covers

The top of each installation shall be protected by a cover, the types of which shall be specified in Schedule S1.16.1 or as instructed by the Investigation Supervisor.

The type of cover required will depend on both the type of instrument and its location. For example, instruments installed in a highway location will require the cover to be flush with ground level whereas those in areas subject to local ponding of surface water would likely need the cover arrangements to be elevated above ground level.

11.3 Fencing

When specified in Schedule S1.16.2, or instructed by the Investigation Supervisor, the Contractor shall install a timber protective fence around the top of an installation. The fence shall comprise at least three wooden stakes, 75 mm square, preserved in accordance with BS 8417, firmly bedded in the ground, stoutly cross-braced and projecting at least 1.0 m above ground level.

In areas with growing crops whose height is expected to exceed 0.75 m longer wooden stakes will be required.

Where livestock are expected to be present, the protective fencing needs to be stock proof and this may require fence posts to be concreted into the ground. Any such special measures should be included in Schedule S1.16.2.

11.4 Installation of groundwater standpipes and piezometers

Standpipes, standpipe piezometers and/or other types of piezometers for monitoring groundwater levels and to facilitate groundwater sampling shall be installed in exploratory holes as specified in Schedules S2 and/or S1.16.3 and S1.16.4 or as instructed by the Investigation Supervisor.

Given suitable ground/groundwater conditions it is often possible to use standpipe piezometers for both ground gas and groundwater sampling/monitoring. Whether this dual purpose can be utilised needs to be assessed by reference to the conceptual model.

Sites with two or more separate groundwater regimes will usually require them to be individually sampled and/or monitored. In principle, more than one instrument can be installed in a single exploratory hole, giving cost savings in forming the hole. However, it is difficult to ensure and prove fully functioning seals between the different response zones. It is therefore recommended that, in general, instruments are limited to one (but in any event no more than two) per hole.

Where multiple aquifers exist or multiple groundwater sampling levels are required, consideration should be given to installing specialist equipment such as multi-port installations. These will require additional Specification items.

The drawings of standpipes and standpipe piezometers in Appendices I and II show generic forms of these installations. Particular installation details (e.g. perforated screen diameter, filter grading, filter length, etc.) should be determined in relation to the site-specific ground/groundwater conditions and the intended purpose of the installation (e.g. groundwater level monitoring, groundwater sampling, permeability testing).

Selection of the standpipe or standpipe piezometer diameter should take into account any requirement for groundwater sampling and ground gas monitoring requirements.

11.4.1 Standpipes

Standpipes shall be as generally described in Appendix I.1 of this Specification and all dimensions and depths shall be recorded at the time of installation.

Simple standpipes should be installed to sample from or determine the general water level in the ground. They may not be suitable for monitoring ground gas.

11.4.2 Standpipe piezometers

Standpipe piezometers shall be as generally described in Appendix I.2 of this Specification and all dimensions and depths shall be recorded at the time of installation.

Standpipe piezometers should be installed to determine the water level within or sample groundwater from a particular stratum.

11.4.3 Other types of piezometers

When required in the Contract, the Contractor shall install piezometers of the hydraulic, electrical or pneumatic type described in BS 5930 and specified in Schedule S1.16.4.

Hydraulic, electrical and pneumatic piezometers have more rapid response times than standpipe piezometers and are therefore more suitable for dynamic measurements (e.g. tidal response). However, electrical and pneumatic piezometers generally cannot be de-aired and cannot be used for permeability tests. Groundwater sampling cannot be effected with these piezometers.

Additional Specification items will be required, tailored to the scope of instrumentation required and its purpose.

11.4.4 Proof of operation

Hydraulic continuity between standpipes/standpipe piezometers and the groundwater shall be proved by the Contractor.

The groundwater level shall be recorded immediately before and after installation of the standpipes/standpipe piezometers.

Recovery of the water level within the standpipe or standpipe piezometer after either raising or lowering it by suitable means (bailing or pumping from the piezometer) can be used to demonstrate the required hydraulic continuity with the groundwater regime. Removal of water from the installation can be part of the development process. See also Clause 11.4.5.

Hydraulic continuity with the groundwater cannot easily be proved with pneumatic and electrical piezometers: their satisfactory operation relies upon correct installation by experienced operatives and check readings during the installation process.

11.4.5 Development

Where specified in Schedule S1.16.5, or instructed by the Investigation Supervisor, groundwater installations shall be developed by air lifting, surging, over-pumping or jetting.

Details of methods of developing groundwater installations are given in BS ISO 14686 (2003).

Particularly where standpipes/standpipe piezometers are to be used for in situ permeability measurements, they need to be developed by air lifting or other suitable methods to:

1. ensure good hydraulic continuity between the installation and the groundwater
2. 'settle down' the filter pack
3. break down any skin of remoulded soil on the borehole wall surface formed during its sinking.

Where standpipes/standpipe piezometers are to be used for groundwater sampling, the installations will also need to be purged/micro-purged prior to sampling; see Clause 12.3.

11.5 Installation of ground gas standpipes

Standpipes for monitoring ground gas concentration and taking samples of ground gas in exploratory holes shall be installed as specified in Schedule S1.16.6 or as instructed by the Investigation Supervisor. They shall be as generally described in Appendix II of this Specification and all dimensions and depths shall be recorded at the time of installation.

See also NG 11.4.

Guidance on the requirements for ground gas monitoring installations is also available in CIRIA Report C665.

11.6 Inclinometers

Where specified in Schedule S1.16.7 or instructed by the Investigation Supervisor, inclinometer tubes shall be installed.

It is not normal practice for the Contractor to supply the Investigation Supervisor with inclinometer reading equipment and software. If equipment and software are required, that must be specified in Schedule S1.16.7.

11.6.1

The borehole into which the inclinometer is to be installed shall be bored/drilled to the depth required at not less than 100 mm diameter, using temporary lining casing if required.

11.6.2

The inclinometer tubing shall be installed in the borehole in lengths not exceeding 3 m which are joined by proprietary methods, supported by centralising spiders at not more than 3 m depth intervals and with the keyways orientated parallel and orthogonal to the line of maximum slope or structure to be monitored.

11.6.3

The annular space around the inclinometer tubing shall be filled with bentonite/cement grout mixed in the proportions of 2:1 by weight, or as specified in Schedule S1.16.7, with the minimum water to provide a slurry which can just be pumped into the hole via a tremie pipe.

The strength of the grout surrounding the installation should match, as closely as possible, the strength of the surrounding ground.

11.6.4

The Contractor shall ensure that no extraneous material is allowed to enter the inclinometer tubing and that damage and deformation of the tubing are prevented.

11.6.5

The Contractor shall provide the Investigation Supervisor with a set of base readings comprising readings at 0.5 m depth intervals over the full depth of the installation. Readings shall be taken with the upper wheels of the probe facing in all four keyway directions.

If multiple sets of base readings are required this should be stated in Schedule S1.16.7.

Any requirement for further readings beyond the base set, either during the intrusive phase of the investigation or requiring return visits to site, should be detailed in Schedule S1.16.7. If return visits to the site are required this should be clearly identified in the Schedule.

11.7 Slip indicators

Where specified in Schedule S1.16.8 or instructed by the Investigation Supervisor, slip indicator tubes shall be installed.

11.7.1

The borehole into which the slip indicator tubing is to be installed shall be bored/drilled to the depth required at not less than 76 mm diameter, using temporary lining casing if required.

11.7.2

Proprietary slip indicator tubing shall be installed in accordance with the manufacturer's instructions.

11.7.3

The annular space around the slip indicator tubing shall be filled with bentonite/cement grout mixed in the proportions of 2:1 by weight or as specified in Schedule S1.16.8, with the minimum water to provide a slurry which can just be pumped into the hole via a tremie pipe.

The strength of the grout surrounding the installation should match, as closely as possible, the strength of the surrounding ground.

11.7.4

A 600 mm long brass slip indicator probe, with a length of nylon twine equal to the installation depth plus 1 m, shall be provided for each installation. The probe shall be lowered to the base of the installation and the remaining twine coiled and securely stored in the space beneath the protective cover.

A set of probe rods shall be supplied to the Investigation Supervisor for his retention.

Any requirement for slip indicator observations to be taken, either during the intrusive phase of the investigation or requiring return visits to site, should be detailed in Schedule S1.16.8. If return visits to site are required this should be clearly identified in the Schedule.

11.8 Extensometers and settlement gauges

Where specified in Schedule S1.16.9 or instructed by the Investigation Supervisor, extensometers and/or settlement gauges shall be installed in accordance with the manufacturer's instructions.

The required type(s) of instruments, details of the installations to be effected and any base readings to be taken by the Contractor should be specified in Schedule S1.16.9.

Similarly, any requirement for further readings beyond the base set, either during the intrusive phase of the investigation or requiring return visits to site, should be detailed in Schedule S1.16.9. If return visits to site are required this should be clearly identified in the Schedule.

11.9   Settlement monuments

Where specified in Schedule S1.16.10 or instructed by the Investigation Supervisor, settlement monuments shall be built by the Contractor.

The required form of the settlement monuments and any base readings to be taken by the Contractor should be specified in Schedule S1.16.10.

Similarly, any requirement for further readings beyond the base set, either during the intrusive phase of the investigation or requiring return visits to site, should be detailed in Schedule S1.16.10. If return visits to site are required this should be clearly identified in the Schedule.

11.10   Removal of installations

Unless otherwise specified in Schedule S1.16.11, installations and their surface protection shall not be removed from the site.

Where the top of an installation (e.g. a stopcock cover and surrounding concrete) needs to be removed to avoid a long-term obstruction, this should be specified in Schedule S1.16.11.

11.11   Other instrumentation

Other instrumentation shall be installed as described in Schedule S1.16.12.

Where additional instrumentation is required, this should be listed in Schedule S1.16.12 with appropriate Specification items.

12 Installation monitoring and sampling

Notes for Guidance

12.1 General

Monitoring of and/or sampling from installations may be required during the intrusive phase of the investigation and/or during return visits to site.

Where concurrent (or immediately sequential) monitoring and sampling of ground gas and groundwater are required from the same installation, the Contractor shall ensure that the operations are carried out such that monitoring does not adversely affect sampling and vice versa.

As far as they are applicable, Clauses 7.1 to 7.6.2 and 7.9.1 to 7.9.3 shall apply to groundwater and ground gas samples taken during return visits to site.

Where combined installations have been installed for ground gas and groundwater, the monitoring/sampling of ground gas must precede that related to groundwater.

Similarly, where concurrent/immediately sequential groundwater level monitoring and sampling in the same installation are required, monitoring should generally precede sampling.

See also NG 12.2, Clause 12.4 and NG 12.4.2.

12.2 Groundwater level readings in installations

Readings of depths to groundwater in standpipes and/or standpipe piezometers shall be made by the Contractor with an approved instrument during the fieldwork period and/or during return visits to site as specified in Schedule S1.17.1, or as directed by the Investigation Supervisor.

It is good practice to also check and record the depth to the installation tip. This is particularly important when there is more than one installation per borehole. When sampling is required at the same time, however, consideration also needs to be given to the disturbance caused to the water column within the instrument if the depth to the installation tip is measured.

Any requirement for readings to be taken during return visits to site should be detailed in Schedule S1.17.1.

12.3 Groundwater sampling from installations

12.3.1 General

Where specified in Schedule S1.17.2 or as directed by the Investigation Supervisor, groundwater samples shall be taken in accordance with BS EN ISO 22475-1 from standpipes and/or standpipe piezometers after they have been installed, developed and generally either purged or micropurged. Sampling may be required during the intrusive phase of the investigation and/or during return visits to site.

BS ISO 5667-11 provides details of the requirements for sampling of groundwater.

Sample volumes, the containers, preservatives and conditions required in transit should be agreed with the testing laboratory before sampling.

Water sample containers should be kept in the dark, filled and refrigerated, without any contact with materials that could affect the water quality.

Samples should be scheduled for testing and dispatched to the testing laboratory in appropriate containers on the day of sampling where possible and, at the latest, within 24 hours of the sample being taken.

Any requirement for sampling during return visits to site should be detailed in Schedule S1.17.2.

See also Clause 11.4.5 and NG 11.4.5.

12.3.2 Purging or micro-purging

Where specified by Schedule S1.17.3 or instructed by the Investigation Supervisor, groundwater installations shall be purged for a period of up to 3 hours prior to groundwater sampling. If further time is required for purging, it shall be paid for at an hourly rate.

During purging, groundwater shall be monitored for conductivity, pH, temperature, dissolved oxygen and Redox potential. Purging shall cease upon stabilisation of these parameters. Alternatively, a minimum of three installation groundwater volumes shall be purged from the well. If the installation pumps dry or site-specific conditions dictate that additional purging is required, the Contractor shall inform the Investigation Supervisor who will decide what actions the Contractor is to carry out.

Purge volumes shall be estimated by the Contractor for each installation.

After purging, the Contractor shall record specific conductivity, pH, temperature, dissolved oxygen and Redox potential.

Micro-purging (to minimise disturbance to the water column) may be specified or instructed by the Investigation Supervisor as an alternative to purging if free-phase contaminants (light or dense non-aqueous phase liquids, LNAPLs and DNAPLs respectively) or VOCs are present or the groundwater column is stratified.

Based on three installation groundwater volumes, the purge volume V is calculated as follows:

$$V = 3\pi(\text{TD} - \text{WL}) \, [r^2 + (R^2 - r^2)p]$$

where r is radius of standpipe; R is radius of filter pack; p is assumed porosity of the filter pack; WL is the depth below ground level to the water surface; and TD is the depth below ground level of the base of the screened section.

The pumping rate during purging should not be greater than the recharge rate to avoid recharging groundwater cascading down the well screen. The pumping rate should also be less than the rate of abstracting water from the installation during its development.

The purged water must be disposed of appropriately.

Where the need for micro-purging can be identified from the desk study results, it should be specified in Schedule S1.17.3. The diameter of the installation will have to be sufficient to install a dedicated pump: bailers, grab samplers and inertial pumps are not suitable.

As noted in NG 12.1, where sampling and groundwater level monitoring are required at the same time, monitoring should normally be carried out first. Since sampling will usually be preceded by purging with a resultant temporary lowering of the borehole water level, it may be necessary to take several water level measurements over a period of time to demonstrate that the equilibrium value has been obtained.

12.4 Monitoring in ground gas standpipes

Ground gas measurements shall be made by the Contractor in ground gas monitoring standpipes where specified in Schedule S1.17.4, or as directed by the Investigation Supervisor. Measurements may be required during the intrusive phase of the investigation and/or during return visits to site.

Any requirement for readings to be taken during return visits to site should be detailed in Schedule S1.17.4.

Gas taps should be kept closed between monitoring events.

12.4.1

The measurements shall include atmospheric pressure, ground gas pressure, flow rate(s) and concentrations of methane, oxygen and carbon dioxide, or as specified in Schedule S1.17.4.

Where the reading instrument does not allow concurrent measurements to be taken, the gas pressure in the installation shall be determined prior to measuring flow rates (including their range and whether the flow is positive or negative). Flow rate measurements shall precede the individual gas concentration measurements.

Ground gas concentrations shall be measured for a minimum of 3 minutes and both the peak and steady-state concentrations recorded. If the concentration is rising/falling at the end of the monitoring period, this shall also be recorded.

12.4.2

The depth to water, atmospheric pressure, atmospheric temperature, ground conditions and weather shall be measured and recorded at the time of taking gas measurements.

Monitoring should include readings taken when the atmospheric pressure is below 1000 mb as well as under falling barometric pressure; see CIRIA C665 (2007).

As noted in NG 12.1, ground gas measurements must precede that of the depth to water.

12.5 Sampling from ground gas installations

Samples shall be taken during the fieldwork period and/or during return visits to site as specified in Schedule S1.17.5, or as directed by the Investigation Supervisor.

Any requirement for sampling during return visits to site should be detailed in Schedule S1.17.5.

12.5.1

Samples of ground gas for chemical analysis shall be obtained from exploratory holes or standpipes in accordance with BS 10175. The sampling method shall relate to the volume of gas available and the type of laboratory analysis to be carried out. The sampler receptacle shall be airtight and may include lockable syringes, Tedlar bags, gas bombs, adsorbent columns or cold traps.

Guidance on groundwater and ground gas sampling is also provided in the SCA Blue Book 'General Principles of sampling water and associated materials' (1996), and 'Guidance on monitoring trace components in landfill gas' (Landfill Directive Technical Guidance Note 04) (Environment Agency, 2004).

12.6 Monitoring of ground movements

The installation and taking of base readings of ground movement monitoring instruments is detailed in Clauses 11.6 to 11.9 and the associated Schedules S1.16.7–S1.16.10.

See also NG 11.6 to NG 11.9.

Where ongoing monitoring of such installations by the Contractor is required, it shall be specified in Schedules S1.16.7–S1.16.10 or instructed by the Investigation Supervisor. Schedules S1.16.7–S1.16.10 shall state whether return visits to site will be required.

12.7 Interface probe tests

Interface probe tests may be specified or instructed by the Investigation Supervisor. The testing is covered by Clause 10.8.

12.8 Other monitoring

Other monitoring shall be carried out as described in Schedule S1.17.6.

Where additional monitoring is required, this should be listed in Schedule S1.17.6 with appropriate Specification items.

12.9 Sampling and testing of surface water bodies

Where specified in Schedule S1.17.7 or instructed by the Investigation Supervisor, surface water bodies shall be sampled and/or site determinations made of dissolved oxygen, redox potential, conductivity, pH and temperature.

BS EN ISO 5667-1 provides guidance on the design of sampling programmes and techniques. Guidance on sampling rivers and streams is given in BS EN ISO 5667-6.

Any requirement for sampling and/or testing necessitating a return visit to site should be detailed in Schedule S1.17.7.

13 Daily records

Notes for Guidance

13.1 General

The Contractor shall prepare for each exploratory hole a daily record which shall be submitted to the Investigation Supervisor at the beginning of the next working day. Information shall be recorded as work proceeds and, except as specified in Schedule S1.18.1, shall include the following where relevant.

The term 'daily record' shall mean the record for each exploratory hole and all other specified measurements, observations and test results deriving from works separate from exploratory holes.

> In practice, a daily record sheet designed for recording the information required for exploratory holes may not be suitable for recording information from some in situ testing, sampling and monitoring, particularly where these activities are independent of exploratory holes. In such cases separate purpose-designed record sheets may be necessary.

13.2 Information for daily records

✓ means information required;

(✓) means information required if applicable.

	Percussion boring (including dynamic sampling)	Rotary drilling (including augering and sonic drilling)	Pitting and trenching	Continuous and semi-continuous sampling	Dynamic probing and static cone testing	Measurements, observations and test results (where separate from other exploratory holes)
1. Contract title and site name	✓	✓	✓	✓	✓	✓
2. Contractor's and crew names	✓	✓	✓	✓	✓	✓
3. CSCS, BDA Audit or similar registration number	✓	✓	✓	✓	✓	
4. Exploratory hole or location number	✓	✓	✓	✓	✓	✓
5. Day and date	✓	✓	✓	✓	✓	✓
6. CAT scan details and type and depth of any services or drains encountered	✓	✓	✓	✓	✓	(✓)
7. Equipment and technique in use	✓	✓	✓	✓	✓	✓
8. Diameter and depth of holes and casing	✓	✓		✓	(✓)	(✓)
9. The depths at which any water was added and the volume of water used	✓					
10. Depth of each change of stratum	✓	✓	✓	✓	(✓)	(✓)
11. Description of each stratum including visual and olfactory (where safe to do so) observations and any evidence of sidewall/basal instability	✓	✓	✓	✓		(✓)
12. The types of samples, the depths from/over which they were taken and length of undisturbed or core sub-samples recovered, the method used and the number of blows required to drive open-tube samples	✓	(✓)	✓	(✓)	(✓)	(✓)
13. The depths and details of all in situ tests	✓	✓	✓		(✓)	(✓)
14. Depths of hard strata and/or obstructions, the justifying progress rate and driving test observations and times o'clock spent on penetration	✓	✓				
15. Records of groundwater readings and times o'clock of the readings	✓	✓	✓	(✓)	(✓)	(✓)
16. Installation details of any standpipes, piezometers or other instrumentation	✓	✓	✓	(✓)	(✓)	(✓)
17. Water level readings in previously installed standpipes and piezometers and times o'clock of the readings	✓	✓	✓	(✓)	(✓)	(✓)
18. Ground gas readings in previously installed standpipes and times o'clock of the readings	✓	✓	✓	(✓)	(✓)	(✓)
19. Details of backfilling and/or infilling	✓	✓	✓	✓	(✓)	(✓)
20. Details of times o'clock spent other than in advancing the borehole, including details and duration of any periods of standing time	✓	✓	✓	✓	✓	✓

	Percussion boring (including dynamic sampling)	Rotary drilling (including augering and sonic drilling)	Pitting and trenching	Continuous and semi-continuous sampling	Dynamic probing and static cone testing	Measurements, observations and test results (where separate from other exploratory holes)
21. Inclination and direction relative to grid north of non-vertical drillholes		✓				
22. Type of drilling fluid		✓			(✓)	(✓)
23. Type of core barrel and bit used		✓				
24. Depth of start and finish of each core run		✓				
25. Core diameters and depths of changes in core diameter	(✓)	✓				
26. Colour and condition of the return drilling fluid and cuttings		✓				(✓)
27. The depth and/or extent of any loss of return of drilling fluid		✓				(✓)
28. Total core recovery and percentage recovery with information as to possible location of core losses, if any, for each core run		✓				
29. The dimensions of the pit or trench in plan and orientation relative to grid north			✓			(✓)
30. The method of pit or trench support and comments on stability			✓			(✓)
31. Sketches of the strata and any foundations or other feature encountered on each face of the pit or trench as appropriate			✓			(✓)
32. Estimate of the quantity of water, if any, pumped from the pit or trench, the type of pump and time spent on pumping			✓			(✓)
33. Details of photographs taken			(✓)			(✓)
34. Results of blow count plotted against depth					(✓)	
35. Results of cone and friction resistance, friction ratio and piezometric pressure as appropriate plotted against depth					(✓)	

13.3 Chain of custody

Copies of all chain of custody records shall be provided to the Investigation Supervisor within 24 hours of the samples being taken.

13.4 Special in situ testing and instrumentation records

The information to be recorded and submitted to the Investigation Supervisor shall be as specified in Schedule S1.18.2.

14 Geotechnical laboratory testing

Notes for Guidance

14.1 Test schedules

14.1.1 Preparation of test schedule

The Investigation Supervisor will prepare a schedule of tests or, if specified in Schedule S1.19.1, the Contractor shall prepare a schedule of tests for approval by the Investigation Supervisor. Unless otherwise agreed, testing schedules will be provided within 5 working days of the receipt of the relevant preliminary logs as detailed in Clauses 16.1 and 16.2.

The Contractor shall inform the Investigation Supervisor within 5 working days from the receipt of the testing schedule if a sample referred to in the schedule is not available for testing.

If the Contractor is required to prepare the schedule of tests this should be stated in Schedule S1.19.1.

Irrespective of whether the Investigation Supervisor or the Contractor is to specify the testing it is necessary to ensure that arrangements are put in place by both parties to ensure that the specified time limits are achieved.

The Contractor should supply a list of samples available in an agreed format for the use of the Investigation Supervisor.

14.1.2 Tests required

Schedule S1.19.2 shall specify the tests required.

It must be accepted that laboratory testing quantities cannot be accurately predicted at tender stage before detailed ground conditions are known. It may be necessary to specify additional testing once the results of the original tests are available. The additional testing may comprise more of the original tests and/or different tests.

14.2 Testing procedures

14.2.1 Testing standards

Where applicable, all preparation, testing and reporting shall be in accordance with the relevant British Standards. Where tests are not covered by British Standards they shall be performed in accordance with the procedures in the references or as described in Schedule S1.19.3.

Specifications for laboratory tests not described in British Standards or in the reference list should be inserted in Schedule S1.19.3.

14.2.2 Calibrations

Calibration of load-displacement or other measuring equipment shall be carried out in accordance with the appropriate British Standards and the manufacturer's recommendations. Evidence of current calibrations shall be supplied to the Investigation Supervisor when requested.

14.2.3 Geotechnical testing on contaminated samples

Where geotechnical testing is required on samples of suspected contaminated material, indicative chemical testing shall be carried out and a safe method of working agreed with the Investigation Supervisor (advised by an environmental specialist if necessary) before any such work is started. It should be noted that this may include, but is not limited to, the safe storage, transportation and handling of all suspect material and its potential reaction with laboratory equipment/materials.

The assessment of whether contaminated samples can be safely handled by the geotechnical laboratory needs to be determined on a sample by sample basis.

14.3   Accreditation

The required schemes and standards to which the laboratory testing shall be accredited shall be specified in Schedule S1.19.4.

It is recommended that where UKAS accreditation is available it is specified.

It is recommended that the precise scope of a laboratory's accreditation be checked prior to engagement.

14.4   Soil testing

Soil testing shall be carried out and reported in accordance with BS 1377/BS EN 1997-2 as appropriate, unless otherwise specified.

Sections of BS 1377 will be progressively replaced by British Standard versions of the CEN ISO/TS Technical Standards 17892 under BS EN 1997-2.

If tests include optional methods and a particular option is required, this should be stated in Schedule S1.19.3.

14.5   Rock testing

Rock testing shall be carried out and reported in accordance with the following references, or appropriate alternative, and as described in Schedule S1.19.5.

If tests include optional methods and a particular option is required, this should be included in Schedule S1.19.5.

Most laboratories will be UKAS accredited for testing in accordance with either ISRM or ASTM methods but not both (although for most tests the ISRM and ASTM procedures are similar and in some cases the same). UKAS accreditation is considered to be more important than the choice between ISRM and ASTM methods.

14.5.1   Classification

1. Natural water content – ISRM (2007)
2. Porosity/density – ISRM (2007)
3. Void index – ISRM (2007)
4. Carbonate content – BS 1881 (1971)
5. Petrographic description – ISRM (2007)

14.5.2   Durability

1. Slake durability index – ISRM (2007)
2. Soundness by solution of magnesium sulphate – BS 812 (1989)
3. Magnesium sulphate test – BS EN 1367-2 (1998)

14.5.3   Hardness

1. Shore sclerometer – ISRM (2007)
2. Schmidt rebound hardness – ISRM (2007)

14.5.4   Aggregates

1. Resistance to fragmentation by the Los Angeles test method – BS EN 1097-2 (1996)
2. Aggregate abrasion value – BS EN 1097-8 (1996)
3. Polished stone value – BS EN 1097-8 (1996)
4. Aggregate frost heave – BS 812 (1989)
5. Resistance to freezing and thawing – BS EN 1367-1 (1998)
6. Resistance to wear Micro-Deval coefficient – BS EN 1097-1 (1996)
7. Particle size distribution – BS EN 933-1 (1997)
8. Flakiness index – BS EN 933-3 (1997)
9. Shape index – BS EN 933-4 (1997)

14.5.5 Strength

1. Uniaxial compressive strength – ISRM (2007)
2. Deformability in uniaxial compression – ISRM (2007)
3. Tensile strength – ISRM (2007)
   Direct tensile strength
   Indirect tensile strength by the Brazilian method
4. Undrained triaxial compression without measurement of porewater pressure – ISRM (2007)
5. Undrained triaxial compression with measurement of porewater pressure – ASTM: SP 402 (1996)
6. Direct shear strength – ISRM (2007)
7. Swelling pressure – ISRM (2007)
   Swelling pressure index under conditions of zero volume change
   Swelling strain index for a radially confined specimen with axial surcharge
   Swelling strain developed in an unconfined rock specimen
8. Point load test – ISRM (2007).

14.5.6 Geophysical

1. Seismic velocity – ISRM (2007).

14.6 Chemical testing for aggressive ground/groundwater for concrete

Where specified or directed by the Investigation Supervisor, the appropriate test suite(s) listed in Schedule S1.19.6 shall be carried out.

During storage and transport, samples shall be protected to ensure that their temperature is kept within the range 2–4°C. Samples shall also be protected from direct heat and sunlight.

Samples shall be tested as soon as possible but, in any event, within 3 weeks after recovery.

The test suites listed in Schedule S1.19.6 cover the requirements for the four types of site (Greenfield without pyrite, Greenfield with pyrite, Brownfield without pyrite and Brownfield with pyrite) defined in BRE Special Digest 1 (2005). Most sites will only require one of the listed test suites to be undertaken. An initial assessment of the category of site (e.g. Brownfield without pyrite) should be made from the desk study results.

In recognition that most testing laboratories will not be able to offer all of the alternative test methods, the final column of each test suite allows for either a particular test method to be specified or the tendering Contractor to indicate which method(s) can be offered. If the latter course is to be followed, it should be stated in Schedule S1.19.6.

Both test suites for Brownfield sites (i.e. pyrite absent and pyrite present) include dependent options of testing for magnesium (when SO_4 >3000 mg/l in water/soil extract or $=3000$ mg/l in groundwater) and testing for nitrate and chloride (when pH <5.5). One alternative is to let the initial test results determine whether testing for magnesium and/or chloride and nitrate is required, with responsibility for carrying out the additional testing either left with the testing laboratory or subject to further instruction from the party scheduling the testing. This approach will likely give the smallest cost of testing but will probably extend the overall testing time and risk sample deterioration. The other alternative is to include for magnesium, chloride and nitrate testing at the outset: the shortest test period will result but at the possible expense of unnecessary testing.

Schedule S1.19.6 does not include testing for the ammonium ion or for aggressive carbon dioxide. It is recommended that, if the desk study results indicate either of these to be of concern, specialist advice is sought.

14.7 Laboratory testing on site

When required in the Contract, tests listed under Schedule S1.19.7 shall be carried out on site.

It should be noted that due to the time required to gain UKAS status, site laboratory testing may not be accredited. Nevertheless, although the mobile field laboratory may not be accredited, consideration may be given to its use to provide preliminary screening to better enable appropriate sample selection and test scheduling from an accredited laboratory.

14.8 Special laboratory testing

Special laboratory testing shall be carried out as described in Schedule S1.19.8.

Where special laboratory testing is required, this should be listed in Schedule S1.19.8 with appropriate Specification items.

15 Geoenvironmental laboratory testing

Notes for Guidance

15.1 Preparation of test schedule

The Investigation Supervisor shall prepare a schedule of tests or, if specified in Schedule S1.20.1, the Contractor shall prepare a schedule of tests for approval by the Investigation Supervisor. The testing schedules shall be provided to the testing laboratory within 24 hours of the samples being taken.

The Contractor shall inform the Investigation Supervisor within a further 24 hours if a sample referred to in the schedule is not available or unsuitable for testing.

If the Contractor is required to prepare the schedules of tests this should be stated in Schedule S1.20.1.

It must be accepted that laboratory testing quantities cannot be accurately predicted at tender stage before detailed ground conditions are known. It may be necessary to specify additional testing once the results of the original tests are available. The additional testing may comprise more of the original tests and/or different tests.

Certain analyses (e.g. biological) are highly time dependent and should be scheduled immediately; the specifier should liaise with the testing laboratory to avoid delays which could invalidate the analytical results.

Irrespective of whether the Investigation Supervisor or the Contractor is to specify the testing, it is necessary to ensure that arrangements are put in place by both parties to ensure that the specified time limits are achieved.

15.2 Accreditation

The required schemes and standards to which the laboratory testing shall be accredited shall be specified in Schedule S1.20.2.

Chemical laboratory testing must be carried out to International Standard BS EN ISO/IEC 17025.

Any laboratory test data on soil samples which is to be submitted to the Environment Agency must conform to the MCERTs standard where applicable. MCERTs is required for, but not limited to, those analytes listed in Annex A of Environment Agency publication 'Performance Standard for Laboratories undertaking Chemical Testing of Soil', Version 3, March 2006. It is important to ensure that the laboratory is accredited for the matrix type being tested.

It is recommended that the precise scope of a laboratory's accreditation should be checked prior to engagement.

15.3 Chemical testing for contaminated ground

Schedule S1.20.3 shall specify which suites of chemical tests and any additional individual tests are required. If appropriate, the Schedule shall also include any detection limits and/or test methods which the Contractor is required to comply with.

Where particular testing turnaround times are required, this shall be included in Schedule S1.20.3.

Both the initial selection of which test suites (and any additional individual tests) based on the desk study findings and any revisions required by the investigation findings should be made by the Investigation Supervisor or the advising site Environmental Scientist.

Beyond that, Schedule S1.20.3 provides for the Investigation Supervisor to specify test methods and/or limits of detection on a test-by-test basis. Alternatively, it can be left to the tendering Contractor to complete either or both of these columns to show what test methods and limits of detection can be offered.

However, detection limits should reflect the guideline/ threshold values against which the test results will be compared, for example Environmental Quality Standards (EQS), Drinking Water Standards or Soil Guidance Values (SGVs), etc. Unless the tendering Contractor is to be informed of these, it therefore mitigates in favour of the Investigation Supervisor specifying the limits of detection.

With regard to test methods, most commercial laboratories offer only a limited range. In practice it will generally be more appropriate for the Contractor/testing laboratory to detail the test methods which can be offered. This is the case where MCERTs accreditation is required; different laboratories may offer alternative methods of testing a particular analyte, each alternative having MCERTs accreditation.

The above considerations mitigate strongly in favour of close cooperation and dialogue between the specialist environmental site staff, Investigation Supervisor and the Contractor/testing laboratory.

It is emphasised that Schedule S1.20.3 includes only a basic list of determinands which are likely to be common to the majority of sites. The schedule must be reviewed (and amended accordingly) on a site-by-site basis to cover all the determinands of concern identified during the desk study and any subsequently obtained information.

Where necessary, additional test suites should be added. Additional Specification items will be required.

Testing turnaround times of 10 days from receipt of the testing schedule are normal. If shorter times are required this should be stated in Schedule S1.20.3. It should however be noted that, due to the test requirements themselves, certain tests (e.g. those for Waste Acceptance Testing) require more than 10 days turnaround.

The specifier should check with the testing laboratory the achievability of the proposed testing regime. This may result in specifying a nominated testing laboratory.

15.4 Waste characterisation

Where specified in Schedule S1.20.4 or directed by the Investigation Supervisor, the Contractor shall assess the waste characterisation status of materials based on the results of contamination testing carried out under Clause 15.3.

Waste characterisation may be required to determine whether materials which are likely to be disposed of will be classed as inert, hazardous or non-hazardous waste.

Environment Agency guidance on waste classification should be consulted. References are included in Section 17.

15.5 Waste Acceptance Criteria testing

Where specified in Schedule S1.20.5 or directed by the Investigation Supervisor, Waste Acceptance Criteria testing comprising one or more of the test suites detailed in Schedule S1.20.5 shall be carried out.

Waste Acceptance Criteria for inert, stable non-reactive hazardous and hazardous waste are defined under statutory regulations.

Waste Acceptance Criteria testing may be required to determine whether materials can be disposed of at a particular landfill site. Such testing may also be required to determine the appropriate methods of dealing with investigation arisings.

Leachate preparation details are set out in Part 3 of BS EN 12457. Test methods are detailed in Tables C3, C4 and C5 of 'Guidance on sampling and testing of wastes to meet landfill waste acceptance procedures' Environment Agency (2005).

Limits of detection must be equal to or better than the Waste Acceptance Criteria for the determinands being considered. In practice, the analytical methods used for WAC testing will be the same as those used in contamination testing, resulting in better limits of detection being achieved than the WAC limits.

15.6 Laboratory testing on site

When specified in Schedule S1.20.6, the tests listed shall be carried out on site.

It should be noted that, due to the time required to gain UKAS or MCERTS status, site laboratory testing may not be accredited. Nevertheless, although the mobile field laboratory may not be accredited, consideration may be given to its use to provide preliminary screening to better enable appropriate sample selection and test scheduling from an accredited laboratory.

15.7 Special laboratory testing

Special laboratory testing shall be carried out as described in Schedule S1.20.7.

Where special laboratory testing is required, this should be listed in Schedule S1.20.7. Appropriate Specification items will be required.

16   Reporting

Notes for Guidance

16.1   Preliminary logs

The Contractor shall prepare a preliminary log of each exploratory hole using an agreed proforma or as shown in the Schedules. For trial pits, a simplified version of the log and elevations showing each face of the pit shall be provided as appropriate. Preliminary logs shall be submitted to the Investigation Supervisor within 7 working days of completion of the explorations to which they refer and shall contain the information required for the exploratory hole logs.

If the Investigation Supervisor requires a particular style of log to be used, an example should be provided with Schedule S1.21.1.

Note that the supply of AGS Format Data (Clause 16.5) can reduce the need for specific formats of exploratory hole logs.

16.2   Exploratory hole logs

16.2.1   General

Unless otherwise specified in Schedule S1.21.2, the exploratory hole logs, which shall be in the same form as the preliminary logs, shall include all the information that follows, such information having been updated as necessary in the light of laboratory testing and further examination of samples and cores.

The logs shall be presented to a single, consistent vertical scale.

16.2.2   Information for exploratory hole logs

✓ means information required;

(✓) means information required if applicable.

If, in addition to the description of each stratum, soil classification is required it should be in accordance with BS EN ISO 14688-2.

Schedule S1.21.2 should state whether fracture index (FI) or fracture spacing (I_f) is required.

	Percussion boring (including dynamic sampling)	Rotary drilling (including augering and sonic drilling)	Pits and trenches	Continuous and semi-continuous sampling	Dynamic probing and static cone testing	Measurements, observations and test results (where separate from other exploratory holes)
1. All the information set out in Clause 13.2	✓	✓	✓	✓	✓	✓
2. Coordinates of hole location to specified grid	✓	✓	✓	✓	✓	(✓)
3. Ground level related to specified datum	✓	✓	✓	✓	✓	(✓)
4. Elevation of each stratum referred to the datum	✓	✓	✓	✓	(✓)	(✓)
5. Description of each stratum in accordance with BS EN ISO 14688-1, BS EN ISO 14689-1 and BS 5930, initials of person who carried out the logging (and responsible Supervisor if under training) and initials of person who reviewed the log	✓	✓	✓	✓	(✓)	(✓)
6. Geological name of each stratum (where possible) in accordance with CIRIA Special Publication SP 149	✓	✓	✓	✓	(✓)	(✓)
7. Details of groundwater observations	✓	✓	✓		(✓)	(✓)
8. Symbolic legend of strata in accordance with BS 5930	✓	✓	✓	✓	(✓)	(✓)
9. Total and solid core recovery as percentage of each core run in accordance with BS 5930		✓				
10. Rock Quality Designation RQD in accordance with BS 5930		(✓)				
11. Fracture index (FI) or fracture spacing (I_f) in accordance with BS 5930		(✓)	(✓)			

16.3 Preliminary laboratory test results

Laboratory test results shall be submitted to the Investigation Supervisor in batches at the completion of each week's testing. Legible photocopies of work sheets are acceptable.

16.4 Drawings

Record drawings are to include the following information:

(a) the project name and identification number in the title block

(b) a sequential number, revision status and date.

It is preferable for drawings to be provided in an appropriate CAD format which should be specified in Schedule S1.21.6.

16.5 Digital data

16.5.1 General

The Contractor shall provide fieldwork, monitoring and laboratory data in digital form in accordance with the current revision of the Association of Geotechnical and Geoenvironmental Specialists (AGS) publication 'Electronic transfer of geotechnical and geoenvironmental data AGS4 ed 4.0' (AGS, 2010) or as specified in Schedule S1.21.3.

The Association of Geotechnical and Geoenvironmental Specialists (AGS) publication 'Electronic transfer of geotechnical and geoenvironmental data AGS4 ed 4.0' (AGS, 2010) provides a specification for the transfer of data between parties involved in any ground investigation. Appropriate software is required to access and use AGS format data. The AGS website (http://www.ags.org.uk) provides more information on both the format and available software.

Digital output data enable efficient processing, presentation, storage and transfer of data. If such data are not required, this should be stated in Schedule S1.21.3.

The format of the data files are provided by the AGS publication. This format provides scope for extending the type and range of data that are contained within any data files. Any variations in the extent of digital data and requirements for preliminary digital data must be stated in Schedule S1.21.3 and S1.21.4, respectively.

If digital data is to be supplied in a single file, this should be stated in Schedule S1.21.3.

If a different version of the AGS data format from the current version is required for consistency with early submissions, this should be specified in Schedules S1.21.3 and S1.21.4. With reference to earlier versions of AGS data format, it is recognised that AGS ed 3.1 and ed 4.0 are likely to co-exist for some years.

Ideally, the digital data should be produced from the same source as that used to produce the report.

16.5.2 Format

The data shall be provided in accordance with the rules provided in the AGS publication, on CD or DVD ROM or other transmission medium as agreed by the Investigation Supervisor. If compression software is to be used in the transmission of the files, the software to be used shall be agreed upon by the Investigation Supervisor.

Abbreviations and codes within the AGS format file shall be from the definitions listed in the AGS publication (see Clause 16.5.1).

All data to correspond with paper records required by the contract shall be included in the AGS format data according to the group definitions listed in the AGS publication (see Clause 16.5.1).

If the Employer or the Investigation Supervisor requires additional data groups, fields or codes or associated files within the AGS format data then these shall be fully specified within Schedule S1.21.3.

The file format for associated files shall be agreed in advance between the Contractor and the Investigation Supervisor.

The data dictionary defining the data groups and headings is given in the AGS publication 'Electronic transfer of geotechnical and geoenvironmental data' (AGS, 2010).

The way that GEOL_GEOL, GEOL_GEOL2 and GEOL_STAT are to be used (by the Employer or Investigation Supervisor) should be defined prior to any generation of AGS data.

Before specifying additional data groups or headings, the Investigation Supervisor is responsible for checking the AGS website (http://www.ags.org.uk) to ensure that data transfer requirements which are not included in the current AGS publication have not already been assigned a code, group or heading.

Associated files would commonly include photographs and CAD format drawings.

16.5.3 Preliminary data

The Contractor shall issue digital copies of preliminary data as specified in Schedule S1.21.4.

A copy of the digital data may in some circumstances accompany every issue of the paper copies. Depending on the contract, however, the Investigation Supervisor may prefer to receive digital data only after a significant amount of data has been collected.

The Investigation Supervisor is likely to be receiving information from a number of sources within the Contractor's organisation, for example field data and laboratory data. The Investigation Supervisor must be prepared to manage the data as it arrives. Any file transmitted during the Contract may contain all or part of the data available at that time. It may contain exploratory hole log data, laboratory data or both.

Preliminary data may be subject to update as necessary in the light of laboratory testing and the further examination of samples and cores. When available, laboratory data should be input.

Common practice is for digital data to be transmitted by email. See also NG 16.10.2.

16.5.4   Data submissions

All AGS format data shall be checked using AGS format checking software. The checking software to be used shall be agreed in advance between the Contractor and the Investigation Supervisor.

It must be recognised that the use of checking software ensures compliance of file format, but not completeness or integrity of file content. Manual checks of information will also be required which are typically part of the report production process.

Checking software should be freely available to both parties and agreed by the Investigation Supervisor.

The details of the data transmission shall also be included in the appropriate fields within the TRAN and/or PROJ group of the data.

The TRAN and/or PROJ groups (edition 4.0 or earlier editions, respectively) in the AGS format data file contains transmission information including data status which must be included in every file submitted.

The digital data provided by the Contractor with the Factual Report or Ground Investigation Report (as applicable) is required to be complete and a total replacement of any previous preliminary data.

The Investigation Supervisor and the Contractor must be aware of the problems posed by the presence of small sets of data in a series of files and the potential for, and the presence of, errors in the datasets. These become very important if the data is being transferred to a database where incoming data is added to existing data. The organisation of the data prior to issue is the responsibility of the Contractor. The Contractor's system must ensure that data originating from different sources within the Contractor's organisation are compatible.

16.6   Form of reports

16.6.1

Schedule S1.21.5 shall specify the type(s) of report required (desk study, if not already in existence and supplied to the Contractor, Ground Investigation Report and Geotechnical Design Report). The Geotechnical Design Report and parts of the Ground Investigation Report following an intrusive investigation will not always be required.

See also NG 3.6.1.

Certain projects may have specific requirements for the format and content of the reports and any such requirements need to be included in Schedule S1.21.5. For example, a particular style of exploratory hole log may be specified; long sections may be required at a particular scale and showing particular information; or the reports may be required in sections analogous to packages of construction work.

Some Conditions of Contract may not cover all the stated requirements of the Specification in respect of a Geotechnical Design Report and the Conditions of Contract may require adjustment accordingly.

Although the use of electronic forms for the report and associated data is encouraged, it is recommended that a minimum of one paper copy of the complete report(s) including the photographs is produced, which should be regarded as the definitive copy.

16.6.2

All reports shall begin with a cover page showing the name of the Contract, a unique project reference number, date, revision status and the names of the Employer, Investigation Supervisor and Contractor. Report pages shall be numbered consecutively.

16.6.3

An electronic copy of the report(s) shall also be submitted to the Investigation Supervisor.

The electronic report shall be submitted in PDF format and include all sections of the report.

Where drawings are included in the PDF format copy of the report, they shall be printed to the same paper size as the original.

It is recommended that all PDF files are created directly from the source documents rather than scanned.

If any contributors to the files have copyrights for their material, permission must be obtained to reproduce the information in electronic format.

In the case of a large report, the report should be submitted in a number of separate PDF files. File sizes should ideally be no larger than 5 MB.

File names shall be descriptive of the file contents and, where required, submitted in a folder structure that also clearly identifies the structure of the report.

Pages in the report shall be rotated to the correct orientation.

Extensive use of bookmarks should be used to enable easy navigation of the PDF file. As a minimum, links should exist within the document between the contents page and the component parts.

Particular requirements for file size or structure should be defined in Schedule S1.21.6.

If specified in Schedule S1.8.19, the electronic copy of the photographs may be submitted as JPG format files on CD or DVD ROM.

16.7   Contents of desk study report

Schedule S1.21.7 shall specify the requirements for a desk study report, if one is not already in existence and supplied to the Contractor.

Full details of the proposed development (as far as they are available) must be included in Schedule S1.4.

It is unlikely that any investigation can be fully and appropriately scoped in the absence of a desk study considering all relevant aspects.

The AGS website (www.ags.org.uk) gives further guidance on desk studies.

16.8   Contents of Ground Investigation Report

The part(s) of the Ground Investigation Report to be compiled by the Contractor shall, as a minimum, comprise all the factual information detailed in Clause 16.8.1. Any additional elements to be compiled by the Contractor shall be detailed in Schedule S1.21.8.

Schedule S1.21.8 must fully detail any elements of the Ground Investigation Report, over and above the factual data, which are to be compiled by the Contractor.

Any known limitations of the investigation results must either be included in the Contractor's Factual Report or communicated to whoever is compiling the Ground Investigation Report.

16.8.1

The factual information to be reported shall comprise:

(a) a statement on the purpose and rationale of the investigation
(b) a description of the work carried out, including reference to the Specification and standards adopted and any deviations from them
(c) exploratory hole logs, including details of any instruments installed
(d) measurements, observations and test results (where separate from other exploratory holes)
(e) laboratory test results
(f) monitoring data
(g) site location plan
(h) detailed site plan showing all exploratory hole locations
(i) a single copy of the photographic volume
(j) any additional information specified in Schedule S1.21.8.

16.8.2

The plans shall be to a stated scale and shall include a scale bar and direction of north.

16.8.3

The Factual Report or Ground Investigation Report (as applicable) shall include a CD or DVD ROM, or other agreed physical media, containing the digital data and associated files specified in the Contract to be in digital form.

16.9 Contents of Geotechnical Design Report

If specified in Schedule S1.21.5, the Contractor shall compile those elements of the Geotechnical Design Report specified in Schedule S1.21.9.

Schedule S1.21.9 must fully detail any elements of the Geotechnical Design Report which are to be compiled by the Contractor.

16.10 Submission of electronic information

16.10.1 Timing

Electronic information shall be provided as specified in Schedule S1.21.10.

Each issue of electronic information shall be sequentially numbered from the start of the contract.

A complete set of digital data (Clause 16.5) shall be submitted with the draft and final Factual Report or Ground Investigation Report (as applicable).

The sequential numbering of data issues must be rigorously adhered to so that no data versions are issued out of sequence. When errors or inconsistencies are noted in the data, by either the Investigation Supervisor or Contractor, they should be corrected by the Contractor and a corrected dataset issued. When a change or addition is made to data within an issue, a complete data group should be reissued (not just the changed fields). This may not require complete replacement of the whole dataset which includes other previous issues.

The Contractor's data management system must ensure that all issues of digital data are compatible, the data status is unambiguous and the issues are numbered in the correct sequential order.

16.10.2 Media

The media used to transmit electronic information shall be specified in Schedule S1.21.11.

The acceptable media for the transmission of information should be specified. For example, email submission of preliminary information may be acceptable. However, submission of final information on secure physical media (CD or DVD ROM) is desirable.

16.10.3 Media labelling

All physical media shall be securely labelled and clearly marked with:

(a) a title that defines the media contents
(b) project identification number
(c) date of issue to the Investigation Supervisor
(d) name of the Contractor
(e) name of the Investigation Supervisor
(f) unique issue sequence number.

Where data are transferred via electronic systems, the information that would be included on a media label shall be provided in associated electronic documentation.

If more than one disk (or other agreed transmission medium) is required to issue AGS format data, then each shall be clearly labelled to indicate the order in which the receiver of the data should read the data. The split of the data into separate files shall be decided by the Contractor following the rules defined in the AGS publication (see Clause 16.5.1).

All media shall be checked for viruses by virus detection software before issue. A statement verifying the virus check shall be included in the covering documentation or media label.

It is critical that disks, or other agreed transmission media, are properly labelled to ensure easy identification.

A media index is also useful in the proper management of disks or other agreed transmission media. The AGS data format publication gives an example of the form of index which can be adopted.

The virus scanning software shall be capable of scanning the included associated files, for example, for macro viruses.

16.10.4 Backup copies of media

The Contractor shall make two identical copies of each media disk containing electronic information.

The first copy will remain the property of the Contractor and will be kept by him until the expiry of the contract maintenance period.

The second copy will be given to the Investigation Supervisor who will be responsible for its long-term retention.

The second copy will be given to the Investigation Supervisor who should, immediately on receipt, make a backup copy for security purposes.

16.11 Approval of report

Draft copies of the required reports shall be submitted to the Investigation Supervisor for approval before submission of the final version.

The required number of copies of the draft and final reports shall be specified in Schedule S1.21.12.

It should be noted that certain approval periods may be stated in the appendix to the Agreement given in the Contract. Required approval periods should be stated in Schedule S1.21.12.

17   References and bibliography

Legislation

Construction (Design and Management) Regulations (2007) Statutory Instruments SI 2007/320.

Control of Pollution Act (1974) and amendment Schedule 23 (1989).

Environmental Protection Act (1990).

Hazardous Waste (England and Wales) Regulations (2005) SI 2005/894.

Management of Health and Safety at Work and Fire Precautions (workplace) (amendments) Regulations (2003) SI 2003/2457.

Manual Handling Operations Regulations 1992 (SI 1992 No. 2793) as amended by Health and Safety (Miscellaneous Amendments) Regulations 2002 (SI 2002 No. 2174).

New Roads and Street Works Act (1991).

Personal Protective Equipment at Work Regulations (1992) (as amended).

Safe Use of Lifting Equipment: Lifting Operations and Lifting Equipment Regulations (LOLER) (1998).

Safe Use of Work Equipment: Provision and Use of Work Equipment Regulations (PUWER) (1998).

Standards and Codes of Practice (published by BSI)

BSI (1988) BS 1881-124: Methods of analysis of hardened concrete. BSI, Milton Keynes.

BSI (1989) BS 812: Testing aggregates. BSI, Milton Keynes. (Superseded by BS EN 932 but remains current.)

BSI (1990) BS 1377: Methods of test for soils for civil engineering purposes. BSI, Milton Keynes. (BS 1377-9: 1990 is partially superseded by BS EN 1997-2: 2007.)

BSI (1996) BS EN 1097: Tests for mechanical and physical properties of aggregates. BSI, Milton Keynes.

BSI (1997) BS EN 932: Testing aggregates. BSI, Milton Keynes.

BSI (1997) BS EN 933: Tests for geometric properties of aggregates. BSI, Milton Keynes.

BSI (1998) BS EN 1367: Tests for thermal and weathering properties of aggregates. BSI, Milton Keynes.

BSI (1999) BS 5930: Code of practice for site investigations. BSI, Milton Keynes. (This publication will be progressively superseded by BS EN 1997-2: 2007. At the time of publication a proposed revision of BS 5930 Standard is being prepared by BSI subcommittee B/52611.)

BSI (2002) BS EN 12457: Characterisation of waste – leaching – compliance test for leaching of granular waste materials and sludges. BSI, Milton Keynes.

BSI (2002) BS EN ISO 14688-1: Geotechnical investigation and testing – Identification and classification of soil. Identification and description. BSI, Milton Keynes. Amended 2007. (Partially supersedes BS 5930: 1999.)

BSI (2003) BS EN ISO 14689-1: Geotechnical investigation and testing – Identification and classification of rock. Identification and description. BSI, Milton Keynes. Amended 2007. (Partially supersedes BS 5930: 1999.)

BSI (2004) BS EN ISO 14001: Environmental Management systems. Requirements with guidance for use. BSI, Milton Keynes.

BSI (2004) BS EN ISO 14688-2: Geotechnical investigation and testing – Identification and classification of soil. Principles for a classification. BSI, Milton Keynes. Amended 2007. (Partially supersedes BS 5930.)

BSI (2005) BS EN ISO 5667-6: Water quality. Sampling. Guidance on sampling of rivers and streams. BSI. Milton Keynes.

BSI (2005) BS EN ISO/IEC 17025: General requirements for the competency of testing and calibration laboratories. BSI, Milton Keynes.

BSI (2005) BS EN ISO 22476-2: Geotechnical investigation and testing. Field testing. Dynamic probing. BSI, Milton Keynes.

BSI (2005) BS EN ISO 22476-3: Geotechnical investigation and testing. Field testing. Standard penetration test. BSI, Milton Keynes.

BSI (2006) BS EN ISO 5667-1: Water quality. Sampling. Guidance on the design of sampling programmes and sampling techniques. BSI, Milton Keynes.

BSI (2006) BS EN ISO 22475-1: Geotechnical investigation and testing – sampling methods and groundwater measurements – Part 1: Technical principles for execution. BSI, Milton Keynes

BSI (2007) BS EN 1997-2: Eurocode 7 – Geotechnical design. Part 2: Ground investigation and testing. BSI, Milton Keynes.

BSI (2007) BS OHSAS 18001: Occupational health and safety management systems. BSI, Milton Keynes.

BSI (2007) BS ISO 18512: Soil Quality: Guidance on long and short term storage of soil samples. BSI, Milton Keynes.

BSI (2008) BS EN ISO 9001: Quality Management Systems – requirements. BSI, Milton Keynes.

BSI (2009) BS ISO 5667-11: Water Quality. Sampling. Guidance on sampling of groundwaters. BSI, Milton Keynes.

BSI (2011) BS 8417: Preservation of wood. BSI, Milton Keynes.

BSI (2011) BS 10175: Investigation of potentially contaminated sites: Code of practice. BSI, Milton Keynes.

BSI (2011) BS EN ISO 22475-2: Geotechnical investigation and testing – sampling methods and groundwater measurements – Part 2: Qualification criteria for enterprises and personnel. BSI, Milton Keynes.

BSI (2011) BS EN ISO 22475-3: Geotechnical investigation and testing – sampling methods and groundwater measurements – Part 3: Conformity assessment of enterprises and personnel by third parties. BSI, Milton Keynes.

Miscellaneous

American Society for Testing Materials (ASTM) (1966) ASTM 402: Equipment for measuring pore pressure in rock specimens under triaxial load. Special Technical Publications 402, ASTM, Pennsylvania.

Association of Geotechnical and Geoenvironmental Specialists (AGS) (1991) Quality management in geotechnical engineering: a practical approach. AGS, Kent.

Association of Geotechnical and Geoenvironmental Specialists (AGS) (2010) Electronic Transfer of Geotechnical and Geoenvironmental Data AGS4 ed 4.0. AGS, Kent.

British Drilling Association (BDA) (2007) Guidance for the safe operation of dynamic sampling rigs and equipment. BDA, London.

British Standards/International Organization for Standardization (2003) BS ISO 14686: Hydrometric determinations. Pumping tests for water wells. Considerations and guidelines for design, performance and use.

Building Research Establishment (BRE) (1995) BR 279 (Bowley MJ): Sulphate and acid attack on concrete in the ground, Recommended procedure for soil analysis. BRE, Watford.

Building Research Establishment (BRE) (2005) BRE Special Digest 1: Concrete in aggressive ground. 3rd Edition. BRE, Watford.

Building Research Establishment (BRE) (2007) BRE Digest 365: Soakaway Design. BRE, Watford.

Butcher AP, McElmeel K and Powell JJM (1995) Dynamic probing and its uses in clay soils. Proceedings of International Conference on Advances in Site Investigation Practice. ICE London, March 1995. Thomas Telford, 383–395.

Clarke GB and Smith A (1992) A model specification for radial displacement measuring pressuremeters. *Ground Engineering* **25(2)**, 28–37.

Construction Industry Research and Information Association (CIRIA) (1998) CIRIA SP 149: A guide to British stratigraphical nomenclature. Powell JH, CIRIA, London.

Construction Industry Research and Information Association (CIRIA) (2002) CIRIA C562: Geophysics in engineering investigations. CIRIA, London.

Construction Industry Research and Information Association (CIRIA) (2007) CIRIA C665: Assessing risks posed by hazardous ground gases to buildings (errata February 2007). CIRIA, London.

Construction Industry Research and Information Association (CIRIA) (2009) CIRIA C681: Unexploded ordnance (UXO) A guide for the construction industry. CIRIA, London.

Darracott BW and McCann DM (1986) Planning engineering geophysical surveys. Engineering Geology Special Publication No. 2. Geological Society, London.

Department for the Environment (DOE) (1994) Sampling Strategies for Contaminated Land. Contaminated Land Research Report 4 (CLR4). DOE,

Department for Transport (DFT) (2006) Traffic Signs Manual Chapter 8-1. Traffic safety measures and signs for road works and temporary situations. DFT, London.

Department for Transport (DFT) (2011) Specifications for the reinstatement of openings in the highways. DFT, London.

Environment Agency (EA) (2000) Technical aspects of site investigation. R&D Technical Report P5-065/TR. EA, Rotherham.

Environment Agency (EA) (2004) Guidance on monitoring trace components in landfill gas. Landfill Directive Technical Guidance Note 04. EA, Rotherham.

Environment Agency (EA) (2005) Guidance on sampling and testing of wastes to meet landfill waste acceptance criteria, Version 4.3a. EA, Rotherham.

Environment Agency (EA) (2006) Performance Standard for Laboratories undertaking chemical testing of soil. Version 3. EA, Rotherham.

Gosling RC and Baldwin M (2010) Development of a thin wall open drive tube sampler. *Ground Engineering* **43(3)**, 37–39.

Health and Safety Executive (HSE) (2000) Avoiding danger from underground services. Guidance Booklets HSG47. HSE, UK.

Health and Safety Executive (HSE) (2002) Safe work in confined spaces. INDG Series 258. HSE, UK.

Hepton P and Gosling RC (2008) The standard penetration test in the UK after Eurocode 7. Amendment to BS1377: Part 9: 1990. *Ground Engineering* **41(11)**, 16–20.

Highways Agency (2011) Manual of contract documents for highway works. (MHCW1). Highways Agency, London.

Institution of Civil Engineers (ICE) (2003) ICE Conditions of Contract for Ground Investigation. Thomas Telford, London.

Institution of Civil Engineers (ICE) (2010) ICE 3009: UK Register of Ground Engineering Professionals. Thomas Telford, London. www.ukrogep.org.uk

International Society for Rock Mechanics (ISRM) (2007) The complete suggested methods for rock characterisation, testing and monitoring: 1974–2006. (Available from ISRM.)

Site Investigation Steering Group (SISG) (2012) *Guidance for Safe Investigation of Potentially Contaminated Land.* ICE Publishing, London.

Standing Committee of Analysts (SCA) (1996) *General Principles of sampling water and associated materials* (second edition). SCA, Rotherham.

Transport Research Laboratories (TRL) TRL447 (Updated) (2005), Sulfate specification for structural backfills (Reid JM, Czerewko MA, Cripps JC). TRL, London.

Further reading

BSI (1980) BS 7022: Geophysical logging of boreholes for hydrogeological purposes. BSI, Milton Keynes.

BSI (2000) BS EN 197-1: Cement. Compositions, specifications and conformity criteria for common cements. BSI, Milton Keynes.

BSI (2002) BS ISO 10381: Soil quality: Sampling. BSI, Milton Keynes.

BSI (2004) BS EN 1997-1: Eurocode 7 – Geotechnical design. Part 1: General rules. BSI, Milton Keynes.

Clark GB (1966) Deformation moduli of rocks. ASTM SP No. 402.

Clarke GB, Allan P, Akbar K and Irvine J (2005) A simple, robust pressuremeter to test glacial till. Proceedings of the 5th International Symposium on Pressuremeter. Paris, France.

Construction Industry Research and Information Association (CIRIA) (1983) CIRIA 25: Site Investigation Manual. (Weltman AJ and Head JA (eds)) CIRIA, London.

Environment Agency (EA) (1997) The physical properties of major aquifers in England and Wales. R&D Publication 8. EA, Rotherham.

Environment Agency (EA) (2001) Piling and penetrative ground improvement methods on land affected by contamination: guidance on pollution prevention. Report NC/99/73. National Groundwater and Contaminated Land Centre. EA, Rotherham.

Environment Agency (EA) (2003) Technical Guidance WM2 Hazardous waste – Interpretation of the definition and classification of hazardous waste. EA, Rotherham.

Environment Agency (EA) (2004) Framework for the Classification of Contaminated Soils as Hazardous Waste. Version 1. EA, Rotherham.

Environment Agency (EA) (2006) Guidance for waste destined for disposal in landfills. Version 2. EA, Rotherham.

Environmental Protection: The Air Quality Limit Values Regulations (2001) SI 2001/2315.

Geological Society Engineering Group (1988) Working Party Report on Engineering Geophysics. *Quarterly Journal of Engineering Geology* **2(1)**, 207–271.

Head KH (1992) *Manual of soil laboratory testing*. Pentech Press, London.

Health and Safety Executive (HSE) (1991) Protection of workers and the general public during the development of contaminated land. Health and Safety: Guidance Booklets 66. HSE, UK.

Mair RJ and Wood DM (1987) *Pressuremeter Testing*. CIRIA, London.

Valentine SJ and Norbury DR (2011) Measurement of total core recovery dealing with core loss and gain. *Quarterly Journal of Engineering Geology and Hydrogeology* **44**, 397–403.

Water, England and Wales: The Water Supply (Water Quality) Regulations (2001) SI 2001/3911 (W.323).

Appendix I: Groundwater standpipes and piezometers

AI.1   Standpipes

1. The installation shall be generally as shown in Drawing AI.1 and described below, with the site-specific requirements being detailed in Schedules S1.16.1, S1.16.2 and S1.16.3 or as instructed by the Investigation Supervisor.

2. The standpipe tubing shall consist of unplasticised polyvinylchloride (uPVC) or high-density polyethylene (HDPE) whose internal diameter is consistent with the specified sampling and/or monitoring requirements.

3. The base of the tubing shall be plugged and the lower section perforated by holes or slots to give an open area of 10–15%. Where specified in Schedule S1.16.3, the slotted section shall be wrapped with a filter fabric.

4. Where the depth of the exploratory hole is greater than the depth to which the filter and tubing are to be installed, then the exploratory hole shall be back-filled with impermeable material (cement/bentonite grout and/or bentonite pellets) up to the base of the filter.

5. If grout is used it shall consist of cement and bentonite in the proportions of 1:1 by weight prepared by thorough mixing with approved equipment and with only sufficient water to form a pumpable mix. The grout shall be placed using a tremie pipe to 1 m below the base of the filter. Sufficient time shall be allowed for the grout to cure (set). When the grout has set, the remaining depth of hole to the level of the base of the filter shall be filled with bentonite pellets to form the lower seal.

6. If water in the exploratory hole becomes contaminated by grout it shall be replaced by clean water, the method being to the approval of the Investigation Supervisor.

7. Where the hole is dry and bentonite pellets are used, sufficient clean water for immediate saturation shall be added concurrently with the bentonite pellets.

8. The filter shall be clean granular material (sand or gravel) and placed in the exploratory hole up to the level of the base of the tubing.

9. The tubing with a centralising device attached within the perforated zone shall be lowered carefully down the exploratory hole to the level of the filter material, and the exploratory hole backfilled to about 1.2 m below ground level with filter material. Bentonite pellets shall be placed on top of the filter to form an upper seal not less than 0.5 m thick. The elevations of the base of the tubing and top and base of the filter shall be recorded.

10. The top of the tubing shall be covered by a plastic cap or similar. The cap shall include an air vent to allow free ingress/egress of air to the top of the standpipe tubing.

11. Arrangements to prevent the ingress of surface water and to protect the top of the tubing shall comprise a suitably sized steel barrel or stopcock cover or as specified in Schedule S1.16.1 or as agreed with the Investigation Supervisor. The protective cover shall be set in concrete and incorporate a gravel drainage layer connected to the air space around the top of the tubing. Protective fencing, where required, shall be in accordance with Schedule S1.16.2.

Drawing AI.1 Schematic drawing of a standpipe installation

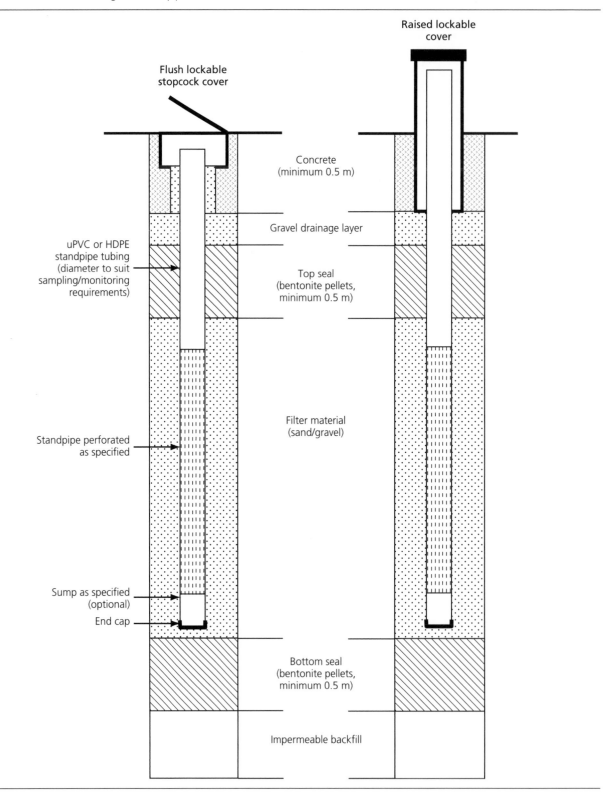

Flush lockable
stopcock cover

Raised lockable
cover

Concrete
(minimum 0.5 m)

Gravel drainage layer

uPVC or HDPE
standpipe tubing
(diameter to suit
sampling/monitoring
requirements)

Top seal
(bentonite pellets,
minimum 0.5 m)

Filter material
(sand/gravel)

Standpipe perforated
as specified

Sump as specified
(optional)

End cap

Bottom seal
(bentonite pellets,
minimum 0.5 m)

Impermeable backfill

AI.2   Standpipe piezometers

1. The installation shall be generally as shown in Drawing AI.2 and described below, with the site-specific requirements being detailed in Schedules S1.16.1, S1.16.2 and S1.16.3 or as instructed by the Investigation Supervisor.

2. The piezometer tip shall consist of a porous ceramic element or slotted pipe with an open area of 10–15% and, if required, wrapped in a filter fabric (all as specified in Schedule S1.16.3).

3. The piezometer tubing shall consist of unplasticised polyvinylchloride (uPVC) or high-density polyethylene (HDPE) whose internal diameter is consistent with the specified sampling and/or monitoring requirements. The tubing shall be supplied and installed in not less than 3 m lengths, except for one shorter length as required to suit the total piezometer depth. The tubing and porous element/slotted section shall be joined by screw thread or screwed couplings.

4. Where the depth of the exploratory hole is greater than the depth to which the filter and tubing are to be installed then the exploratory hole shall be backfilled with impermeable materials (cement/bentonite grout and/or bentonite pellets) to the base of the filter as described in Appendix AI.1 5, 6 and 7.

5. The filter shall be clean granular material (sand or gravel) placed as described in 6, 7 and 8 below.

6. That portion of the filter below the porous element shall be placed first and, if necessitated by the absence of casing, methods such as tremie pipe shall be used to ensure that no filter material adheres to the soil in the sides of an unlined exploratory hole. Where there is water in an exploratory hole, the Contractor shall allow sufficient time for all the sand to settle.

7. The porous element shall be placed in the hole using centralisers to ensure that the vertical axis of the porous element is coincident with the vertical axis of the exploratory hole. The remaining sand filter shall then be added as described in 6 above. The final elevation of the top of the filter shall be recorded.

8. Where the piezometer is to be used for a permeability test the filter material shall be placed in measured equal small quantities. After each addition of filter material, and allowing time for it to settle if placed through water, the depth to its upper surface shall be measured and recorded in order to permit the shape of the filter to be assessed.

9. Bentonite pellets shall be placed on top of the filter to form an upper seal not less than 0.5 m thick. The remainder of the exploratory hole shall be filled with cement/bentonite grout or bentonite pellets to within 0.5 m of ground level.

10. The top of the piezometer tubing shall be covered by a plastic cap or similar. The cap shall include an air vent to allow free ingress/egress of air to the top of the standpipe tubing.

11. Arrangements to prevent the ingress of surface water and to protect the top of the piezometer tubing shall be as described in Appendix AI.1 11.

Drawing AI.2 Schematic drawing of a standpipe piezometer installation

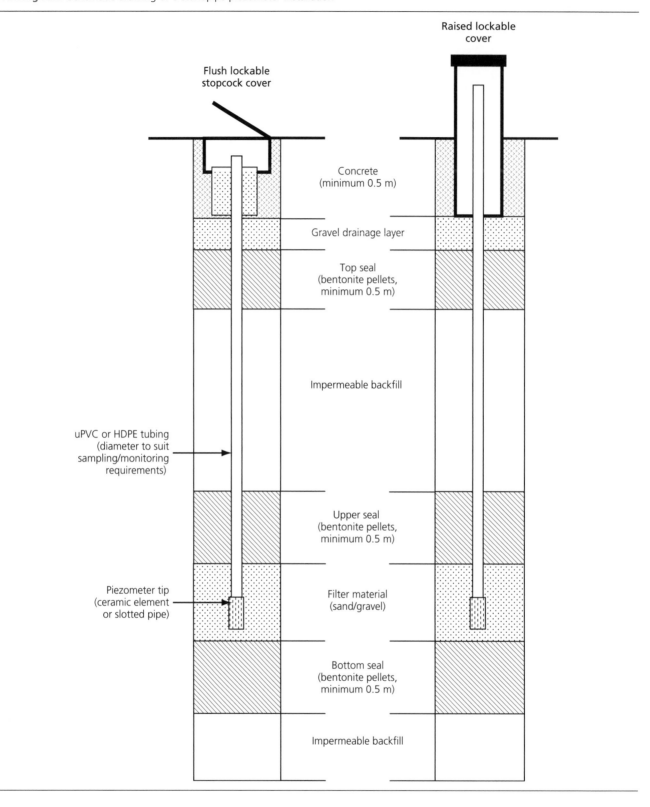

Raised lockable
cover

Flush lockable
stopcock cover

Concrete
(minimum 0.5 m)

Gravel drainage layer

Top seal
(bentonite pellets,
minimum 0.5 m)

Impermeable backfill

uPVC or HDPE tubing
(diameter to suit
sampling/monitoring
requirements)

Upper seal
(bentonite pellets,
minimum 0.5 m)

Piezometer tip
(ceramic element
or slotted pipe)

Filter material
(sand/gravel)

Bottom seal
(bentonite pellets,
minimum 0.5 m)

Impermeable backfill

Appendix II: Ground gas monitoring standpipe

AII.1 Ground gas monitoring standpipe

1. The installation shall be generally as shown in Drawing AII.1 and described below, with the site-specific requirements being detailed in Schedules S1.16.1, S1.16.2 and S1.16.6 or as instructed by the Investigation Supervisor.

2. The tubing shall consist of unplasticised polyvinylchloride (uPVC) or high-density polyethylene (HDPE). HDPE is the preferred material as it is more resistant to attack by aggressive chemicals. Each length of tubing shall be joined by screw thread or threaded couplers. Glue or adhesive shall not be used to join tubing. The base of the tubing shall be plugged and the tubing perforated by holes or slots to give an open area of 10–15%. The depth to the top of the perforated tubing shall be as specified in Schedule S1.16.6 or as instructed by the Investigation Supervisor.

3. The filter shall be clean non-calcareous quartz-based single-sized gravel, 6–10 mm in diameter.

4. Where the depth of the exploratory hole is greater than the depth to which the filter and tubing are to be installed, then the exploratory hole shall be back-filled with impermeable materials (cement/bentonite grout and/or bentonite pellets) to the base of the filter as described in Appendix AI.1 *5, 6* and *7*.

5. The tubing shall be lowered carefully down the exploratory hole to the level of the filter gravel, and the exploratory hole backfilled with filter gravel to the top of the perforated section. Where tubing is required to be installed to a considerable depth, the use of centralising devices should be considered.

6. The top of the tubing shall be covered by a screw-on gas tap, rubber bung or push-on cap with a gas valve as indicated on Drawing AII.1.

7. That part of the borehole above the perforated section shall be backfilled with bentonite pellets placed on top of the filter to form an upper seal not less than 0.5 m thick. Where the hole is dry, sufficient clean water for immediate saturation shall be added concurrently with the bentonite pellets.

8. Arrangements to prevent the ingress of surface water and to protect the top of the piezometer tubing shall be as described in Appendix AI.1 *11*.

Drawing AII.1 Schematic drawing of a ground gas monitoring installation

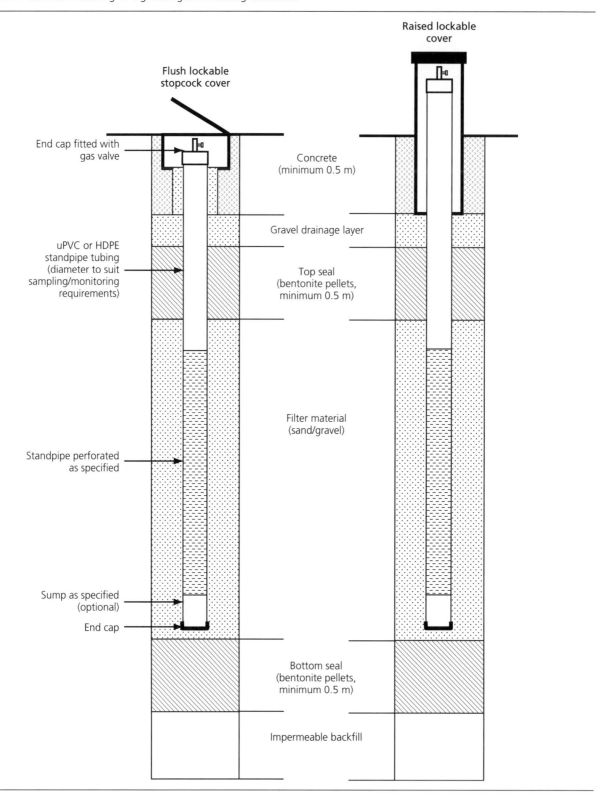

Flush lockable
stopcock cover

Raised lockable
cover

End cap fitted with
gas valve

Concrete
(minimum 0.5 m)

Gravel drainage layer

uPVC or HDPE
standpipe tubing
(diameter to suit
sampling/monitoring
requirements)

Top seal
(bentonite pellets,
minimum 0.5 m)

Filter material
(sand/gravel)

Standpipe perforated
as specified

Sump as specified
(optional)

End cap

Bottom seal
(bentonite pellets,
minimum 0.5 m)

Impermeable backfill

UK Specification for Ground Investigation
ISBN: 978-0-7277-3506-5

Schedules and Notes for Guidance

Specification

The Specification shall be the *UK Specification for ground investigation* published by ICE Publishing, with information, amendments and additions as described in the Schedules.

Schedule 1. Information and site-specific requirements
Schedule 2. Exploratory holes
Schedule 3. Investigation Supervisor's facilities
Schedule 4. Specification amendments
Schedule 5. Specification additions

Notes for Guidance

1. Information and requirements specific to the particular contract are to be inserted in the Schedules. The intention is that all extra information is entered in the Schedules so that the remainder of the Specification may be incorporated unchanged or may be simply referenced.

2. The Schedules should normally be produced in electronic form using the published documents but, if appropriate, may be completed by hand or retyped for presentation purposes. For consistency, Schedule clause numbers should remain unaltered. If there are no particular requirements in a section, the words 'Not required' should be inserted against the section header and the underlying string of Schedules may be omitted. For example, against Percussion Boring enter 'Not required' and delete Schedules S1.9.1– S1.9.3 inclusive.

Schedule 1: Information and site-specific requirements

General comments

Notes for Guidance

1. Schedules S1.1–Sl.7 must be completed for all investigations and preferably Schedule 2, cross-referenced to the drawings. Those parts of the remaining Schedules which are applicable to the specific investigation also need to be completed.

2. Schedules S1.8–S1.21 inclusive should be used to provide information and Specification requirements which are particular to the site-specific investigation. When completing the schedules, reference should be made to the Specification and accompanying Notes for Guidance: the latter which include advice on the information to be included in the Schedules are not generally repeated here.

3. Schedule S2 should list all the planned exploratory holes, together with details of the expected in situ testing and monitoring installations to be installed.

4. Schedule S3 should detail all the facilities/services to be provided by the Contractor for the sole use of the Investigation Supervisor. This Schedule may be omitted if the investigation is let as a Design and Construct with the Contractor carrying out all aspects of the work.

5. Schedules S4 and S5 should be used for amendments and additions to the actual Specification clauses.

S1.1   Name of Contract

A concise and unique name is required for contract and reporting purposes. The name should include the nearest town where possible.

S1.2   Investigation Supervisor

The name, contact details and other relevant information for the Investigation Supervisor should be inserted.

Detailed information needs to be provided here or referenced in the contract amendments in order to clarify/define the role of the Investigation Supervisor in relation to the selected Conditions of Contract.

S1.3   Description of site

The description of the site should include its location (with national grid reference), boundaries, topography, current use, site classification (green, yellow or red), known or expected contamination, any access restrictions (physically difficult access or the need for passes to a restricted entry site) and all other pre-construction information required by CDM (2007).

S1.4 Main works proposed and purpose of this contract

1. A description of the Main Works should be provided including proposed land use, locations and descriptions of proposed groundworks, earthworks, roads and structures together with the type(s) of foundations intended, if known.
2. The text should state whether the investigation comprises a desk study or is a preliminary, main or supplementary intrusive investigation and whether it is for geotechnical, environmental or combined geo-environmental purposes.

S1.5 Scope of investigation

1. A brief outline is required of the work to be done under the contract, stating the type of exploratory holes (boring, drillings, trial pits, probings, etc.). It should also be stated whether sampling and testing (in situ and laboratory) and monitoring during/after completion of fieldwork are required, what monitoring instruments are to be installed and what types of report are to be compiled (desk study, factual, Geotechnical Investigation Report or Geotechnical Design Report).
2. Schedules which are not used for a particular investigation should be listed.
3. Any restrictions on the methods of investigation or their timing due to the presence of protected species of flora or fauna need to be stated.
4. All other general requirements where further schedules are not used in detail.

S1.6 Geology and ground conditions

The following general assessment of the geology of the site and ground conditions has been inferred from available information. No assurance is given to its accuracy.

A summarised description is required of the geology and ground conditions expected to exist based on information obtained from maps and memoirs of the British Geological Survey, other readily accessible publications and records and any previous investigations. Difficult ground or groundwater conditions, mine workings, etc. should also be noted. Where hazardous or contaminated ground is known to exist, full details must be made available.

S1.7 Schedule of drawing(s) and documents

The drawing number, title and scale of each contract drawing should be listed; landowners and tenants may be listed where appropriate. Setting out points, temporary benchmarks (TBMs) and benchmark data should be shown when such data are available and provided. Agreed access points and routes to and from exploratory hole locations should also be shown on the drawings.

Other documents which should be provided include the available information on services and the desk study report if one exists. Reference should also be made to other relevant documents which may be inspected at the Investigation Supervisor/Employer's Office, for example previous site investigations on or immediately adjacent to the site and aerial photographs.

It is recommended that drawings are provided in CAD format.

S1.8 General requirements (Specification Section 3) Particular restrictions/ relaxations

Contract specific restrictions/relaxations, if any, shall be inserted below.

1. Any restrictions on the order of carrying out the work (unnecessary restrictions should not be imposed on the Contractor) or section(s) of the investigation which are to be completed at a particular time or within a particular period need to be stated.
2. Any restrictions on the methods of investigation or their timing due to the presence of protected species of flora or fauna need to be stated.

S1.8.1 Quality management system (Clause 3.3)

S1.8.2 Professional Attendance (Clause 3.5.2)

The provision of any part- or full-time professional attendance needs to be detailed here and appropriate items included in/deleted from the Bill of Quantities.

Reference should be made to Specification Note for Guidance NG 3.5.2 for details of the technical activities comprising Professional Attendance. Any amendments to the activities listed in NG 3.5.2 also need to be detailed in Schedule S1.8.2.

S1.8.3 Provision of ground practitioners and other personnel (Clauses 3.6.1 and 3.6.2)

When known at the time of tender, the requirements for ground practitioners to provide advice or assistance to the Investigation Supervisor during the course of the works or for the preparation of the Ground Investigation Report and/or the Geotechnical Design Report and/or the provision of other personnel to assist in the running of the investigation need to be detailed in Schedule S1.8.3.

**S1.8.4   Hazardous ground, land affected by
contamination and notifiable and
invasive weeds (Clauses 3.7.1 and 3.22)**

Details of notifiable and/or invasive weeds need to be
included in Schedule S1.8.4.

**S1.8.5   Additional information on services not
shown on Contract drawings
(Clause 3.7.2)**

Reference should be made to relevant statutory distances,
or safe distances if these exceed statutory distances, from
any known or suspected services unless included in the
Special Requirements of the Conditions of Contract.

**S1.8.6   Known/suspected mine workings,
mineral extractions, etc. (Clause 3.7.3)**

S1.8.7   Protected species (Clause 3.7.4)

S1.8.8   Archaeological remains (Clause 3.7.5)

S1.8.9   Security of site (Clause 3.11)

**S1.8.10 Traffic management measures
(Clause 3.12)**

All forms of traffic management should be included (not just highways) as well as the required pedestrian safety controls.

S1.8.11 Restricted working hours (Clause 3.13)

S1.8.12 Trainee site operatives (Clause 3.14.1)

**S1.8.13 Contamination avoidance and/or aquifer
protection measures required
(Clauses 3.15.2 and 3.15.3)**

**S1.8.14 Maximum period for boring, pitting or
trenching through hard material, hard
stratum or obstruction
(Clauses 2.8, 4.3 and 6.4)**

S1.8.15 Reinstatement requirements (Clause 3.16)

S1.8.16 Hygiene facilities required (Clauses 2.20 and 3.16.1)

S1.8.17 Unavoidable damage to be reinstated by Contractor (Clause 3.16.1)

S1.8.18 Accuracy of exploratory hole locations (Clauses 3.19 and 3.20)

The required accuracy must be compatible with that of the benchmark and survey reference point information provided to the Contractor.

S1.8.19 Photography requirements (Clause 3.25)

Further particular Contract restrictions/ relaxations shall be entered below, using sequential numbers to those above

Particular requirements and details should be given.

S1.9 Percussion boring (Specification Section 4) Particular restrictions/relaxations

Contract specific restrictions/relaxations, if any, shall be inserted below.

S1.9.1 Permitted methods and restrictions (Clauses 4.1 to 4.4)

Sampling requirements should be detailed under the relevant schedules of S1.12.

S1.9.2 Backfilling (Clause 4.5)

S1.9.3 Dynamic sampling (Clause 4.6)

Further particular Contract restrictions/relaxations shall be entered below, using sequential numbers to those above

Particular requirements and details should be given.

S1.10 Rotary drilling (Specification Section 5) Particular restrictions/ relaxations

Contract specific restrictions/relaxations, if any, shall be inserted below.

S1.10.1 Augering requirements and restrictions (Clauses 5.1)

S1.10.2 Particular rotary drilling techniques (Clause 5.2)

Any requirements for minimum hole or core diameter, drilling/coring methods/equipment and flush medium should be specified in the Schedule.

S1.10.3 Drilling fluid type and collection (Clause 5.3)

S1.10.4 Rotary core drilling equipment and core diameter (Clauses 5.4.1 and 5.4.2)

Core diameter can either be stipulated where experience is available or the Contractor asked to identify the core diameter proposed to be used to achieve the core recovery within the known ground conditions.

S1.10.5 Core logging (Clause 5.4.6)

S1.10.6 Core sub-samples for laboratory testing (Clause 5.4.7)

> Details of the method of taking, preserving and transporting core sub-samples should be specified. These will vary depending on whether the logging and associated sub-sampling is carried out on site or at the Contractor's offices, the type of material, what laboratory tests are required and the delay between sub-sampling and testing.

S1.10.7 Address for delivery of selected cores (Clauses 5.4.8 and 5.4.9)

S1.10.8 Rotary open-hole drilling general requirements (Clause 5.5.1)

S1.10.9 Rotary open-hole drilling for locating mineral seams, mine workings, etc. (Clause 5.5.2)

> A purpose-designed form may be necessary to record the additional information required by the referenced Specification clause, over and above that listed in the daily record under Specification Clause 13.2.

S1.10.10 Open-hole resonance (sonic) drilling (Clause 5.6.1)

**S1.10.11 Resonance (sonic) drilling with sampling
or continuous coring (Clause 5.6.2)**

S1.10.12 Backfilling (Clause 5.7)

**S1.10.13 Core photographic requirements
(Clause 5.8)**

**Further particular Contract restrictions/
relaxations shall be entered below,
using sequential numbers to those above**

Particular requirements and details should be given.

S1.11 Pitting and trenching (Specification Section 6) Particular restrictions/relaxations

Contract specific restrictions/relaxations, if any, shall be inserted below.

S1.11.1 Indirect detection of buried services and inspection pits (Clauses 3.8.3 and 6.1)

If CAT scanning and/or service inspection pits are not required, this should be stated and the accompanying risk assessments made available to the Contractor.

S1.11.2 Restrictions on plant or pitting/trenching methods (Clauses 6.2 and 6.3)

S1.11.3 Entry of personnel (Clause 6.5)

S1.11.4 Alternative pit and trench dimensions (Clause 6.7)

S1.11.5 Abstracted groundwater from land affected by contamination (Clause 6.9.2)

S1.11.6 Backfilling (Clause 6.10)

S1.11.7 Photographic requirements (Clause 6.12)

S1.11.8 Artificial lighting (Clause 6.12.2)

**S1.11.9 Provision of pitting equipment and crew
for Investigation Supervisor's use
(Clause 6.13)**

Schedule S1.11.9 must include details of the depth of pits to
be excavated, any required ground support measures and
whether a ground engineer is required for sampling/
logging.

**Further particular Contract restrictions/
relaxations shall be entered below,
using sequential numbers to those above**

Particular requirements and details should be given.

S1.12 Sampling and monitoring during intrusive investigation (Specification Section 7) Particular restrictions/relaxations

Contract specific restrictions/relaxations, if any, shall be inserted below.

S1.12.1 Address for delivery of selected geotechnical samples (Clause 7.6.1)

S1.12.2 Retention and disposal of geotechnical samples (Clause 7.6.2)

See also NG S1.12.10.

S1.12.3 Frequency of sampling for geotechnical purposes (Clauses 7.6.3–7.6.11)

S1.12.4 Open-tube and piston sample diameters (Clause 7.6.5)

S1.12.5 Retention of cutting shoe samples (Clause 7.6.5)

S1.12.6   Delft and Mostap sampling (Clause 7.6.12)

S1.12.7   Groundwater level measurements during exploratory hole construction (Clause 7.7)

S1.12.8   Special geotechnical sampling (Clause 7.8)

S1.12.9   Address for delivery of selected samples (Clause 7.9.2)

S1.12.10 Retention and disposal of contamination/ WAC samples (Clause 7.9.3)

The different requirements (and therefore cost implications) for storing geotechnical and contamination/WAC test samples should be noted (see Specification Notes for Guidance NG 7.6.2 and NG 7.9.3, the latter being different to the requirements of most Conditions of Contract).

S1.12.11 Frequency of sampling (Clause 7.9.4)

S1.12.12 Sampling method (Clause 7.9.5)

Whether contamination/WAC samples are to be taken by an environmental scientist, etc. or by others working under the supervision or under the direction of the environmental scientist, etc. needs to be defined.

S1.12.13 Headspace testing (Clause 7.9.8)

A purpose-designed form may be necessary to record the additional information required by the referenced Specification clause, over and above that listed in the daily record under Specification Clause 13.2.

Further particular Contract restrictions/relaxations shall be entered below, using sequential numbers to those above

Particular requirements and details should be given.

S1.13 Probing and cone penetration testing (Specification Section 8) Particular restrictions/relaxations

Contract specific restrictions/relaxations, if any, shall be inserted below.

S1.13.1 Type(s) and reporting of dynamic probing (Clauses 8.1.1 and 8.1.2)

S1.13.2 Capacity and equipment requirements for cone penetration testing (Clause 8.2.1)

S1.13.3 Reporting of cone penetration testing parameters (Clause 8.2.4)

A purpose-designed form may be necessary to record the additional information required by the referenced Specification clause, over and above that listed in the daily record under Specification Clause 13.2.

S1.13.4 Seismic cone equipment requirements (Clause 8.3.1)

S1.13.5 Interpretation of seismic cone tests (Clause 8.3.4)

S1.13.6 Other cone or specialist probes (Clause 8.4)

Further particular Contract restrictions/ relaxations shall be entered below, using sequential numbers to those above

Particular requirements and details should be given.

S1.14 Geophysical testing (Specification Section 9) Particular restrictions/ relaxations

Contract specific restrictions/relaxations, if any, shall be inserted below.

S1.14.1 Geophysical survey objectives (Clause 9.1.1)

S1.14.2 Requirement for Ground Specialist geophysicist (Clause 9.1.1)

S1.14.3 Trials of geophysical methods (Clause 9.1.1)

S1.14.4 Types of geophysics required (Clause 9.1.1)

S1.14.5 Information provided (Clause 9.2)

S1.14.6   Horizontal data density (Clause 9.3)

S1.14.7   Level datum (Clause 9.4)

S1.14.8   Geophysical survey report (Clause 9.7)

A purpose-designed form may be necessary to record the additional information required by the referenced Specification clause, over and above that listed in the daily record under Specification Clause 13.2.

Further particular Contract restrictions/ relaxations shall be entered below, using sequential numbers to those above

Particular requirements and details should be given.

S1.15 In situ testing (Specification Section 10) Particular restrictions/ relaxations

Contract specific restrictions/relaxations, if any, shall be inserted below.

S1.15.1 Tests in accordance with British Standards (Clause 10.3)

S1.15.2 Hand penetrometer and hand vane for shear strength (Clause 10.4.1)

S1.15.3 Self-boring pressuremeter and high-pressure dilatometer testing and reporting (Clause 10.5.1)

S1.15.4 Driven or push-in pressuremeter testing and reporting requirements (Clause 10.5.2)

S1.15.5 Menard pressuremeter tests (Clause 10.5.3)

S1.15.6 Soil infiltration test (Clause 10.6)

A purpose-designed form may be necessary to record the additional information required by the referenced Specification clause, over and above that listed in the daily record under Specification Clause 13.2.

S1.15.7 Special in situ testing and reporting requirements (Clause 10.7)

S1.15.8 Interface probes (Clause 10.8)

A purpose-designed form may be necessary to record the additional information required by the referenced Specification clause, over and above that listed in the daily record under Specification Clause 13.2.

S1.15.9 Contamination screening tests (Clause 10.9)

A purpose-designed form may be necessary to record the additional information required by the referenced Specification clause, over and above that listed in the daily record under Specification Clause 13.2.

S1.15.10 Metal detection (Clause 10.10)

Further particular Contract restrictions/ relaxations shall be entered below, using sequential numbers to those above

Particular requirements and details should be given.

S1.16 Instrumentation (Specification Section 11) Particular restrictions/ relaxations

Contract specific restrictions/relaxations, if any, shall be inserted below.

S1.16.1 Protective covers for installations (Clause 11.2)

S1.16.2 Protective fencing (Clause 11.3)

S1.16.3 Standpipe and standpipe piezometer installations (Clauses 11.4.1 and 11.4.2)

S1.16.4 Other piezometer installations (Clause 11.4.3)

S1.16.5 Development of standpipes and standpipe piezometers (Clause 11.4.5)

S1.16.6 Ground gas standpipes (Clause 11.5)

S1.16.7 Inclinometer installations (Clause 11.6)

S1.16.8 Slip indicators (Clause 11.7)

S1.16.9 Extensometers and settlement gauges (Clause 11.8)

Details of required type(s) of extensometers and settlement gauges and proposed installations need to be specified.

S1.16.10 Settlement monuments (Clause 11.9)

Details of required type(s) of settlement monuments and proposed installations need to be specified.

S1.16.11 Removal of installations (Clause 11.10)

S1.16.12 Other instrumentation (Clause 11.11)

Further particular Contract restrictions/ relaxations shall be entered below, using sequential numbers to those above

Particular requirements and details should be given.

S1.17 Installation monitoring and sampling (Specification Section 12) Particular restrictions/relaxations

Contract specific restrictions/relaxations, if any, shall be inserted below.

S1.17.1 Groundwater level readings in installations (Clause 12.2)

S1.17.2 Groundwater sampling from installations (Clause 12.3.1)

S1.17.3 Purging/micro-purging (Clause 12.3.2)

S1.17.4 Ground gas monitoring (Clause 12.4)

S1.17.5 Sampling from ground gas installations (Clause 12.5)

S1.17.6 Other monitoring (Clause 12.8)

S1.17.7 Sampling and testing of surface water bodies (Clause 12.9)

A plan needs to be provided showing the required testing positions.

Further particular Contract restrictions/ relaxations shall be entered below, using sequential numbers to those above

Particular requirements and details should be given.

S1.18 Daily records (Specification Section 13) Particular restrictions/ relaxations

Contract specific restrictions/relaxations, if any, shall be inserted below.

S1.18.1 Information for daily records (Clause 13.1)

S1.18.2 Special in situ tests and instrumentation records (Clause 13.4)

Further particular Contract restrictions/ relaxations shall be entered below, using sequential numbers to those above

Particular requirements and details should be given.

S1.19 Geotechnical laboratory testing (Specification Section 14) Particular restrictions/relaxations

Contract specific restrictions/relaxations, if any, shall be inserted below.

S1.19.1 Investigation Supervisor or Contractor to schedule testing (Clause 14.1.1)

S1.19.2 Tests required (Clause 14.1.2)

S1.19.3 Specifications for tests not covered by BS 1377 and options under BS 1377 (Clauses 14.2.1 and 14.4)

S1.19.4 UKAS accreditation to be adopted (Clause 14.3)

S1.19.5   Rock testing requirements (Clause 14.5)

**S1.19.6   Chemical testing for aggressive ground/
groundwater for concrete (Clause 14.6)
(Test Suites A–D are overleaf)**

The Schedules for test suites A–D allow for the Investigation Supervisor to specify the test methods required or for the Contractor to detail which methods can be offered.

The Schedule should also define whether dependent option tests in Suites C and D are to be carried out in any event or only if the option trigger level are reached. See Specification NG 14.5.

S1.19.7   Laboratory testing on site (Clause 14.7)

S1.19.8   Special laboratory testing (Clause 14.8)

**Further particular Contract restrictions/
relaxations shall be entered below,
using sequential numbers to those above**

Particular requirements and details should be given.

SCHEDULE 1.19.6 (Derived from BRE Special Digest SD1)

CHEMICAL TESTS ON POTENTIALLY AGGRESSIVE GROUND/GROUNDWATER

SUITE A Greenfield site (pyrite absent)			
Sample type	**Determinand**	**Recommended test methods**	**Test method specified/offered**[1]
Soil	pH in 2.5:1 water/soil extract	BR 279 Electrometric	
		BS 1377 Part 3, Method 9	
	SO$_4$ in 2:1 water/soil extract	BR 279 Gravimetric method, cation exchange or ion chromatography	
		BS 1377 Part 3 Method 5.3 + 5.5	
		TRL 447 Test 1	
Groundwater	pH	BR 279 Electrometric	
		BS 1377 Part 3, Method 9	
	SO$_4$	BR 279 Gravimetric method, cation exchange or ion chromatography	
		BS 1377 Part 3 Method 5.4 + 5.5	
		Commercial lab in-house procedure – determination of sulphur by ICP-AES[2]	

SUITE B Greenfield site (pyrite present)			
Soil	pH in 2.5:1 water/soil extract	BR 279 Electrometric	
		BS 1377 Part 3, Method 9	
	SO$_4$ in 2:1 water/soil extract	BR 279 Gravimetric method, cation exchange or ion chromatography	
		BS 1377 Part 3 Method 5.3 + 5.5	
		TRL 447 Test 1	
	Acid soluble SO$_4$	BR 279 Gravimetric method	
		BS 1377 Part 3, Method 5.2 + 5.5	
		TRL 447 Test 2	
	Total sulphur	BR 279 Ignition in oxygen	
		TRL 447 Test 4A	
		TRL 447 Test 4B	
Groundwater	pH	BR 279 Electrometric	
		BS 1377 Part 3, Method 9	
	SO$_4$	BR2 79 Gravimetric method, cation exchange or ion chromatography	
		BS 1377 Part 3 Method 5.4 + 5.5	
		Commercial lab in-house procedure – determination of sulphur by ICP-AES[2]	

[1] **Either** Investigation Supervisor to specify method required **or** Contractor to detail method(s) offered.
[2] ICP-AES: inductively coupled plasma atomic emission spectroscopy.

SCHEDULE 1.19.6 (Derived from BRE Special Digest SD1)

CHEMICAL TESTS ON POTENTIALLY AGGRESSIVE GROUND/GROUNDWATER

SUITE C Brownfield site (pyrite absent)			
Sample type	Determinand	Recommended test methods	Test method specified/offered[1]
Soil	pH in 2.5:1 water/soil extract	BR 279 Electrometric	
		BS 1377 Part 3, Method 9	
	SO_4 in 2:1 water/soil extract	BR 279 Gravimetric method, cation exchange or ion chromatography	
		BS 1377 Part 3 Method 5.3 + 5.5	
		TRL 447 Test 1	
	Mg (only required if water soluble SO_4 >3000 mg/l)	BR 279 AAS[2] method	
		Commercial lab in-house procedure – variant of BR 279 using ISP-AES[3]	
	NO_3 in 2:1 water/soil extract (only required if pH <5.5)	BR 279	
	Cl in 2:1 water/soil extract (only required if pH <5.5)	BR 279	
		BS 1377 Part 3, Method 7.2	
Groundwater	pH	BR 279 Electrometric	
		BS 1377 Part 3, Method 9	
	SO_4	BR 279 Gravimetric method, cation exchange or ion chromatography	
		BS 1377 Part 3 Method 5.4 + 5.5	
		Commercial lab in-house procedure – determination of sulphur by ICP-AES[3]	
	Mg (only required if water soluble SO_4 ⩾3000 mg/l)	BR 279 AAS method[2]	
		Commercial lab in-house procedure – Mg in solution by ICP-AES[3]	
	NO_3 (only required if pH <5.5)	BR 279	
	Cl (only required if pH <5.5)	BR 279	
		BS 1377 Part 3, Method 7.2	

[1] **Either** Investigation Supervisor to specify method required **or** Contractor to indicate method(s) offered.
[2] AAS: atomic absorption spectrometry.
[3] ICP-AES: inductively coupled plasma atomic emission spectroscopy.

SCHEDULE 1.19.6 (Derived from BRE Special Digest SD1)

CHEMICAL TESTS ON POTENTIALLY AGGRESSIVE GROUND/GROUNDWATER

SUITE D Brownfield site (pyrite present)			
Sample type	Determinand	Recommended test methods	Test method specified/offered[1]
Soil	pH in 2.5:1 water/soil extract	BR 279 Electrometric	
		BS 1377 Part 3, Method 9	
	SO_4 in 2:1 water/soil extract	BR 279 Gravimetric method, cation exchange or ion chromatography	
		BS 1377 Part 3 Method 5.3 + 5.5	
		TRL 447 Test 1	
	Acid soluble SO_4	BR 279 Gravimetric method	
		BS 1377 Part 3, Method 5.2 + 5.5	
		TRL 447 Test 2	
	Total sulphur	BR 279 Ignition in oxygen	
		TRL 447 Test 4A	
		TRL 447 Test 4B	
	Mg (only required if water soluble SO_4 >3000 mg/l)	BR 279 AAS[2] method	
		Commercial lab in-house procedure – variant of BR 279 using ISP-AES[3]	
	NO_3 in 2:1 water/soil extract (only required if pH <5.5)	BR 279	
	Cl in 2:1 water/soil extract (only required if pH <5.5)	BR 279	
		BS 1377 Part 3, Method 7.2	
Groundwater	pH	BR 279 Electrometric	
		BS 1377 Part 3, Method 9	
	SO_4	BR 279 Gravimetric method, cation exchange or ion chromatography	
		BS 1377 Part 3 Method 5.4 + 5.5	
		Commercial lab in-house procedure – determination of sulphur by ICP-AES[3]	
	Mg (only required if water soluble SO_4 ≥3000 mg/l)	BR 279 AAS method[2]	
		Commercial lab in-house procedure – Mg in solution by ICP-AES[3]	
	NO_3 (only required if pH <5.5)	BR 279	
	Cl (only required if pH <5.5)	BR 279	
		BS 1377 Part 3, Method 7.2	

[1] **Either** Investigation Supervisor to specify method required **or** Contractor to indicate method(s) offered.
[2] AAS: atomic absorption spectrometry.
[3] ICP-AES: inductively coupled plasma atomic emission spectroscopy.

S1.20 Geoenvironmental laboratory testing (Specification Section 15) Particular restrictions/relaxations

Contract specific restrictions/relaxations, if any, shall be inserted below.

S1.20.1 Investigation Supervisor or Contractor to schedule testing (Clause 15.1)

S1.20.2 Accreditation required (Clause 15.2)

S1.20.3 Chemical testing for contamination (Clause 15.3) (Test Suites E–G are overleaf)

Schedule S1.20.3 should include the details of any nominated testing laboratories which are to be used.

Schedule S1.20.3 should include any required testing turnaround times.

The test suites provided under Schedule S1.20.3 must be reviewed (and amended accordingly) on a site-by-site basis to cover all the determinands of concern identified during the desk study or subsequently obtained information.

The Schedules for Test Suites E–G allow for the Investigation Supervisor to specify the test methods (except testing under MCERTs), limit of detection and accreditation required or for the Contractor to detail what can be offered under each of these categories.

Testing of estuarine and/or marine sediments which are expected to be dredged is likely to require different sample preparation and/or testing methods to enable more accurate limits of detection to be achieved.

SCHEDULE 1.20.3

CHEMICAL LABORATORY TESTING FOR CONTAMINATION

Nominated test laboratory ? _____

Required testing turnaround times ? _____

NB 1. This proforma Schedule MUST be reviewed in the light of site-specific desk study results and amended accordingly to include any additional determinands likely to be required.

2. Limits of detection should reflect the guideline/threshold values against which the test results will be compared.

SUITE E – Soil samples			
Determinand (Procurer to list required determinands)	**Limit of detection** required/offered[1]	**Test method** required/offered[1]	**Accreditation** required/offered[1]
Arsenic			
Boron			
Cadmium			
Chromium (total)			
Copper			
Lead			
Mercury			
Nickel			
Zinc			
pH			
Water soluble sulphate (as SO_4)			
Organic matter			
Total petroleum hydrocarbons			
Speciated polyaromatic hydrocarbons (USEPA 16)			
Phenol			
Cyanide (total)			
Asbestos			

[1] **Either** Investigation Supervisor to specify the test method (except testing under MCERTs), limit of detection and accreditation required **or** Contractor to detail what can be offered under each of these categories. See also Specification Note for Guidance 15.3.

SCHEDULE 1.20.3

CHEMICAL LABORATORY TESTING FOR CONTAMINATION

Nominated test laboratory ? _____

Required testing turnaround Times ? _____

NB 1. This proforma Schedule MUST be reviewed in the light of site-specific desk study results and amended accordingly to include any additional determinands likely to be required.

2. Limits of detection should reflect the guideline/threshold values against which the test results will be compared.

SUITE F – Water samples			
Determinand (Procurer to list required determinands)	**Limit of detection required/offered[1]**	**Test method required/offered[1]**	**Accreditation required/offered[1]**
Arsenic			
Boron			
Cadmium			
Chromium (total)			
Copper			
Lead			
Mercury			
Nickel			
Zinc			
pH			
Sulphate (as SO$_4$)			
Total petroleum hydrocarbons			
Speciated polyaromatic hydrocarbons (USEPA 16)			
Phenol			
Cyanide (total)			

[1] **Either** Investigation Supervisor to specify the test method, limit of detection and accreditation required **or** Contractor to detail what can be offered under each of these categories. See also Specification Note for Guidance 15.3.

SCHEDULE 1.20.3

CHEMICAL LABORATORY TESTING FOR CONTAMINATION

Nominated test laboratory ? _____

Required testing turnaround Times ? _____

NB 1. This proforma Schedule MUST be reviewed in the light of site-specific desk study results and amended accordingly to include any additional determinands likely to be required.

2. Limits of detection should reflect the guideline/threshold values against which the test results will be compared.

SUITE G – Ground gas samples			
Determinand (Procurer to list required determinands)	**Limit of detection required/offered[1]**	**Test method required/offered[1]**	**Accreditation required/offered[1]**
Oxygen			
Nitrogen			
Carbon dioxide			
Carbon monoxide			
Hydrogen			
Hydrogen sulphide			
Methane			
Ethane			
Propane			
Butane			
Iso-butane			

[1] **Either** Investigation Supervisor to specify the test method, limit of detection and accreditation required **or** Contractor to detail what can be offered under each of these categories. See also Specification Note for Guidance 15.3.

S1.20.4 Waste characterisation (Clause 15.4)

**S1.20.5 Waste Acceptance Criteria testing
(Clause 15.5)
(Test Suites H–J are overleaf)**

The Schedules for Test Suites H–J allow for the Investigation Supervisor to specify the test methods, limit of detection and accreditation required or for the Contractor to detail what can be offered under each of these categories.

S1.20.6 Laboratory testing (Clause 15.6)

S1.20.7 Special laboratory testing (Clause 15.7)

**Further particular Contract restrictions/
relaxations shall be entered below,
using sequential numbers to those above**

Particular requirements and details should be given.

SCHEDULE 1.20.5

CHEMICAL TESTING FOR WASTE ACCEPTANCE CRITERIA TESTING (from STWAPs 2003)

SUITE H – Inert waste landfill			
Determinand	**Limit of detection required/offered**[1]	**Test method required/offered**[1]	**Accreditation required/offered**[1]
Soil analyses			
Total organic carbon			
BTEX			
PCBs (7 congeners)			
Mineral oil (C_{10}–C_{40})			
PAHs			
Leachate analyses			
Arsenic			
Barium			
Cadmium			
Chromium (total)			
Copper			
Mercury			
Molybdenum			
Nickel			
Lead			
Antimony			
Selenium			
Zinc			
Chloride			
Fluoride			
Sulphate (as SO_4)			
Total dissolved solids			
Phenol Index			
Dissolved organic carbon at own pH or pH 7.5–8.0			

[1] **Either** Investigation Supervisor to specify the test method, limit of detection and accreditation required **or** Contractor to detail what can be offered under each of these categories. See also Specification Note for Guidance 15.5.

SCHEDULE 1.20.5

CHEMICAL TESTING FOR WASTE ACCEPTANCE CRITERIA TESTING (from STWAPs 2003)

SUITE I – Stable non-reactive hazardous waste in non-hazardous landfill			
Determinand	**Limit of detection required/offered**[1]	**Test method required/offered**[1]	**Accreditation required/offered**[1]
Soil analyses			
Total organic carbon			
pH			
Leachate analyses			
Arsenic			
Barium			
Cadmium			
Chromium (total)			
Copper			
Mercury			
Molybdenum			
Nickel			
Lead			
Antimony			
Selenium			
Zinc			
Chloride			
Fluoride			
Sulphate (as SO_4)			
Total dissolved solids			
Phenol Index			
Dissolved organic carbon			

[1]**Either** Investigation Supervisor to specify the test method, limit of detection and accreditation required **or** Contractor to detail what can be offered under each of these categories. See also Specification Note for Guidance 15.5.

SCHEDULE 1.20.5

CHEMICAL TESTING FOR WASTE ACCEPTANCE CRITERIA TESTING (from STWAPs 2003)

SUITE J – Hazardous waste landfill			
Determinand	**Limit of detection required/offered**[1]	**Test method required/offered**[1]	**Accreditation required/offered**[1]
Soil analyses			
Total organic carbon			
Loss on ignition			
Leachate analyses			
Arsenic			
Barium			
Cadmium			
Chromium (total)			
Copper			
Mercury			
Molybdenum			
Nickel			
Lead			
Antimony			
Selenium			
Zinc			
Chloride			
Fluoride			
Sulphate (as SO_4)			
Total dissolved solids			
Phenol Index			
Dissolved organic carbon			

[1] **Either** Investigation Supervisor to specify the test method, limit of detection and accreditation required **or** Contractor to detail what can be offered under each of these categories. See also Specification Note for Guidance 15.5.

S1.21 Reporting (Specification Section 16) Particular restrictions/relaxations

Contract specific restrictions/relaxations, if any, shall be inserted below.

S1.21.1 Form of exploratory hole logs (Clauses 16.1 and 16.2.1)

S1.21.2 Information on exploratory hole logs (Clause 16.2.2)

The Schedule should state whether fracture index or fracture spacing is to be used on the log and whether soil classification is required.

S1.21.3 Variations to final digital data supply requirements (Clause 16.5.1)

S1.21.4 Preliminary digital data (Clause 16.5.3)

S1.21.5 Type(s) of report required (Clause 16.6)

**S1.21.6 Electronic report requirements
(Clause 16.6.3)**

**S1.21.7 Format and contents of Desk Study
Report (Clause 16.7)**

**S1.21.8 Contents of Ground Investigation Report
(or specified part thereof) (Clause 16.8)**

Schedule S1.21.8 must fully detail what elements of the Ground Investigation Report are to be compiled by the Contractor.

**S1.21.9 Contents of Geotechnical Design Report
(or specified part thereof) (Clause 16.9)**

Schedule S1.21.9 must fully detail any elements of the Geotechnical Design Report which are to be compiled by the Contractor.

**S1.21.10 Times for supply of electronic information
(Clause 16.10.1)**

**S1.21.11 Electronic information transmission
media (Clause 16.10.2)**

S1.21.12 Report approval (Clause 16.11)

The number of copies of draft and final reports needs to be defined.

Report approval times need to be compatible with those specified in the Appendix to the Form of Tender.

Further particular Contract restrictions/ relaxations shall be entered below, using sequential numbers to those above

Particular requirements and details should be given.

Schedule 2: Exploratory holes

S2.1   Hole number

Notes for Guidance

This is a unique identification for each hole. If a suffix or prefix is used, there should be no space between letters and numbers to assist with digital data, for example BH62 or TP49A. Each type of exploratory hole should have a unique number series, for example boreholes 1 onwards, trial pits 100 onwards, cone penetration tests 200 onwards, etc. The type shall preferably use AGS format type codes for the exploratory hole.

It is also recommended that, where there have been previous investigations on the site, entirely separate exploratory hole numbering sequences are used for the proposed investigation.

S2.2   Type

Reference to the type of hole should be given if not covered by the hole number.

S2.3   Scheduled depth

This is the depth anticipated, but it is subject to variation depending on the ground conditions encountered. Note that under most Conditions of Contract the Contractor may vary the depth under certain circumstances. The required depth of investigation is also heavily dependent on the anticipated type of foundation, for example a piled foundation will require a much greater depth of investigation than a shallow founded structure. See also Annex B3 of EC7 Part 2.

S2.4   National grid reference

A provisional national grid reference should be given where possible, in advance of exploration, for setting-out purposes.

S2.5   Approximate ground level

The approximate ground level may be determined from Ordnance Survey contour maps for tabulation prior to surveying for level.

S2.6   Remarks

Where known in advance, an indication should be given of any in situ tests or instrument installations, for example pressuremeter tests, standpipe piezometer installations for water and/or gas, specialist sampling for laboratory tests, etc., together with any further controlling detail, for example depths and spacings of tests.

Hole number	Type	Scheduled depth (m)	National grid reference		Approximate ground level (mOD)	Remarks
			Easting (m)	Northing (m)		

Schedule 3: Investigation Supervisor's facilities

S3.1   Accommodation

Notes for Guidance

The accommodation requirements will vary depending on the size and duration of the Contract and the number of the Investigation Supervisor's staff involved.

S3.2   Furnishings

S3.3   Services

The need for steady current electricity may relate to the use of on-site computers. Portable telephones are likely to be necessary on larger sites and where fixed lines are not available. Cleaning of the office should be included and other facilities such as copiers, paper supply, etc.

S3.4   Equipment

The Investigation Supervisor may require equipment such as tapes, penetrometer, hand vane, hand probing equipment, computer hardware and software, etc. Details should be given, and also the period for which it is required. If on-site computer equipment is required, the robustness of such equipment in dusty site conditions should be considered.

S3.5   Transport

If vehicles are required for the Investigation Supervisor's use, the number and type should be specified. The following example clause illustrates factors to be specified.

The Contractor shall provide (number) plain-coloured (vehicle type) transport for the exclusive use of the Investigation Supervisor for any purpose in connection with the site operations. The vehicles shall be delivered and maintained in good roadworthy condition. They shall be licensed and insured for use on the public highway and shall have comprehensive insurance cover for any qualified driver over 21 years of age authorised by the Investigation Supervisor, together with any authorised passengers and the carriage of goods or samples. The Contractor shall provide fuel, oil and maintenance in conformity with the vehicle manufacturer's recommendation and shall clean the vehicles inside and outside as required. A suitable replacement shall be provided for any vehicle out of service for more than 24 hours.

S3.6 Personal Protective Equipment for Investigation Supervisor

Essential clothing should be listed, bearing in mind the possibility of working in contaminated ground. If clothing is to be retained by the Investigation Supervisor this should be stated.

It should be noted, however, that current practice is for essential PPE to be provided by the Investigation Supervisor's Employer.

Schedule 4: Specification amendments

Notes for Guidance

Clauses which do not apply to the required work are covered by Clause 3.1 and should not be deleted.

Where an applicable clause contains an inappropriate word or phrase this may be amended, for example 'Clause 2.9 Line 3 delete x insert y'. If much of the clause is inappropriate, the entire clause may be deleted and replaced, for example, by 'Delete Clause 2.9 and insert new Clause 2.9A' with the new clause wording inserted in column 4.

The following clauses are amended			
Section number	**Clause number**	**Delete the following**	**Substitute the following**

Schedule 5: Specification additions

Notes for Guidance

Where a required activity or condition is not covered by a Specification clause, an additional clause may be added at the end of the relevant section or as a sub-clause if a related topic exists, for example 'add Clause 3.16.5 Crazy Paving...'.

Details of special sampling, in situ testing and laboratory testing may be given clause numbers relating to the relevant section. If the addition is extensive or does not relate to an existing section, a new section or an additional Appendix may be added.

The following clauses are added to the Specification		
Section number	**Clause number**	**Clause wording**

UK Specification for Ground Investigation
ISBN: 978-0-7277-3506-5

doi: 10.1680/uksgi.35065.135

Annex 1 Bill of Quantities for Ground Investigation

Preamble

1.

In this Bill of Quantities the sub-headings and item descriptions identify the work covered by the respective items. The exact nature and extent of the work to be performed shall be ascertained by reference to the Conditions of Contract, the Specification and the Schedules and Appendices to the Specification, as appropriate. The rates and prices entered in the Bill of Quantities shall be deemed to be the full inclusive value of the work covered by the several items, including the following unless stated otherwise:

(a) Contract management and superintendence, labour and all costs in connection therewith
(b) the supply of materials, goods, storage, facilities and services and all costs in connection therewith, including wastage and delivery to site
(c) plant and all costs in connection therewith
(d) fixing, erecting and installing or placing of materials and goods in position
(e) all temporary works
(f) all general obligations, requirements, liabilities and risks involved in the execution of the investigation as set forth or implied in the documents on which the tender is based
(g) establishment charges, overheads and profit
(h) bringing plant and sampling, in situ testing and monitoring equipment to the site of each exploratory hole, erecting, dismantling and removing on completion
(i) on completion, removal of all equipment and services from site and disposal of arisings.

Notes for Guidance

1. The Bill of Quantities is presented as a comprehensive list of items which are conveniently correlated to the Specification items.
2. It is intended that the numbering of items will remain unaltered. Additional items may be added to correspond with contract-specific Specification requirements. If necessary, a subsidiary numbering system may be introduced where this extends an existing item (for example B2.1 Extra over Item Bl for moving over a distance exceeding 500 m – nr). Otherwise, any contract-specific additional items should be detailed in the space provided at the end of each Bill.
3. Work items should have required quantities inserted. Items against which no quantities are entered shall be deemed not to be required. If lump-sum items are not required, this should be stated against the item in the Bill of Quantities. Provisional sums should be inserted as required to cover items not detailed in the Specification and Bill of Quantities and which are to be charged by the Contractor as agreed with the Investigation Supervisor. Provisional sums should normally be entered by the Investigation Supervisor but alternatively by the Contractor in a 'design and investigate' form of contract.
4. The use of 'rate only' items is discouraged. Where there is a reasonable probability that an item will be required, a realistic assessment of the quantity should be made and entered in the Bill of Quantities. However, the nature of ground investigation is such that some modifications and/or additions to the work content may be identified as the investigation proceeds.

5. The Bill of Quantities should be prepared in electronic form using the published documents. There is also an option to re-draft and omit items not required, but preferably retaining the same item numbering system to reduce cross-referencing errors. Where a series of items is to be omitted, for example drilling without cores (Items C21–C33 inclusive), this may be done by first entering the words 'Not required' in the header/subheader line under the Quantity column and then deleting the individual lines for Items C21–C33 inclusive.

6. Any apparent conflict between the Bill of Quantities and other contract documentation should be clarified with the Investigation Supervisor during the tender period.

7. The preamble supplements the Specification to define general and particular activities to be included in the rates. Additional numbered preambles may be included as necessary at the end of the Preambles.

2.

Unless identified as Not required, all items in section A of the Bill of Quantities (general items, provisional services and additional items), and also all items in subsequent sections against which quantities are entered shall be priced.

The rate entered for Item A2 does not include for setting up at the first exploratory hole location.

3.

If lump-sum items are not required by the Contractor, this shall be stated against the rate item in the Bill of Quantities and £0.00 entered in the amount. Where rates are not priced they shall have £0.00 placed against them and £0.00 entered in the amount.

4.

When full- or part-time professional attendance on site is required in accordance with Clause 3.5.2, this shall normally be paid for under Item A7 of the Bill of Quantities.

Unless otherwise detailed in Schedule S1.8.2, the on-site professional attendance services provided by the technical staff shall comprise the technical supervision of site activities, site liaison, logistics, logging, in situ testing and sampling, photography and the preparation of daily records and preliminary logs (except where any of the above activities are carried out by site operatives and boring/drilling operatives).

When individuals are not carrying out their specific duties or are otherwise away from site, then daily rates will not apply and these costs will be deemed to be covered under general items.

If it is deemed appropriate and site supervision or other professional attendances are required but are to be included in the general rates, then this should be stated in Schedule S1.8.2, Preamble Item 1 adjusted accordingly and Item A7 shown as 'Not required'.

Work on highways, waterways and railways, etc. may require additional professional safety staff. These individuals must either be provided by the Employer or provision included in the Bill of Quantities either under Item A7, further subdivided for each individual, or Appendix A, subject to the understanding of need at the time of preparation of the job-specific documentation.

5.

The rate entered under Item A3 shall include for the provision of any additional PPE, ground surface protection measures, additional welfare and hygiene facilities and plant and equipment decontamination facilities required as a direct result of the contamination or hazard(s) detailed in Schedule S1.8.4 and/or S1.8.6.

6.

The item for photographs shall allow for the standing time of associated plant and supply of negatives, enprints and bound volume or electronic equivalents.

7.

Rates for moving plant and equipment to the site of each exploratory hole shall allow for the formation of access routes and working areas and making good avoidable damage to access routes and working areas on completion as required by the Contract.

Agreed access points and routes should be defined on the Drawing(s) at the time of tender.

Any access difficulties, including restrictions where passes are required, should be detailed in the description of the site in Schedule S1.3.

Unavoidable damage should normally be accommodated as a direct compensation payment by the Employer to land owners/occupiers.

Damage to land or property in the vicinity of the exploratory hole and on access routes in excess of that which is unavoidable should be made good at the Contractor's expense.

8.

The rates for moving rotary drilling plant to the site of each hole shall include for setting up over a previously formed borehole, including for any additional costs arising from pulling casings left in the ground or providing temporary casings.

Unless the requirement of rotary drilling is that all holes are a 'follow on', a separate item shall usually be entered in the Bill of Quantities for setting up over a previously formed borehole.

It is often preferable to undertake a separate rotary hole and allow for extra meterage for drillholes to be undertaken alongside the previously formed borehole.

9.

Payment for forming exploratory holes shall be based on:

(a) full thickness of strata investigated and described in accordance with the Specification
(b) depths measured from ground level
(c) depth measured from original ground level where an inspection pit has been excavated
(d) that part of a drillhole below the bottom of a borehole where a drill hole has been ordered to continue from the bottom of a borehole
(e) core recovery of at least 90% in any core run, unless the Investigation Supervisor is satisfied it cannot be achieved
(f) volume calculated as measured length times measured depth times specified width for trial and observation trenches.

10.

Rates for forming exploratory holes shall allow for:

(a) temporary casing installation, where necessary, and removal
(b) dealing with surface water
(c) backfilling with arisings
(d) taking information and supply of daily record for works carried by site operatives
(e) additional site supervision of non-qualified operatives.

Damage to land or property in the vicinity of the exploratory hole and on access routes in excess of that which is unavoidable should be made good at the Contractor's expense.

Compensation to land owners/occupiers for unavoidable damage should be provided by the Employer.

Backfilling with arisings should include for any required topping-up of the backfill during the fieldwork and maintenance periods.

11.

Rates for aquifer protection measures shall allow for the measures detailed in Schedule S1.8.13.

Where both aquifer protection measures and cross-contamination measures at a single soil boundary or more than one set of aquifer measures are required in a single hole, additional bill items may be required.

12.

Standing time shall be measured as the duration of time for which plant, equipment and personnel are standing on the instruction of the Investigation Supervisor or in accordance with the Specification.

Standing time shall be paid for interruption of the formation of exploratory holes to record groundwater entry in accordance with Clause 7.7. The rates for standing time shall include for:

(a) plant equipment and personnel
(b) consequential costs
(c) changes in the programme of working
(d) recording information and preparing daily record.

13.

The rates for daily provision of dynamic sampling and probing, hand augering and pitting and trenching crews and equipment at locations as directed by the Investigation Supervisor shall allow for compliance with the requirements of the Contract, including preparation of records (unless the Investigation Supervisor takes responsibility for the logging and preparation of records).

The rates for dynamic sampling Items B15–B17 and B19 shall include for the provision of liners.

Dynamic probing/sampling and hand augering can be carried out without the full-time presence of a ground practitioner. Conversely, trial pitting/trenching would normally require the full-time presence of a ground practitioner for sampling and logging purposes. This may not be the case when the pitting/trenching is being directed by the Investigation Supervisor; the Supervisor may opt to perform the sampling and logging tasks and should then also prepare the records.

A clear definition of what needs to be included in the provision of these services to work under the instructions of the Investigation Supervisor is therefore essential, in particular, whether a ground practitioner for sampling/logging is required as part of the field crew but charged for under Item A7. The requirements may vary on a site-specific basis and must therefore be clearly defined in Schedule S1.11.9.

14.

The rates for sampling shall allow for the standing time of associated plant. The rates for sampling shall also include for the costs of the sample containers and transport and storage of the samples up to the specified time limits.

The rate for taking a U100 or UT100 sample does not include for recovery of a sample from the cutting shoe.

The rates for each of Items E14.1–E15.3 shall include for all necessary containers and collected samples for an individual determination of the specified contamination or WAC suite.

15.

The rates for in situ testing shall allow for the standing time of associated plant and for interpretation and presentation of the results on preliminary logs/exploratory hole logs or on separate agreed report forms using the same dates of presentation as the exploratory hole to which they refer.

In the case of the self-boring pressuremeter, high-pressure dilatometer or Menard pressuremeter, the rates shall also allow for the mutual standing of the respective boring/drilling plant and specialist testing equipment and crews during the combined process.

Where in situ testing is paid for on an hourly basis, the time measured shall be the actual time taken to carry out the test in accordance with the Investigation Supervisor's instruction and/or the Specification but excluding the time taken to erect and dismantle test equipment where this is itemised separately.

The rate for carrying out an SPT (whether using a split spoon or solid cone) does not include for recovery of an associated sample.

16.

The rates for cone penetration tests Items F15 and F21 shall allow for provision of daily records and for interpretation and presentation of the results on agreed report forms/exploratory hole logs in accordance with BS 1377 and Schedules 1.13.3 or 1.13.4.

For the seismic cone, the recorded and presented data shall include the specified CPT data recorded between seismic test depths.

The rates for dynamic probing shall allow for undertaking and reporting torque measurements at the prescribed vertical intervals.

17.

The rates for installation of instruments shall allow for:

(a) clearing and keeping the hole free of unwanted materials
(b) all costs associated with equipment, installation, specified seals, surround and backfill materials excluding backfill below the instrument
(c) proving correct functioning
(d) delays due to installations, including the setting time for grout
(e) recording information and preparing daily record and additional reports.

18.

The rates for monitoring and sampling of installations during the fieldwork period shall allow for:

(a) purging and dealing with disposal of recovered water
(b) all costs associated with consumables and provision of data recording equipment to site
(c) proving correct calibration and recalibration
(d) recording information, preparing, updating and submitting additional reports successively and at the completion of monitoring, including notification of any unexpected readings and/or variation in readings
(e) delays due to interruptions of other site activities.

The rates for monitoring and sampling of installations during the post-fieldwork period shall allow for:

(a) items (a)–(d) above
(b) all costs associated with remobilising the appropriate (number and experience) staff to site and all travelling and accommodation expenses.

Item (b) may be omitted if these costs are recovered as a per day or per visit item or alternatively under Appendix A.

The rates for recording of water level, ground gas or other monitoring measurements shall allow for notices of re-entry to the Investigation Supervisor, owners or occupiers affected by the location or access route.

19.

The rates for laboratory testing shall include for:

(a) the supply of a copy of the preliminary test results to the Investigation Supervisor
(b) notification of unavailable test samples, failed tests and/or deviating samples (e.g. samples not correctly preserved)
(c) the cost of determining a parameter (e.g. moisture content or density) where that parameter forms part of the information to be reported for the specified test (e.g. undrained shear strength, consolidation test or unconfined compressive strength)
(d) the disposal of samples in accordance with the relevant regulations.

20.

The provisional sum, Item A6, for the off-site disposal of contaminated waste shall include for temporary storage and for organising the transport and disposal by a suitably licenced waste disposal contractor. Payment shall be made only against receipted invoices.

The costs of laboratory testing to determine the nature of the waste shall be covered by laboratory testing rates for tests actually completed and to an agreed schedule. Those sums shall be offset against the Provisional sum Item A6.

Prior to laboratory test results becoming available, the cost of disposing of arisings cannot be accurately estimated and it is recommended that a Provisional Sum is included in the Bill of Quantities, the monetary value being assessed using the results of the site-specific desk study.

The costs of temporary on-site storage of contaminated waste can be significant.

21.

Appendix A to the Bill of Quantities (Rates for Ground Practitioners and other Personnel) shall be priced. The rates given will be used by the Investigation Supervisor to make an initial estimate of costs, where applicable, of employing the Contractor's staff in accordance with Clauses 3.5.2, 3.6.1 and/or 3.6.2 of the Specification.

It is recommended that Appendix A is included in all contracts to provide a tendered basis for works in accordance with Clauses 3.5.2, 3.6.1 and/or 3.6.2 that may be required by the Investigation Supervisor or Employer during the course of the contract.

If not required, the words 'Not required' should be entered and the respective items in the Appendix deleted.

22.

Items for the supply of the master and copies of the Desk Study Report, Ground Investigation Report and/or Geotechnical Design Report shall include for the printing and supply of the specified number of draft and final copies (Specification Clause 16.11 and Schedule S1.21.12). All other duties in compiling, preparing and checking the draft and final reports shall normally be paid for either under Item A7 of the Bill of Quantities or using the rates given under Appendix A.

In respect of the costs of compilation, preparation and checking of reports, Bill of Quantities Item A7 is only likely to be suitable when the reporting requirements can be fully detailed in Schedule S1.8.3 at the time of tender. If the requirements cannot be fully detailed at that time, it will be more appropriate for payment to be based on the rates given under Appendix A.

If the costs of compilation, preparation and checking of the draft and final reports are to be included in the general rates, then this should be stated in Schedule S1.21.12 and Preamble Item 1 adjusted accordingly.

23.   Units of measurement

The following abbreviations shall be used for the units of measurements

Millimetres: mm
Metre: m
Kilometre: km
Square millimetres: mm^2
Square metre: m^2
Cubic metre: m^3
Square metre per day: m^2/day
Linear metre: lin.m
Kilogramme: kg
Tonne: t
Sum: sum
Number: nr
Hour: h
Week: wk
Vehicle week: v.wk
Item: item
Day: day
Specimen day: sp.day
Person day: p.day

Preamble amendments and additions shall be entered below, using sequential numbers to those above

The following clauses are amended or added to the Preamble.

Bill of Quantities

The following pages constitute the Bill of Quantities.

Bill of Quantities Section A: General items, provisional services and additional items – Notes for Guidance

Items A2–A5 may be subdivided where the investigation requires the involvement of several separate Contractors or it is preferable to separately itemise different investigatory techniques.

The same approach of subdividing Items A2–A5 can be used where a site includes both Yellow and Red Category areas, for example Items A2–A5 can be retained for Yellow areas and A2.1–A5.1 for the Red areas. However, a Red Categorisation may well require additional items to be included in other Bills, for example those for percussion boring, rotary drilling, sampling, etc. to cover for the additional costs arising from the Red Categorisation.

If the whole of a site is a Red Catgeory, the same subdivisions as suggested above can be used but with Items A2–A5 (Yellow Category) shown as 'Not required'.

Depending on the nature of a Red Category site it may be necessary to include further additional items such as off-site monitoring and health motoring of site personnel: items could be numbered A5.2, A5.3, etc.

Item A6 does not include for laboratory testing to determine the nature of the contaminated arisings. The required testing should be covered by relevant rates under Bill L. It is recommended that a provisional sum is always included under Item A6 and rates under Bill L are obtained in order to cover for unforeseen contamination not revealed by the desk study.

Subject to the following notes, Item A7 enables full identification of professional staff which the Contractor is required to provide.

Items A7.1–A7.6 are primarily intended for detailing the requirements for Professional Attendance in accordance with Specification Clause 3.5.2. Each of the items may be subdivided where different disciplines of ground practitioners or specific duties for those personnel are required. An estimate of the appropriate number of person days should be entered under Quantity against each grade of practitioner.

Items A7.1–A7.6 may also be used to detail the requirements for ground practitioners and other personnel for work in accordance with Specification Clauses 3.6.1 and 3.6.2, provided that the extent of the work can be defined at the time of tender. However, it may be necessary to add additional items in order to adequately describe the categories of other personnel, for example traffic safety officer, archaeologist, etc. and the grade of person required.

Where the provision of staff for work in accordance with Specification Clauses 3.5.2, 3.6.1 and 3.6.2 cannot be adequately specified at tender, Appendix A can be used to obtain the Contractor's rates for selected disciplines and/or grades of staff. Appendix A can then be used as the charge basis for employing the Contractor's staff as and when required.

Item A7 may also be used to cover daily rate costs for the provision of the Investigation Supervisor (and any required assistants) when provided from the Contractor's staff.

Item A16 may be revised to 'sum' if the traffic safety and management requirements are simple and can be fully defined in Schedule S1.8.10. In many cases it will be appropriate to add additional items (A16.1, A16.2, etc.) to cover for the provision and maintainance of the measures. In any event, Schedule S1.8.8 should provide the maximum possible detail of the required traffic management measures.

In connection with Items A19–A24, Schedules S1.21.8 and S1.21.9 should specify the required parts of the Ground Investigation Report and Geotechnical Design Report, respectively. In respect of the former, frequently the Contractor may only be required to provide a factual report.

Bill of Quantities

Bill A   General items, provisional services and additional items

Number	Item description	Unit	Quantity	Rate	Amount £
A	**General items, provisional services and additional items**				
A1	Offices and stores for the Contractor	sum			
A2	Establish on site all plant, equipment and services for a Green Category site	sum			
A3	Extra over Item A2 for a Yellow Category site	sum			
A4	Maintain on site all site safety equipment for a Yellow Category site	week			
A5	Decontamination of equipment during and at end of intrusive investigation for a Yellow Category site	sum			
A6	Appropriate storage, transport and off-site disposal of contaminated arisings and any PPE equipment, excluding laboratory testing	provisional sum			
A7	Provide professional attendance in accordance with Clause 3.5.2				
A7.1	Provide Technician	p.day			
A7.2	Provide graduate ground engineer	p.day			
A7.3	Provide Experienced Ground Engineer	p.day			
A7.4	Provide Registered Ground Engineering Professional	p.day			
A7.5	Provide Registered Ground Engineering Specialist	p.day			
A7.6	Provide Registered Ground Engineering Advisor	p.day			
A8	Establish the location and elevation of the ground at each exploratory hole	sum			
A9	Preparation of Health and Safety documentation and Safety Risk Assessment	sum			
A10	Facilities for the Investigation Supervisor	sum			
A11	Vehicle(s) for the Investigation Supervisor	v.wk			
A12	Fuel for vehicle for the Investigation Supervisor	provisional sum			
A13	Investigation Supervisor's telephone and facsimile charges	provisional sum			
A14	Deliver selected cores and samples to the specified address	provisional sum			
A15	Special testing and sampling required by Investigation Supervisor	provisional sum			
A16	Traffic safety and management	provisional sum			
A17	One master copy of the Desk Study Report	sum			
A18	Additional copies of the Desk Study Report	nr			
A19	One master copy of the Ground Investigation Report (or specified part thereof)	sum			
A20	Additional copies of the Ground Investigation Report (or specified part thereof)	nr			
A21	Electronic copy of Ground Investigation Report (or specified part thereof)	sum			
A22	One master copy of the Geotechnical Design Report (or specified part thereof)	sum			

Number	Item description	Unit	Quantity	Rate	Amount £
A23	Additional copies of the Geotechnical Design Report (or specified part thereof)	nr			
A24	Electronic copy of Geotechnical Design Report (or specified part thereof)	sum			
A25	Digital data in AGS transfer format	sum			
A26	Hard-copy photographs	nr			
A27	Photographic volume	nr			
A28	Long-term storage of geotechnical samples (Appendix B)	provisional sum			
A29	Long-term storage of geoenvironmental samples (Appendix B)	provisional sum			
	Contract specific additional bill items				

Total section A carried to summary _____

Bill of Quantities Section B: Percussion boring – Notes for Guidance

For certain sites it is optional to introduce an extra over rate as Item B1.1 for moving boring plant and equipment over distances exceeding, say, 500 m to give more flexibility in the Investigation Supervisor's direction of field operations; similarly for Item B13.

Dynamic sampling may be measured on a per hole and metreage basis or alternatively on a time basis; the Investigation Supervisor will normally adopt one of these methods. Quantities shall be entered for only one method. Measurement on a time basis is often appropriate to permit flexibility for adequate examination, sampling and testing in less certain or complex ground condition or in areas of difficult access.

If dynamic probing is to be carried out at the site of each sampling hole this should be stated in Schedule S1.9.3 and be allowed for in the rates entered under Items B13–B18 or B19 as appropriate.

If two or more dynamic sampling units are required, this should be stated in Schedule S1.9.3. The requirement for window or windowless sampling should also be indicated in Schedule S1.9.3 and the costs for liners included within Items B15–B17 or B19 as appropriate.

If dynamic sampling rigs are used to carry out conventional sampling (SPTs and U100 driven samples) additional Bill Items will be required.

Bill of Quantities

Bill B   Percussion boring

Number	Item description	Unit	Quantity	Rate	Amount £
B	**Percussion boring**				
B1	Move boring plant and equipment to the site of each exploratory hole and set up	nr			
B2	Extra over Item BI for setting up on a slope of gradient greater than 20%	nr			
B3	Break out surface obstruction where present at exploratory borehole	h			
B4	Advance borehole between existing ground level and 10 m depth	m			
B5	As Item B4 but between 10 and 20 m depth	m			
B6	As Item B4 but between 20 and 30 m depth	m			
B7	As Item B4 but between 30 and 40 m depth	m			
B8	As Item B4 but between 40 and 50 m depth	m			
B9	Advance borehole through hard stratum or obstruction	h			
B10	Provide aquifer protection measures at a single aquiclude/aquifer boundary or cross-contamination control measures at a single soil boundary in a borehole	nr			
B11	Backfill borehole with cement/bentonite grout or bentonite pellets	m			
B12	Standing time for borehole plant, equipment and crew	h			
	Dynamic sampling				
B13	Move dynamic sampling equipment to the site of each exploratory hole and set up	nr			
B14	Extra over Item BI3 for setting up on a slope of gradient greater than 20%	nr			
B15	Advance dynamic sample hole between existing ground level and 5 m depth	m			
B16	As Item B15 but between 5 and 10 m depth	m			
B17	As Item B15 but between 10 and 15 m depth	m			
B18	Standing time for dynamic sampling equipment and crew	hr			

Number	Item description	Unit	Quantity	Rate	Amount £
B19	Provision of dynamic sampling equipment and crew for sampling as directed by the Investigation Supervisor; maximum depth 15 m	day			
B20	Backfill dynamic sampling hole with cement/bentonite grout or bentonite pellets	m			
	Contract specific additional bill items				

Total section B carried to summary _____

Bill of Quantities Section C: Rotary drilling – Notes for Guidance

Hand augering may be measured on a meterage basis or alternatively on a time basis; the Investigation Supervisor will normally adopt one of these methods. Quantities shall be entered for only one method. Measurement on a time basis is often appropriate to permit flexibility for adequate examination and sampling in less certain or complex ground conditions. If two or more hand augering crews are required, this should be stated in Schedule 1.

For certain sites it is optional to introduce an extra over rate as Item C15.1 for moving rotary drilling plant and equipment (or C59.1 for sonic drilling plant and equipment) over distances exceeding, say, 500 m to give more flexibility in the Investigation Supervisor's direction of field operations.

Hole and core diameters will be defined in the Schedules. If more than one hole or core diameter is required, the Bill of Quantities must identify this with different items repeated as required for each core size. The separate Bill items for the semi-rigid core liner should always have quantities corresponding to the lengths of rotary or sonic drilling to obtain cores, unless the Investigation Supervisor wishes to restrict the drilling method used.

Bill of Quantities

Bill C   Rotary drilling

Number	Item description	Unit	Quantity	Rate	Amount £
C	**Rotary drilling**				
	Hand augering				
C1	Bring hand auger equipment to the position of each exploratory hole	nr			
C2	Bore with hand auger from existing ground level to 2 m depth	m			
C3	As Item C2 but between 2 and 4 m depth	m			
C4	Standing time for hand auger equipment and crew	h			
C5	Provision of hand augering equipment and crew for augering as directed by the Investigation Supervisor; maximum depth 4 m	day			
C6	Backfill hand auger hole with cement/bentonite grout or bentonite pellets	m			
	Continuous flight and hollow-stem flight augering				
C7	Move mechanical augering plant and equipment to the site of each exploratory hole and set up	nr			
C8	Extra over Item C7 for setting up on a slope of gradient greater than 20%	nr			
C9	Break out surface obstructions where present at auger hole	h			
C10	Standing time for rotary auger equipment and crew	h			
C11	Auger in materials other than hard strata at the specified diameter between existing ground level and 10 m depth	m			
C12	As Item C11 but between 10 and 20 m depth	m			
C13	As Item C11 but between 20 and 30 m depth	m			
C14	Backfill auger hole with cement/bentonite grout or bentonite pellets	m			
	Rotary drilling with and without core recovery				
C15	Move rotary drilling plant and equipment to the site of each exploratory drillhole and set up	nr			
C16	Extra over Item C15 for setting up on a slope of gradient greater than 20%	nr			
C17	Extra over Item C15 for setting up drilling plant for inclined drillhole	nr			
C18	Break out surface obstructions where present at exploratory drillhole	h			

Number	Item description	Unit	Quantity	Rate	Amount £
C19	Standing time for rotary drilling plant, equipment and crew	h			
C20	Provide aquifer protection measures at a single aquiclude/aquifer boundary in a drillhole	nr			
	Drilling without cores				
C21	Rotary drill in materials other than hard strata at the specified diameter, from which cores are not required, between existing ground level and 10 m depth	m			
C22	As Item C21 but between 10 and 20 m depth	m			
C23	As Item C21 but between 20 and 30 m depth	m			
C24	As Item C21 but between 30 and 40 m depth	m			
C25	As Item C21 but between 40 and 50 m depth	m			
C26	Extra over Items C21 to C25 for inclined rotary drillhole	m			
C27	Rotary drill in hard strata at the specified diameter, from which cores are not required, between existing ground level and 10 m depth	m			
C28	As Item C27 but between 10 and 20 m depth	m			
C29	As Item C27 but between 20 and 30 m depth	m			
C30	As Item C27 but between 30 and 40 m depth	m			
C31	As Item C27 but between 40 and 50 m depth	m			
C32	Extra over Items C27 to C31 for inclined drillhole	m			
C33	Backfill rotary drillhole with cement/bentonite grout or bentonite pellets	m			
	Drilling to obtain cores				
C34	Rotary drill in materials other than hard strata to obtain cores of the specified diameter between existing ground level and 10 m depth	m			
C35	As Item C34 but between 10 and 20 m depth	m			
C36	As Item C34 but between 20 and 30 m depth	m			
C37	As Item C34 but between 30 and 40 m depth	m			
C38	As Item C34 but between 40 and 50 m depth	m			
C39	Extra over Items C34 to C38 for use of semi-rigid core liner	m			
C40	Extra over Items C34 to C38 for coring inclined rotary drillhole	m			
C41	Rotary drill in hard strata to obtain cores of the specified diameter between existing ground level and 10 m depth	m			
C42	As Item C41 but between 10 and 20 m depth	m			
C43	As Item C41 but between 20 and 30 m depth	m			
C44	As Item C41 but between 30 and 40 m depth	m			
C45	As Item C41 but between 40 and 50 m depth	m			
C46	Extra over Items C41 to C45 for use of semi-rigid liner	m			
C47	Extra over Items C41 to C45 for coring inclined rotary drillhole	m			
C48	Backfill rotary drillhole with cement/bentonite grout or bentonite pellets	m			
C49	Core box to be retained by client	nr			
	Rotary percussive drilling				
C50	Move rotary percussive drilling plant and equipment to the site of each drill hole and set up	nr			
C51	Extra over Item C50 for setting up on a slope of gradient greater than 20%	nr			

Number	Item description	Unit	Quantity	Rate	Amount £
C52	Rotary percussive drill at the specified diameter in any material between existing ground level and 10 m depth	m			
C53	As Item C52 but between 10 and 20 m depth	m			
C54	As Item C52 but between 20 and 30 m depth	m			
C55	As Item C52 but between 30 and 40 m depth	m			
C56	As Item C52 but between 40 and 50 m depth	m			
C57	Standing time for rotary percussive drilling plant, equipment and crew	h			
C58	Backfill rotary percussive drillhole with cement/bentonite grout or bentonite pellets	m			
	Resonance (sonic) drilling				
C59	Move sonic drilling plant and equipment to the site of each exploratory drillhole and set up	nr			
C60	Extra over Item C59 for setting up on a slope of gradient greater than 20%	nr			
C61	Extra over Item C59 for setting up sonic drilling plant for inclined drillhole	nr			
C62	Break out surface obstructions where present at exploratory drillhole	h			
C63	Standing time for sonic drilling plant, equipment and crew	h			
	Sonic drilling without cores				
C64	Sonic drill in materials other than hard strata at the specified diameter, from which cores are not required, between existing ground level and 10 m depth	m			
C65	As Item C64 but between 10 and 20 m depth	m			
C66	As Item C64 but between 20 and 30 m depth	m			
C67	As Item C64 but between 30 and 40 m depth	m			
C68	As Item C64 but between 40 and 50 m depth	m			
C69	Extra over Items C64 to C68 for inclined sonic drillhole	m			
C70	Sonic drill in hard strata at the specified diameter, from which cores are not required, between existing ground level and 10 m depth	m			
C71	As Item C70 but between 10 and 20 m depth	m			
C72	As Item C70 but between 20 and 30 m depth	m			
C73	As Item C70 but between 30 and 40 m depth	m			
C74	As Item C70 but between 40 and 50 m depth	m			
C75	Extra over Items C70 to C74 for inclined sonic drillhole	m			
C76	Backfill sonic drillhole with cement/bentonite grout or bentonite pellets	m			
	Sonic drilling to obtain cores				
C77	Sonic drill in materials other than hard strata to obtain cores of the specified diameter between existing ground level and 10 m depth	m			
C78	As Item C77 but between 10 and 20 m depth	m			
C79	As Item C77 but between 20 and 30 m depth	m			
C80	As Item C77 but between 30 and 40 m depth	m			
C81	As Item C77 but between 40 and 50 m depth	m			

Number	Item description	Unit	Quantity	Rate	Amount £
C82	Extra over Items C77 to C81 for use of semi-rigid core liner	m			
C83	Extra over Items C77 to C81 for coring inclined sonic drillhole	m			
C84	Sonic drill in hard strata to obtain cores of the specified diameter between existing ground level and 10 m depth	m			
C85	As Item C84 but between 10 and 20 m depth	m			
C86	As Item C84 but between 20 and 30 m depth	m			
C87	As Item C84 but between 30 and 40 m depth	m			
C88	As Item C84 but between 40 and 50 m depth	m			
C89	Extra over Items C84 to C88 for use of semi-rigid liner	m			
C90	Extra over Items C84 to C88 for coring inclined sonic drillhole	m			
C91	Backfill sonic drillhole with cement/bentonite grout or bentonite pellets	m			
	Contract specific additional bill items				

Total section C carried to summary _____

Bill of Quantities Section D: Pitting and trenching – Notes for Guidance

Trial pits and trenches and observation pits and trenches may be measured on a linear metre basis (for pits) and a m³ basis (for trenches) or alternatively on a time basis. Normally the Investigation Supervisor will adopt one of these methods. Quantities shall be entered for only one method for each pit or trench. Measurement on a time basis is often appropriate to permit flexibility for adequate examination, sampling and testing in less certain or complex ground conditions. If two or more pitting crews are required, this should be stated in Schedule S1.11.2.

Pits and trenches exceeding 4.5 m in depth require the mobilisation of more significant plant and an extra over item is included for moving to the site of each pit or trench accordingly. An additional item in A2 may also be considered appropriate for mobilisation to site.

Rates for Items D29–D35 inclusive will vary on a site-specific basis depending on what services are to be provided by the Contractor as part of the field crew: Schedule S1.11.9 should detail the site-specific services. Where professional attendance is required for logging of the pit or trench, then this should be recovered under Item A7.

Bill of Quantities

Bill D   Pitting and trenching

Number	Item description	Unit	Quantity	Rate	Amount £
D	**Pitting and trenching**				
	Inspection pits				
D1	Excavate inspection pit by hand to 1.2 m depth	nr			
D2	Extra over Item Dl for breaking out surface obstructions	h			
	Trial pits and trenches				
D3	Move equipment to the site of each trial pit or trench of not greater than 4.5 m depth	nr			
D4	Extra over Item D3 for setting up on a slope of gradient greater than 20%	nr			
D5	Extra over Item D3 for trial pit or trench between 4.5 and 6 m depth	nr			
D6	Excavate trial pit between existing ground level and 3.0 m depth	m			
D7	As Item D6 but between 3.0 and 4.5 m depth	m			
D8	As Item D6 but between 4.5 and 6 m depth	m			
D9	Excavate trial trench between existing ground level and 3.0 m depth	m³			
D10	As Item D9 between 3.0 and 4.5 m in depth	m³			
D11	As Item D9 between 4.5 and 6 m depth	m³			
D12	Extra over Items D6 to D11 inclusive for breaking out hard material or surface obstructions	h			
D13	Standing time for excavation plant, equipment and crew for machine dug trial pit or trench	h			
	Observation pits and trenches				
D14	Move equipment to the site of each observation pit or trench of not greater than 4.5 m depth	nr			
D15	Extra over Item D14 for setting up on a slope of gradient greater than 20%	nr			
D16	Extra over Item D14 for trial pit or trench between 4.5 and 6 m depth	nr			
D17	Excavate observation pit between existing ground level and 3.0 m depth	m			
D18	As Item D17 but between 3.0 and 4.5 m depth	m			

Number	Item description	Unit	Quantity	Rate	Amount £
D19	As Item D 17 but between 4.5 and 6 m depth	m			
D20	Extra over Item D17 for hand excavation	m			
D21	Excavate observation trench between existing ground level and 3.0 m depth	m^3			
D22	As Item D21 but between 3.0 and 4.5 m depth	m^3			
D23	As Item D21 but between 4.5 and 6 m depth	m^3			
D24	Extra over Item D21 for hand excavation	m^3			
D25	Extra over Items D17 to D19 and D21 to D23 for breaking out hard strata or obstructions	h			
D26	Extra over Items D17 and D21 for breaking out hard strata or obstructions by hand	h			
D27	Standing time for excavation plant, equipment and crew for machine dug observation pit or trench	h			
D28	Standing time for excavation plant, equipment and crew for hand dug observation pit or trench	h			
	Daily provision of pitting crew and equipment				
D29	Provision of excavation plant equipment and crew for machine dug trial pits or trenches as directed by the Investigation Supervisor; maximum depth 3.0 m	day			
D30	As Item D29 but between 3.0 and 4.5 m depth	day			
D31	As Item D29 but between 4.5 and 6.0 m depth	day			
D32	Provision of excavation plant, equipment and crew for machine dug observation pit or trench as directed by the Investigation Supervisor; maximum depth 3.0 m	day			
D33	As Item D32 but between 3.0 and 4.5 m depth	day			
D34	As Item D32 but between 4.5 and 6.0 m depth	day			
D35	As Item D32 but for hand excavation	day			
D36	Extra over Items D32 to D34 for breaking out hard strata or obstructions	day			
	General				
D37	Bring pump to the position of each exploratory pit or trench	nr			
D38	Pump water from pit or trench	h			
D39	Extra over Item D38 for temporary storage, treatment and disposal of contaminated water	Provisional sum			
D40	Leave open observation pit or trench	m^2/day			
D41	Leave open trial pit or trench	m^2/day			
	Contract specific additional bill items				

Total section D carried to summary _____

Bill of Quantities Section E: Sampling and monitoring during intrusive investigation – Notes for Guidance

Use of thin-walled samplers (OS-T/W) or piston samplers (PS-T/W) is recommended where the sample is to be used for laboratory strength and/or compressibility testing. The UT100 can be considered but the driving mechanism and the number of blows to retrieve the sample should be taken into account.

Item E8 relates to sub-samples obtained from rotary recovered cores by conventional or reasonance methods.

The rates for Items E14.1–E15.3 should include for plastic tubs, glass bottles or any combination of these as required for the laboratory analysis of the contaminants concerned.

Where other laboratory tests or test suites are required on a site-specific basis, additional Bill items will be needed to cover for the provision of the appropriate containers.

Bill of Quantities

Bill E   Sampling and monitoring during intrusive investigation

Number	Item description	Unit	Quantity	Rate	Amount £
E	**Sampling and monitoring during intrusive investigation**				
	Samples for geotechnical purposes				
E1	Small disturbed sample	nr			
E2	Bulk disturbed sample	nr			
E3	Large bulk disturbed sample	nr			
E4.1	Open-tube sample using thick-walled (OS-TK/W) sampler	nr			
E4.2	Open-tube sample using thin-walled (OS-T/W) sampler	nr			
E5	Piston sample	nr			
E6	Groundwater sample	nr			
E7	Ground gas sample	nr			
E8	Cut, prepare and protect core sub-sample	nr			
	Continuous or semi-continuous sampling				
E9	Move Delft continuous or Mostap semi-continuous sampling plant and equipment to the site of each exploratory hole and set up	nr			
E10	Extra over Item E9 for setting up on a slope of gradient greater than 20%	nr			
E11	Break out surface obstruction where present at exploratory hole	h			
E12	Advance sampler between existing ground level and 10 m depth	m			
E13	As Item E12 but between 10 and 20 m depth	m			
	Containers for contamination assessment and WAC testing				
E14.1	Provision of containers and collection of samples for contamination Suite E (S1.20.3)	nr			
E14.2	Provision of containers and collection of samples for contamination Suite F (S1.20.3)	nr			
E14.3	Provision of containers and collection of samples for contamination Suite G (S1.20.3)	nr			
E15.1	Provision of containers and collection of samples for WAC Suite H (S1.20.5)	nr			

Number	Item description	Unit	Quantity	Rate	Amount £
E15.2	Provision of containers and collection of samples for WAC Suite I (S1.20.5)	nr			
E15.3	Provision of containers and collection of samples for WAC Suite J (S1.20.5)	nr			
	Contract specific additional bill items				

Total section E carried to summary _____

Bill of Quantities Section F: Probing and cone penetration testing – Notes for Guidance

If dynamic probing is to be carried out at the site of each dynamic sampling hole, Items F1–F6 or F7 should not be used and the cost of the probing included in the rates defined under Items B13–B18 or B19 as appropriate.

Bill of Quantities

Bill F   Probing and cone penetration testing

Number	Item description	Unit	Quantity	Rate	Amount £
F	**Probing and cone penetration testing**				
	Dynamic probing				
F1	Bring dynamic probe equipment to the site of each test location	nr			
F2	Extra over Item F1 for setting up on a slope of gradient greater than 20%	nr			
F3	Carry out dynamic probe test from existing ground level to 5 m depth	m			
F4	As Item F3 but between 5 and 10 m depth	m			
F5	As Item F3 but between 10 and 15 m depth	m			
F6	Standing time for dynamic probe test equipment and crew	h			
F7	Provision of dynamic probing equipment and crew for probing as directed by the Investigation Supervisor; maximum depth 15 m	day			
	Cone penetration testing				
F8	Bring static cone penetration test equipment to the site of each test location	nr			
F9	Extra over Item F8 for setting up on a slope of gradient greater than 20%	nr			
F10	Carry out static cone penetration test measuring both cone and sleeve resistance from existing ground level to 10 m depth	m			
F11	As Item F10 but between 10 and 20 m depth	m			
F12	As Item F10 but between 20 and 30 m depth	m			
F13	As Item F10 but between 30 and 40 m depth	m			
F14	Extra over Items F10 to F13 for use of piezocone	m			
F15	Extra over Items F10 to F13 for interpretation of CPT/CPTU data	m			
F16	Carry out dissipation test up to 1 hour duration	nr			
F17	Extra over Item F16 for test duration exceeding 1 hour	h			
F18	Standing time for static cone penetration test equipment and crew	h			
F19	Extra over Items F10 to F13 for use of seismic cone	m			
F20	Carry out seismic cone test	nr			
F21	Extra over Item F20 for interpretation of seismic cone data	nr			
F22	Standing time for seismic cone test equipment and crew	h			
	Contract specific additional bill items				

Total section F carried to summary _____

Bill of Quantities Section G: Geophysical testing – Notes for Guidance

The recommended basis for pricing land-based mapping is linear (line) metres. In order to compare alternative tenders it will be necessary for the intended line spacings either to be specified or defined by the tenderers. Line metres is also adopted for land-based profiling techniques. Here the inter-sensor spacings need either to be specified or defined by the tenderers.

Slim-line down-hole methods can be subdivided as subitems of G5 to cover specific suites that can be run on the one sonde; the recovered cost being the metres run for that sonde, not per determinand.

Daily rate is adopted for overwater geophysics as the majority of methods can be carried out simultaneously. However, performance and acceptance criteria will need to be agreed.

Bill of Quantities

Bill G   Geophysical testing

Number	Item description	Unit	Quantity	Rate	Amount £
G	**Geophysical testing**				
	Land-based mapping techniques				
G1	Collect and process conductivity, magnetic or gravimetric data	lin.m			
G2	Collect and process microgravity data at each measuring station	nr			
	Land-based profiling techniques				
G3	Collect and process resistivity, seismic or ground probing radar data	lin.m			
	Land-based borehole techniques				
G4	Move down-hole logging equipment to the site of each exploratory hole and set up	nr			
G5	Carry out down-hole calliper, natural gamma, resistivity (where hole is uncased), fluid temperature, conductivity and fluid flow logging	m			
	Overwater				
G6	Collect and process echo sounding, side-scan sonar, magnetic, conductivity, seismic reflection, seismic refraction, resistivity imaging or ground-probing radar data	day			
	Contract specific additional bill items				

Total section G carried to summary _____

Bill of Quantities Section H: In situ testing – Notes for Guidance

The types of work included are those most often used. Additional techniques should be added when required and included as additions to the Specification and schedules.

The nuclear method of determining in situ density is one which can be carried out rapidly and is therefore more appropriately priced on a time basis.

Items H24–H38 (self-boring pressuremeter), H39–H53 (high-pressure dilatometer), H54–H68 (driven or push-in pressuremeter) and H69–H80 (Menard pressuremeter) provide stand-alone coverage of the works involved without the need to cross-refer to relevant items from Bill B (percussion boring) and/or Bill C (rotary drilling). The stand-alone coverage also allows for the use of other hole-forming plant not covered by Bills B and C.

Bill of Quantities

Bill H   In situ testing

Number	Item description	Unit	Quantity	Rate	Amount £
H	**In situ testing**				
H1	Standard penetration test in borehole	nr			
H2	Standard penetration test in rotary drillhole	nr			
H3	In situ density testing				
H3.1	Small pouring cylinder method	nr			
H3.2	Large pouring cylinder method	nr			
H3.3	Water replacement method	nr			
H3.4	Core cutter method	nr			
H3.5	Nuclear method	day			
H4	California Bearing Ratio test	nr			
H5	Vane shear strength test in borehole	nr			
H6	Penetration vane test, penetration from ground level	nr			
H7	Hand penetrometer test (set of 3 readings)	nr			
H8	Hand vane test (set of 3 readings)	nr			
	Other tests				
H9	Apparent resistivity of soil	nr			
H10	Redox potential	nr			
	Permeability testing				
H11	Set up and dismantle variable head permeability test in borehole	nr			
H12	Set up and dismantle constant head permeability test in borehole	nr			
H13	Carry out permeability test in borehole	h			
H14	Set up and dismantle variable head permeability test in standpipe/ standpipe piezometer	nr			
H15	Set up and dismantle constant head permeability test in standpipe/ standpipe piezometer	nr			
H16	Carry out permeability test in standpipe/standpipe piezometer	h			
H17	Set up and dismantle variable head permeability test in rotary drillhole	nr			
H18	Set up and dismantle constant head permeability test in rotary drillhole	nr			
H19	Carry out permeability test in rotary drillhole	h			
H20	Set up and dismantle single packer permeability test	nr			
H21	Set up and dismantle double packer permeability test	nr			

Number	Item description	Unit	Quantity	Rate	Amount £
H22	Carry out single packer permeability test	h			
H23	Carry out double packer permeability test	h			
	Self-boring pressuremeter				
H24	Move and set up self-boring pressuremeter and exploratory hole-forming equipment to site of each exploratory hole	nr			
H25	Extra over Item H24 for setting up on a slope of gradient greater than 20%	nr			
H26	Advance exploratory hole to pressuremeter test location between ground level and 10 m depth	m			
H27	As Item H26 but between 10 and 20 m depth	m			
H28	As Item H26 but between 20 and 30 m depth	m			
H29	Advance exploratory hole through hard stratum or obstruction	h			
H30	Self-bore to form test pocket between ground level and 10 m depth	m			
H31	As item H30 but between 10 and 20 m depth	m			
H32	As item H30 but between 20 and 30 m depth	m			
H33	Carry out pressuremeter test, provision of data and report, test duration not exceeding 1.5 hours	nr			
H34	Extra over Item H33 for test duration in excess of 1.5 hours	h			
H35	Carry out additional calibrations as instructed by the Investigation Supervisor				
H35.1	Displacement transducers	nr			
H35.2	Pore pressure transducers	nr			
H35.3	Total pressure transducers	nr			
H35.4	Membrane stiffness	nr			
H36	Carry out membrane compression calibrations as instructed by the Investigation Supervisor	nr			
H37	Backfill exploratory hole for pressuremeter with cement/bentonite grout	m			
H38	Standing time for self-boring pressuremeter and crew	h			
	High pressure dilatometer				
H39	Move and set up high-pressure dilatometer and exploratory hole-forming equipment to site of each exploratory hole	nr			
H40	Extra over Item H39 for setting up on a slope of gradient greater than 20%	nr			
H41	Advance exploratory hole to dilatometer test depth between ground level and 10 m depth	m			
H42	As Item H41 but between 10 and 20 m depth	m			
H43	As Item H41 but between 20 and 30 m depth	m			
H44	Advance exploratory hole through hard stratum or obstruction	h			
H45	Rotary core to form dilatometer test pocket between ground level and 10 m depth	m			
H46	As item H45 but between 10 and 20 m depth	m			
H47	As item H45 but between 20 and 30 m depth	m			
H48	Carry out dilatometer test, provision of data and report, test duration not exceeding 1.5 hours	nr			
H49	Extra over Item H48 for test duration in excess of 1.5 hours	h			

Number	Item description	Unit	Quantity	Rate	Amount £
H50	Carry out additional calibrations as instructed by the Investigation Supervisor				
H50.1	Displacement Transducers	nr			
H50.2	Total Pressure Transducers	nr			
H50.3	Membrane stiffness	nr			
H51	Carry out membrane compression calibrations as instructed by the Investigation Supervisor	nr			
H52	Backfill exploratory hole for high-pressure dilatometer with cement/bentonite grout	m			
H53	Standing time for dilatometer equipment and crew	h			
	Driven or push-in pressuremeter				
H54	Move and set up pressuremeter and exploratory hole-forming equipment to site of each exploratory hole	nr			
H55	Extra over Item H54 for setting up on a slope of gradient greater than 20%	nr			
H56	Advance exploratory hole to pressuremeter test location between ground level and 10 m depth	m			
H57	As Item H56 but between 10 and 20 m depth	m			
H58	As Item H56 but between 20 and 30 m depth	m			
H59	Advance exploratory hole through hard stratum or obstruction	h			
H60	Install pressuremeter at base of exploratory hole between ground level and 10 m depth	m			
H61	As Item H60 but between 10 and 20 m depth	m			
H62	As Item H60 but between 20 and 30 m depth	m			
H63	Carry out pressuremeter test, provision of data and report, test duration not exceeding 1.5 hours	nr			
H64	Extra over Item H63 for test duration in excess of 1.5 hours	h			
H65	Carry out additional calibrations as instructed by the Investigation Supervisor				
H65.1	Displacement transducers	nr			
H65.2	Pore pressure transducers	nr			
H65.3	Total pressure transducers	nr			
H65.4	Membrane stiffness	nr			
H66	Carry out membrane compression calibrations as instructed by the Investigation Supervisor	nr			
H67	Backfill exploratory hole for pressuremeter with cement/bentonite grout	m			
H68	Standing time for driven or push-in self-boring pressuremeter and crew	h			
	Menard pressuremeter				
H69	Move and set up pressuremeter and exploratory hole-forming equipment to site of each exploratory hole	nr			
H70	Extra over Item H69 for setting up on a slope of gradient greater than 20%	nr			
H71	Advance exploratory hole to pressuremeter test location between ground level and 10 m depth	m			
H72	As Item H71 but between 10 and 20 m depth	m			

Number	Item description	Unit	Quantity	Rate	Amount £
H73	As Item H71 but between 20 and 30 m depth	m			
H74	Advance exploratory hole through hard stratum or obstruction	h			
H75	Rotary core to form pressuremeter test pocket between ground level and 10 m depth	m			
H76	As Item H75 but between 10 and 20 m depth	m			
H77	As Item H75 but between 20 and 30 m depth	m			
H78	Carry out Menard pressuremeter test	nr			
H79	Backfill exploratory hole for pressuremeter with cement/bentonite grout	m			
H80	Standing time for Menard pressuremeter and crew	h			
	Soil infiltration test				
H81	Provide equipment and carry out set of 3 infiltration tests at selected location up to 1 day, including hire of excavation equipment	nr			
H82	Extra over Item H81 for additional days	day			
H83	Calculation of infiltration rate for each tested location	nr			
	Miscellaneous site testing				
H84	Reading of free product level in borehole using an interface probe	nr			
H85	Provide contamination screening test kits per sample	nr			
H86	Carry out headspace testing by FID/PID	nr			
	Contract specific additional bill items				

Total section H carried to summary _____

Bill of Quantities Section I: Instrumentation – Notes for Guidance

The types of instrumentation included are those most often used. Additional instrumentation should be added when required and included as additions to the Specification.

Additional Items will be required to cover extensometers, settlement gauges and settlement monuments. The form and content of the additional items will depend on the Specification details set out in Schedules S1.16.9 and S1.16.10.

Forming the exploratory hole for standpipe, standpipe piezometer, inclinometer and slip indicator installations by boring/drilling should have meterage included under Bill B or C.

Where standpipes for sampling and monitoring groundwater and ground gas monitoring standpipes are in the form of a combined installation, they should be measured once under appropriate Items I6, I7 or I8.

Chemical testing necessary to enable the safe disposal of the purged water, Item I15.9, should be charged and included per number under Bill K.

Item I18 covers only for the base set of readings following installation of the instrument. Subsequent sets of readings during the fieldwork period or during the post fieldwork period and requiring a return visit to site should be charged under Bill items J3 or J12 as appropriate.

Bill of Quantities

Bill I   Instrumentation

Number	Item description	Unit	Quantity	Rate	Amount £
I	**Instrumentation**				
	Standpipes and piezometers				
I1	Backfill exploratory hole with cement/bentonite grout below standpipe or standpipe piezometer	m			
I2	Provide and install standpipe (19 mm)	m			
I3	Provide and install standpipe piezometer (19 mm)	m			
I4	Provide and install standpipe piezometer (50 mm)	m			
I5	Provide and install standpipe piezometer (75 mm)	m			
I6	Provide and install ground gas monitoring standpipe (19 mm)	m			
I7	Provide and install ground gas monitoring standpipe (50 mm)	m			
I8	Provide and install ground gas monitoring standpipe (75 mm)	m			
I9	Provide and install headworks for ground gas monitoring standpipe, standpipe or standpipe piezometer	nr			
I10	Provide and install protective cover (flush)	nr			
I11	Provide and install protective cover (raised)	nr			
I12	Extra over Item I10 for heavy duty cover in highways	nr			
I13	Supply and erect protective fencing around standpipe or piezometer installation	nr			
I14	Supply and erect 1.5 m high marker post	nr			
I15	Standpipe and piezometer development				
I15.1	Supply equipment and personnel to carry out development by surging	nr			
I15.2	Develop standpipe or piezometer by surging	h			
I15.3	As Item I15.1 but by airlift pumping	nr			

Number	Item description	Unit	Quantity	Rate	Amount £
I15.4	As Item I15.2 but by airlift pumping	h			
I15.5	As Item I15.1 but by over pumping	nr			
I15.6	As Item I15.2 but by over pumping	h			
I15.7	As Item I5.1 but by jetting	nr			
I15.8	As Item I15.2 but by jetting	h			
I15.9	Disposal of development water, not including chemical testing	Provisional sum			
	Inclinometer				
I16	Supply and install inclinometer tubing in exploratory hole, not including hole formation	m			
I17	Hire of inclinometer readout unit	day			
I18	Carry out base set of inclinometer readings per installation and installation report	h			
I19	Provide and install protective cover (flush)	nr			
I20	Provide and install protective cover (raised)	nr			
	Slip indicators				
I21	Supply and install slip indicators in exploratory hole, including brass probe and not including hole formation	m			
I22	Provide and install protective cover (flush)	nr			
I23	Provide and install protective cover (raised)	nr			
	Contract specific additional bill items				

Total section I carried to summary _____

Bill of Quantities Section J: Installation monitoring and sampling – Notes for Guidance

A set of base inclinometer readings is defined in Specification Clause 11.6.5 but may be varied on a site-specific basis by means of Schedule S1.16.7. Further readings during or after fieldwork should comply with this requirement unless otherwise stated in the Schedule.

When readings of standpipes, piezometers, inclinometers, etc. are required to be continued after the fieldwork period, the alternative of measuring this work on Appendix A rates may be appropriate.

Bill of Quantities

Bill J   Installation monitoring and sampling (during fieldwork period)

Number	Item description	Unit	Quantity	Rate	Amount £
J	**Installation monitoring and sampling** (during fieldwork period)				
J1	Reading of water level in standpipe or standpipe piezometer during fieldwork period	nr			
J2	Ground gas measurement in gas monitoring standpipe during fieldwork period	nr			
J3	Set of inclinometer readings (as defined in Specification Clause 11.6.5 or Schedule S1.16.7) per installation during fieldwork period and report results	nr			
J4	Check for ground slippage in slip indicator installation during fieldwork period	nr			
J5	Water sample from standpipe or standpipe piezometer during fieldwork period, including purging or micro-purging up to 3.0 hours	nr			
J6	Extra over Item J5 for purging or micro-purging in excess of 3.0 hours	h			
J7	Ground gas sample from gas monitoring standpipe during fieldwork period	nr			
J8	Reading of free product level in standpipe using an interface probe during fieldwork period	nr			
	Installation monitoring and sampling (post fieldwork period)				
J9	Return visit to site following completion of fieldwork to take readings in, or recover samples from, installations	nr			
J10	Extra over Item J9 for reading of water level in standpipe or standpipe piezometer during return visit	nr			
J11	Extra over Item J9 for ground gas measurement in ground gas monitoring standpipe during return visit	nr			
J12	Extra over Item J9 for set of inclinometer readings (as defined in Specification Clause 11.6.5 or Schedule S1.16.7) per installation during return visit and report results	nr			
J13	Extra over Item J9 to check for ground slippage in slip indicator installation during return visit to site	nr			
J14	Extra over Item J9 for water sample from standpipe or standpipe piezometer during return visit to site, including purging or micro-purging up to 3.0 hours	nr			
J15	Extra over Item J14 for purging or micro-purging in excess of 3.0 hours	h			
J16	Extra over Item J9 for ground gas sample from gas monitoring standpipe during return visit to site	nr			
J17	Extra over Item J9 for reading of free product level in standpipe using an interface probe during return visit to site	nr			

Number	Item description	Unit	Quantity	Rate	Amount £
	Surface water body sampling and testing				
J18	Surface water body sample taken during fieldwork period	nr			
J19	Surface water body sample taken during return visit to site	nr			
J20	Determination of dissolved oxygen, conductivity, pH and temperature of surface water body during fieldwork period	nr			
J21	Determination of dissolved oxygen, conductivity, pH and temperature of surface water body during return visit to site	nr			
	Contract specific additional bill items				

Total section J carried to summary _____

Bill of Quantities Section K: Geotechnical laboratory testing – Notes for Guidance

Items for laboratory testing on soil are listed to correspond with appropriate sections of BS 1377.

Where significant quantities of geotechnical testing of contaminated ground samples are also anticipated, consideration may be given to the inclusion of an additional Bill which repeats the relevant geotechnical tests to enable the Contractor to better identify any additional costs involved.

Items K9.1–K9.4 accord with the test suites offered by many testing laboratories in respect of the aggressivity of soil and groundwater to below ground concrete. Items K2.3–K2.10 cover the same chemical tests but are listed individually to permit the separate selection of required tests.

Bill of Quantities

Bill K   Geotechnical laboratory testing

Number	Item description	Unit	Quantity	Rate	Amount £
K	**Geotechnical laboratory testing**				
K1	Classification				
K1.1	Moisture content	nr			
K1.2	Liquid limit, plastic limit and plasticity index	nr			
K1.3	Volumetric shrinkage	nr			
K1.4	Linear shrinkage	nr			
K1.5	Density by linear measurement	nr			
K1.6	Density by immersion in water or water displacement	nr			
K1.7	Dry density and saturation moisture content for chalk	nr			
K1.8	Particle density by gas jar or pycnometer	nr			
K1.9	Particle size distribution by wet sieving	nr			
K1.10	Particle size distribution by dry sieving	nr			
K1.11	Sedimentation by pipette	nr			
K1.12	Sedimentation by hydrometer	nr			
K2	Chemical and electrochemical				
K2.1	Organic matter content	nr			
K2.2	Mass loss on ignition	nr			
K2.3	Sulphate content of acid extract from soil	nr			
K2.4	Sulphate content of water extract from soil	nr			
K2.5	Sulphate content of groundwater	nr			
K2.6	Carbonate content by rapid titration	nr			
K2.7	Carbonate content by gravimetric method	nr			
K2.8	Water soluble chloride content	nr			
K2.9	Acid soluble chloride content	nr			
K2.10	Total sulphur content	nr			
K2.11	Total dissolved solids	nr			
K2.12	pH value	nr			
K2.13	Resistivity	nr			
K2.14	Redox potential	nr			
K3	Compaction related				
K3.1	Dry density/moisture content relationship using 2.5 kg rammer	nr			
K3.2	Dry density/moisture content relationship using 4.5 kg rammer	nr			
K3.3	Dry density/moisture content relationship using vibrating rammer	nr			

Number	Item description	Unit	Quantity	Rate	Amount £
K3.4	Extra over Items K3.1, K3.2 and K3.3 for use of CBR mould	nr			
K.3.5	Maximum and minimum dry density for granular soils	nr			
K3.6	Moisture Condition Value at natural moisture content	nr			
K3.7	Moisture Condition Value/moisture content relationship	nr			
K3.8	Chalk crushing value	nr			
K3.9	California Bearing Ratio on re-compacted disturbed sample	nr			
K3.10	Extra over Item K3.9 for soaking	day			
K4	Compressibility, permeability and durability				
K4.1	One-dimensional consolidation properties, test period 5 days	nr			
K4.2	Extra over Item K4.1 for test period in excess of 5 days	day			
K4.3	Measurements of swelling pressure, test period 2 days	nr			
K4.4	Measurement of swelling, test period 2 days	nr			
K4.5	Measurement of settlement on saturation, test period 1 day	nr			
K4.6	Extra over Items K4.3 to K4.5 for test period in excess of 2 or 1 day (s)	day			
K4.7	Permeability by constant head method	nr			
K4.8	Dispersibility by pinhole method	nr			
K4.9	Dispersibility by crumb method	nr			
K4.10	Dispersibility by dispersion method	nr			
K4.11	Frost heave of soil	nr			
K5	Consolidation and permeability in hydraulic cells				
K5.1	Consolidation properties of a 76 mm diameter specimen using a hydraulic cell, test period 4 days	nr			
K5.2	As Item K5.1 but using a 100 mm diameter specimen	nr			
K5.3	As Item K5.1 but using a 150 mm diameter specimen	nr			
K5.4	As Item K5.1 but using a 250 mm diameter specimen	nr			
K5.5	Extra over Items K5.1–K5.4 for test period in excess of 4 days	day			
K5.6	Permeability of a 76 mm diameter specimen in hydraulic consolidation cell, test period 4 days	nr			
K5.7	As Item K5.6 but using a 100 mm diameter specimen	nr			
K5.8	As Item K5.6 but using a 150 mm diameter specimen	nr			
K5.9	As Item K5.6 but using a 250 mm diameter specimen	nr			
K5.10	Extra over Items K5.6–K5.9 for test period in excess of 4 days	day			
K5.11	Isotropic consolidation properties in a triaxial cell, test period 4 days	nr			
K5.12	Extra over Item K5.11 for test periods in excess of 4 days	day			
K5.13	Permeability in a triaxial cell, test period 4 days	nr			
K5.14	Extra over Item K5.13 for test period in excess of 4 days	day			
K6	Shear strength (total stress)				
K6.1	Shear strength by the laboratory vane method (set of 3)	nr			
K6.2	Shear strength by hand vane (set of 3)	nr			
K6.3	Shear strength by hand penetrometer (set of 3)	nr			
K6.4	Shear strength of a set of three 60 mm × 60 mm square specimens by direct shear, test duration not exceeding 1 day per specimen	nr			
K6.5	Extra over Item K6.4 for test durations in excess of 1 day per specimen	sp.day			

Number	Item description	Unit	Quantity	Rate	Amount £
K6.6	Shear strength of a single 300 mm × 300 mm square specimen by direct shear, test duration not exceeding 1 day	nr			
K6.7	Extra over Item K6.6 for test durations in excess of 1 day	day			
K6.8	Residual shear strength of a set of three 60 mm × 60 mm square specimens by direct shear, test duration not exceeding 4 days per specimen	nr			
K6.9	Extra over Item K6.8 for test durations in excess of 4 days per specimen	sp.day			
K6.10	Residual shear strength of a 300 mm square specimen by direct shear, test duration not exceeding 4 days	nr			
K6.11	Extra over Item K6.10 for test duration in excess day of 4 days	day			
K6.12	Residual shear strength using the small ring shear apparatus at three normal pressures, test duration not exceeding 4 days	nr			
K6.13	Extra over Item K6.12 for test duration in excess of 4 days	day			
K6.14	Unconfined compressive strength of 38 mm diameter specimen	nr			
K6.15	Undrained shear strength of a set of three 38 mm diameter specimens in triaxial compression without the measurement of pore pressure	nr			
K6.16	Undrained strength of a single 100 mm diameter specimen in triaxial compression without the measurement of pore pressure	nr			
K6.17	Undrained shear strength of single 100 mm diameter specimen in triaxial compression with multi-stage loading and without measurement of pore pressure	nr			
K7	Shear strength (effective stress)				
K7.1	Consolidated undrained triaxial compression test with measurement of pore pressure (set of three 38 mm specimens), test duration not exceeding 4 days per specimen	nr			
K7.2	As K7.1 but single-stage or multi-stage test using 100 mm diameter specimen	nr			
K7.3	Consolidated drained triaxial compression test with measurement of volume change (set of three 38 mm specimens), test duration not exceeding 4 days per specimen	nr			
K7.4	As Item K7.3 but single-stage or multi-stage test using 100 mm diameter specimen, test duration not exceeding 4 days	nr			
K7.5	Extra over Items K7.1 and K7.3 for test duration in excess of 4 days per specimen	sp.day			
K7.6	Extra over Items K7.2 and K7.4 for test duration in excess of 4 days	day			
K8	Rock testing				
K8.1	Natural water content of rock sample	nr			
K8.2	Porosity/density using saturation and calliper techniques	nr			
K8.3	Porosity/density using saturation and buoyancy	nr			
K8.4	Slake durability index	nr			
K8.5	Soundness by magnesium sulphate	nr			
K8.6	Magnesium sulphate test	nr			
K8.7	Shore scleroscope	nr			
K8.8	Schmidt rebound hardness	nr			
K8.9	Resistance to fragmentation	nr			
K8.10	Aggregate abrasion value	nr			

Number	Item description	Unit	Quantity	Rate	Amount £
K8.11	Polished stone value	nr			
K8.12	Aggregate frost heave	nr			
K8.13	Resistance to freezing and thawing	nr			
K8.14	Uniaxial compressive strength	nr			
K8.15	Deformability in uniaxial compression	nr			
K8.16	Indirect tensile strength by Brazilian test	nr			
K8.17	Undrained triaxial compression without measurements of porewater pressure	nr			
K8.18	Undrained triaxial compression with measurement of porewater pressure	nr			
K8.19	Direct shear strength of a single specimen	nr			
K8.20	Swelling pressure test	nr			
K8.21	Measurement of point load strength index of rock specimen (set of ten individual determinations)	nr			
K8.22	Single measurement of point load strength on irregular rock lump or core sample (either axial or diametral test)	nr			
	Ground/groundwater aggressivity				
K9.1	Suite A (Greenfield site – pyrite absent Schedule 1.19.6)	nr			
K9.2	Suite B (Greenfield site – pyrite present Schedule 1.19.6)	nr			
K9.3	Suite C (Brownfield site – pyrite absent Schedule 1.19.6)	nr			
K9.4	Suite D (Brownfield site – pyrite present Schedule 1.19.6)	nr			
	Contract specific additional bill items				

Total section K carried to summary _____

Bill of Quantities Section L: Geoenvironmental laboratory testing – Notes for Guidance

The tests included in each of Suites E, F and G under Items L1.1–L1.3 inclusive need to be reviewed and, if necessary, amended in light of the results of the site-specific desk study. It is likely that other determinands will need to be included for many investigations.

Additional test suites or individual tests may be added as Items L1.4, etc. where required.

Bill of Quantities

Bill L   Geoenvironmental laboratory testing

Number	Item description	Unit	Quantity	Rate	Amount £
L	**Geoenvironmental laboratory testing**				
	Contamination testing				
L1.1	Suite E (Soil samples Schedule S1.20.3)	nr			
L1.2	Suite F (Water samples Schedule S1.20.3)	nr			
L1.3	Suite G (Gas samples Schedule S1.20.3)	nr			
	Waste acceptance criteria testing				
L2.1	Suite H (Inert waste landfill Schedule S1.20.5)	nr			
L2.2	Suite I (Stable, non-reactive hazardous waste in non-hazardous waste landfill Schedule S1.20.5)	nr			
L2.3	Suite J (Hazardous waste landfill Schedule S1.20.5)	nr			
	Contract specific additional bill items				

Total section L carried to summary _____

Summary of Bill of Quantities

	£
A. General items, provisional services and additional items	
B. Percussion boring	
C. Rotary drilling	
D. Pitting and trenching	
E. Sampling and monitoring during intrusive investigation	
F. Probing and cone penetration testing	
G. Geophysical testing	
H. In situ testing	
I. Instrumentation	
J. Installation monitoring and sampling	
K. Geotechnical laboratory testing	
L. Geoenvironmental laboratory testing	
Total tender	

Appendix A. Rates for Ground Practitioners and other Personnel

Rates shall be entered for the various grades of staff listed, who will be employed by agreement with the Investigation Supervisor to provide advice or assistance during the course of the investigation and/or the preparation of the Ground Investigation Report and/or the Geotechnical Design Report all in accordance with Specification Clauses 3.6.1 and 3.6.2 and Schedule S1.8.3.

These services exclude the contract management, superintendence and technical direction required under the Conditions of Contract and the requirements of Specification Clause 3.5.1, which shall be included in the general rates and prices of the main Bill of Quantities (see Clause 1 of the Preamble to the Bill of Quantities).

Notes for Guidance

The disciplines and/or grades of ground practitioners and other personnel required to assist or advise the Investigation Supervisor will need to be determined on a site-specific basis. The list may be subdivided or repeated for the main services required where due consideration is to be given to the separate costs of the advisory services or report preparation.

Where the professional attendances required by Specification Clause 3.5.2 can be adequately specified at tender, they should be detailed in Schedule S1.8.2 and covered by the rates and prices entered in the main Bill of Quantities Items A7.1–A7.6.

Where the provision of staff for work in accordance with Specification Clauses 3.5.2, 3.6.1 and 3.6.2 cannot be adequately specified at tender, Appendix A can be used to obtain the Contractor's rates for selected disciplines and/or grades of staff. Appendix A can then be used as the charge basis for employing the Contractor's staff as and when required.

Item	Item description	Unit	Rate
1	Technician	h	
2	Graduate ground engineer	h	
3	Experienced ground engineer	h	
4	Registered Ground Engineering Professional	h	
5	Registered Ground Engineering Specialist	h	
6	Registered Ground Engineering Advisor	h	
7	Expenses incurred by staff on site visits or who are resident by agreement with the Investigation Supervisor	day	
8	Rate per kilometre[1] from Contractor's premises and return for Items 1, 2 and 3	km[1]	
9	As above but for Items 4, 5 and 6	km[1]	
10	All other expenses incurred in conjunction with a site visit where a return journey is made on the same day for Items 1, 2 and 3	visit	
11	As above but for Items 4, 5 and 6	visit	
12	All other expenses incurred in connection with visit where an overnight stay is necessary for Items 1, 2 and 3	overnight	
13	As above but for Items 4, 5 and 6	overnight	

[1]Where considered more appropriate, 'mile' may be used.

Estimate of costs under Appendix A to the Bill of Quantities where the provision of the Contractor's staff for work in accordance with Specification Clauses 3.5.2, 3.6.1 and 3.6.2 cannot be adequately specified at tender. **(To be assessed by the Investigation Supervisor)**

£

Appendix B. Long-term sample storage

Rates shall be entered for

Item	Item description	Unit	Rate/month
Geotechnical samples			
1	Dynamic (windowless) samples	nr	
2	Rotary drilling core in core box	nr	
3	Rotary drilling core sub-samples	nr	
4	Bulk samples	nr	
5	Large bulk samples	nr	
6	Open-tube samples (thick-wall sampler)	nr	
7	Open-tube samples (thin-wall sampler)	nr	
8	Disturbed samples	nr	
9	Groundwater samples	nr	
10	Delft samples	nr	
11	Mostap samples	nr	
12	Piston samples	nr	
Contamination samples			
13	Soil samples in plastic tubs	nr	
14	Soil samples in glass containers	nr	
15	Groundwater samples	nr	
16	Gas samples	nr	

Where samples comprise more than one container, the rate entered shall be per container.

Estimate of costs under Appendix B to the Bill of Quantities for long-term storage of samples where required in Schedules S1.12.2 and S1.12.10. **(To be assessed by the Investigation Supervisor)**

£

UK Specification for Ground Investigation
ISBN: 978-0-7277-3506-5

ICE Publishing: All rights reserved
doi: 10.1680/uksgi.35065.175

Example uses of the Schedules and Bills of Quantities

General comments

Three examples of the use of the Schedules and Bill of Quantities are given.

Example A assumes that a simple single-storey construction is to be built on a previously undeveloped green category site.

Examples B and C both relate to a more complex site which has been previously developed and is likely to have been contaminated, but where alternative proposed developments lead to differing investigation requirements. The site is categorised as yellow.

The proposed development for Example B is standard two-storey residential housing where relatively shallow foundations are likely to suffice. Only a limited depth of investigation is required.

For Example C the site is to be subject to an industrial development including heavy machinery, likely to require piled foundations extending into the bedrock.

Although the site is the same for Examples B and C, the differing proposed developments necessitate some significant differences in the ground investigations required. The two examples are also used to illustrate other options available in the documentation.

In Example B it is assumed that the Contractor is to provide only the factual report element of the Ground Investigation Report and that the costs involved in compiling that report can reasonably be assessed at tender. It is therefore assumed that these costs are to be included within the Bill Item A7, although the Contractor is required to include his estimate of these costs in his tender.

In Example C it is assumed that the Contractor is to compile the full Ground Investigation Report in compliance with Eurocode 7. In recognition that compiling such a report is likely to involve significant uncertainties, it is assumed that the costs for reporting will be recovered through the use of the rates provided by the Contractor in Appendix A.

Examples B and C also illustrate the flexibility offered by Schedules S1.19.6 (Chemical tests for potentially aggressive ground/groundwater) and S1.20.3 (Chemical laboratory testing for contamination). Either the testing requirements can be fully or partially specified to the Contractor or the onus can be placed on the Contractor to complete the Schedules to detail what can be offered.

Example A

Particulars of this example

The hypothetical site is assumed to be a small approximately level green field which is surrounded by an existing secure fence. The desk study findings have revealed that the site is highly unlikely to be crossed by any services or have been contaminated, is probably underlain by a firm becoming stiff clay and for several decades has been free from any large trees. The walkover survey has confirmed no visible evidence of contamination or notifiable weeds.

In this example it is assumed that the site is to be developed with a small light-weight single-storey building to be used as a village hall. The development and ground conditions require a simple investigation, predominantly of trial pits, and a factual Report provided which will be used by the developer's Engineer to complete the design of foundations and associated ground engineering aspects. The Contractor is required to enter rates in Bill item A7 for completion of the Factual Report. In respect of testing for the aggressiveness of the ground to concrete, the Contractor is to detail in Schedule S1.19.6 Suite A what test methods can be offered.

The Employer has instructed the same Engineer to provide the Investigation Supervisor. The Contractor is to supply an Experienced Geotechnical Engineer full time on site; 2 days has been entered in Bill A for this purpose with a further half-day allowance for compiling the factual report, but the Contractor shall only be paid for the actual time spent.

Notwithstanding that the site is expected to be free of contamination, attention is drawn to Schedule S1.20.3 and the specified part of Bill L, which are to be completed to cover the eventuality that unforeseen contamination is found to exist on the site. A Provisional sum is included in Item A6 to cover for the costs of dealing with unforseen contamination.

The developers' design engineer has considerable local experience of building construction and road pavement design, and large bulk samples from the trial pits for CBR testing are not required. As a result of that local experience, it is not expected that the Contractor will be required to give further assistance to the Investigation Supervisor or the Engineer's designer; the Contractor is therefore not required to complete either Appendices A or B.

Schedule 1: Information and site-specific requirements

S1.1 Name of Contract
Proposed Village Hall, South Hamlet

S1.2 Investigation Supervisor
Mr A N Other of XYZ Associates, Site Investigation House, Anytown AB1 2CD, Someshire shall be both Project Manager and Investigation Supervisor for the Contract.

Contact No. 07123-456789 (mobile)
Email 'another@xyzassociates.co.uk'

The Conditions of Contract shall be the NEC3 Engineering and Construction Contract (2005), Option B and Option W1.

S1.3 Description of site
The site, centred at approximate National Grid Coordinates AB 101 202, comprises approximately 0.5 hectares of generally level ground. It is surrounded by a permanent secure fence with a padlocked gated access from the adjacent Main Street. Keys for the padlocked gate will be available from the Investigation Supervisor. No below-ground or above-ground services are known to exist within the site boundary.

The desk study indicates that there is no evidence of previous development, no reason to suspect that the site has been contaminated and an absence of any large trees for several decades. The walkover survey showed the site to be currently covered by rough grass and confirmed no visible evidence of either contamination or notifiable weeds.

The site classification is GREEN.

S1.4 Main works proposed and purpose of this contract
The proposed construction is a new single-storey village hall of approximately 800 square metres plan area. The new hall is to be of lightweight construction and it is expected that it will be supported on shallow strip footing foundations imposing a net increase in ground loading of about 20 kN/m run. It is expected that foundation excavation arisings will be used to form low landscaping features around the hall and no materials will be disposed of off-site during the construction. The proposed development includes the construction of new vehicular entrance from Main Street and parking for approximately 20 cars immediately adjacent to the eastern side of the building. Services to the new building are to run along the line of the new vehicular entrance.

The aims of this main geotechnical investigation are to provide assessments of the ground conditions for foundation design, to determine the chemical conditions in respect of below-ground concrete and to confirm that groundwater will not be encountered within foundation depth.

The proposed outline and likely foundation plan for the new hall is shown on Drg No. XYZ_001 Rev 0.

S1.5 Scope of investigation
The proposed investigation comprises 1 No cable percussion borehole to 7 m depth and 6 No trial pits to a maximum depth of 3.5 m. However, the borehole shall attain a minimum penetration of 2 m into bedrock or until identification is certain, whichever is the greater.

Undisturbed driven thin-wall tube samples, SPTs and small disturbed samples are required in the boring. Small disturbed and bulk samples will be required from the trial pits. Geotechnical laboratory testing will be scheduled by the Investigation Supervisor on selected samples.

No monitoring instruments are required but the borehole shall be left open overnight to confirm the standing groundwater level.

A soil infiltration test is to be performed in a trial pit to be selected by the Investigation Supervisor.

Only the factual part of the Ground Investigation Report is to be provided by the Contractor.

There are no restrictions on the timing of the fieldwork part of the investigation.

The following Schedules are not required for this investigation:

S1.10 (Rotary drilling)
S1.13 (Probing and cone penetration testing)
S1.14 (Geophysical testing)
S1.16 (Instrumentation)
S1.17 (Instrumentation monitoring and sampling)

The associated Bills C, F, G, I and J are also not required.

S1.6 Geology and ground conditions

The following general assessment of the geology of the site and ground conditions has been inferred from available information. No assurance is given to its accuracy.

The downward succession is expected to comprise thin topsoil overlying firm glacial clay, becoming stiff with depth, overlying weathered Sherwood Sandstone bedrock at about 3 m below existing ground level. The groundwater table is expected to be at or just below rockhead.

S1.7 Schedule of drawing(s) and documents

The documentation includes:

The Site Plan (in AutoCAD format), Drg No. XYZ_001 Rev 0, Scale 1:500 which shows the location and layout of the proposed construction works, the fenced site boundary, the immediately surrounding existing residential properties, the setting-out points which are provided to the Contractor and the available information on services which are all shown to lie outside the site boundary.

Copies of the service plans obtained from the gas, electricity and telecoms utilities.

Copies of the risk assessments.

The Desk Study Report No. XYZ.

Specific routes across the site have not been indicated on the drawings, but the Contractor shall restrict movements to/from individual locations in order to minimise site damage.

Aerial photographs of the site may be viewed at the Investigation Supervisor's offices.

S1.8 General requirements (Specification Section 3) Particular restrictions/relaxations

Contract specific restrictions/relaxations, if any, shall be inserted below.

S1.8.1 Quality management system (Clause 3.3)

Quality management to BS EN ISO 9001, BS EN ISO 14001 and BS OHSAS 18001 required.

S1.8.2 Professional Attendance (Clause 3.5.2)

The Contractor shall provide an experienced ground engineer full time on site for the supervision of all site activities, logging trial pits, taking samples from the trial pits, take photographs and providing daily records and preliminary logs (except where daily records are for activities carried out by boring operatives).

S1.8.3 Provision of ground practitioners and other personnel (Clauses 3.6.1 and 3.6.2)

The Contractor is to prepare the specified factual part of the Ground Investigation Report.

No other personnel (see Specification Cl 3.6.2) are to be provided by the Contractor during the course of the site operations.

The Contractor is not required to complete Appendix A.

S1.8.4 Hazardous ground, land affected by contamination and notifiable and invasive weeds (Clauses 3.7.1 and 3.22)

None.

S1.8.5 Additional information on services not shown on Contract drawings (Clause 3.7.2)

None.

S1.8.6 Known/suspected mine workings, mineral extractions, etc. (Clause 3.7.3)

None.

S1.8.7 Protected species (Clause 3.7.4)

None.

S1.8.8 Archaeological remains (Clause 3.7.5)

None.

S1.8.9 Security of site (Clause 3.11)

Existing fencing not to be breached. Site access is to be via the existing gate which is to be kept locked except when entering and leaving the site.

Any exploratory hole left open overnight is to be fenced off with reflective two-rail rigid barriers.

S1.8.10 Traffic management measures (Clause 3.12)

Not required.

S1.8.11 Restricted working hours (Clause 3.13)

All work to be between 0800 and 1800 hours.

S1.8.12 Trainee site operatives (Clause 3.14.1)

Not permitted.

S1.8.13 Contamination avoidance and/or aquifer protection measures required (Clauses 3.15.2 and 3.15.3)

Not required.

S1.8.14 Maximum period for boring, pitting or trenching through hard material, hard stratum or obstruction (Clauses 2.8, 4.3 and 6.4)

2 hours.

Powered breakers will not be required to extend the depths of trial pits if hard material is encountered within the scheduled depth.

S1.8.15 Reinstatement requirements (Clause 3.16)

As specified.

S1.8.16 Hygiene facilities required (Clauses 2.20 and 3.16.1)

No facilities required in excess of the minimum welfare facilities.

S1.8.17 Unavoidable damage to be reinstated by Contractor (Clause 3.16.1)

Not required.

S1.8.18 Accuracy of exploratory hole locations (Clauses 3.19 and 3.20)

As specified.

S1.8.19 Photography requirements (Clause 3.25)

As specified plus a minimum of 2 photographs of the site (taken from opposing directions) prior to the start of investigation works and an analogous set of photographs on completion of the investigation.

Further particular Contract restrictions/relaxations shall be entered below, using sequential numbers to those above

None.

S1.9 Percussion boring (Specification Section 4) Particular restrictions/relaxations

Contract specific restrictions/relaxations, if any, shall be inserted below.

S1.9.1 Permitted methods and restrictions (Clauses 4.1 to 4.4)

As specified.

S1.9.2 Backfilling (Clause 4.5)

Backfill to be bentonite pellets.

S1.9.3 Dynamic sampling (Clause 4.6)

Not required.

Further particular Contract restrictions/relaxations shall be entered below, using sequential numbers to those above

None.

S1.10 Rotary drilling (Specification Section 5) Particular restrictions/relaxations

Not required.

S1.11 Pitting and trenching (Specification Section 6) Particular restrictions/relaxations

Contract specific restrictions/relaxations, if any, shall be inserted below.

S1.11.1 Indirect detection of buried services and inspection pits (Clauses 3.8.3 and 6.1)

Notwithstanding the apparent absence of any below-ground services, all exploratory hole locations shall be CAT scanned prior to any excavation. In addition, an inspection pit to a depth of 1.2 m below existing ground level, as specified, is required at the proposed borehole location.

S1.11.2 Restrictions on plant or pitting/trenching methods (Clauses 6.2 and 6.3)

Notwithstanding the apparent absence of any below-ground services, excavation is to be carried out as described in Specification Note for Guidance 6.2.

Topsoil is to be stockpiled separately from other excavation arisings.

S1.11.3 Entry of personnel (Clause 6.5)

No personnel to enter trial pit excavations.

S1.11.4 Alternative pit and trench dimensions (Clause 6.7)

As specified except as detailed in Schedule S1.15.6.

S1.11.5 Abstracted groundwater from land affected by contamination (Clause 6.9.2)

No contamination expected.

S1.11.6 Backfilling (Clause 6.10)

Excavation arisings to be placed in layers not more than 0.3 m thick (measured on loose arisings) and compacted using excavator bucket. Bedrock arisings shall be placed at the base of the pit.

All trial pits shall be backfilled on the same day as they are excavated. The only exception to backfilling on the same day as excavation is the trial pit used for the soakaway test if the rate of soakage requires the pit to be left open for more than one working day. Overnight fencing around the trial pit as detailed in Schedule S1.8.9 is then required.

S1.11.7 Photographic requirements (Clause 6.12)

All pits to be photographed to show a general view of the pit and excavation arisings plus separate views of each excavated face.

S1.11.8 Artificial lighting (Clause 6.12.2)

Required if there is insufficient daylight to provide clear images of the strata exposed in each trial pit face.

S1.11.9 Provision of pitting equipment and crew for Investigation Supervisor's use (Clause 6.13)

Not required.

Further particular Contract restrictions/relaxations shall be entered below, using sequential numbers to those above

None.

S1.12 Sampling and monitoring during intrusive investigation (Specification Section 7) Particular restrictions/relaxations

Contract specific restrictions/relaxations, if any, shall be inserted below.

S1.12.1 Address for delivery of selected geotechnical samples (Clause 7.6.1)

Not required.

S1.12.2 Retention and disposal of geotechnical samples (Clause 7.6.2)

As specified.

S1.12.3 Frequency of sampling for geotechnical purposes (Clauses 7.6.3–7.6.11)

In borehole:

Small disturbed samples at 0.4 m depth intervals in inspection pit. Thereafter, thin-wall open-tube driven sample followed immediately by an SPT with the sequence repeated at 1.0 m depth intervals to the base of the glacial clay deposits. Soil from the cutting shoe of an open tube shall be retained as a small disturbed sample.

In the underlying bedrock SPTs at 0.75 m depth intervals. The maximum blow count for SPTs in bedrock shall be extended to 100 blows.

In trial pits:

Sampling as specified in Clause 7.6.11.

S1.12.4 Open-tube and piston sample diameters (Clause 7.6.5)

100 mm diameter samples to be taken using thin-wall sampler type UT100 (OS-T/W).

S1.12.5 Retention of cutting shoe samples (Clause 7.6.5)

As specified in Schedule S1.12.3.

S1.12.6 Delft and Mostap sampling (Clause 7.6.12)

Not required.

S1.12.7 Groundwater level measurements during exploratory hole construction (Clause 7.7)

As specified.

S1.12.8 Special geotechnical sampling (Clause 7.8)

Not required.

S1.12.9 Address for delivery of selected samples (Clause 7.9.2)

Not required.

S1.12.10 Retention and disposal of contamination/WAC samples (Clause 7.9.3)

Not required.

S1.12.11 Frequency of sampling (Clause 7.9.4)

Not required.

S1.12.12 Sampling method (Clause 7.9.5)

Not required.

S1.12.13 Headspace testing (Clause 7.9.8)

Not required.

Further particular Contract restrictions/relaxations shall be entered below, using sequential numbers to those above

None.

S1.13 Probing and cone penetration testing (Specification Section 8) Particular restrictions/relaxations

Not required.

S1.14 Geophysical testing (Specification Section 9) Particular restrictions/relaxations

Not required.

S1.15 In situ testing (Specification Section 10) Particular restrictions/relaxations

Contract specific restrictions/relaxations, if any, shall be inserted below.

S1.15.1 Tests in accordance with British Standards (Clause 10.3)

Standard Penetration Tests but extended to 100 blows for tests in bedrock.

S1.15.2 Hand penetrometer and hand vane for shear strength (Clause 10.4.1)

Not required.

S1.15.3 Self-boring pressuremeter and high-pressure dilatometer testing and reporting (Clause 10.5.1)

Not required.

S1.15.4 Driven or push-in pressuremeter testing and reporting requirements (Clause 10.5.2)

Not required.

S1.15.5 Menard pressuremeter tests (Clause 10.5.3)

Not required.

S1.15.6 Soil infiltration test (Clause 10.6)

One soil infiltration test will be required as specified in BRE 365 in a trial pit location to be selected by the Investigation Supervisor on completion of the first five trial pits. The likely dimensions of the trial pit for the soil infiltration test trial will be approximately 2 m long, 1 m wide and 3 m deep (but of sufficient depth to penetrate into the top of the bedrock).

S1.15.7 Special in situ testing and reporting requirements (Clause 10.7)

Not required.

S1.15.8 Interface probes (Clause 10.8)

Not required.

S1.15.9 Contamination screening tests (Clause 10.9)

Not required.

S1.15.10 Metal detection (Clause 10.10)

Not required.

Further particular Contract restrictions/relaxations shall be entered below, using sequential numbers to those above

None.

S1.16 Instrumentation (Specification Section 11) Particular restrictions/relaxations

Not required.

S1.17 Installation monitoring and sampling (Specification Section 12) Particular restrictions/relaxations

Not required.

S1.18 Daily records (Specification Section 13) Particular restrictions/relaxations

Contract specific restrictions/relaxations, if any, shall be inserted below.

S1.18.1 Information for daily records (Clause 13.1)

As specified.

S1.18.2 Special in situ tests and instrumentation records (Clause 13.4)

Not required.

Further particular Contract restrictions/relaxations shall be entered below, using sequential numbers to those above

None.

S1.19 Geotechnical laboratory testing (Specification Section 14) Particular restrictions/relaxations

Contract specific restrictions/relaxations, if any, shall be inserted below.

S1.19.1 Investigation Supervisor or Contractor to schedule testing (Clause 14.1.1)

Investigation Supervisor to schedule testing based on the daily records.

S1.19.2 Tests required (Clause 14.1.2)

Natural moisture content,
liquid limit, plastic limit and plasticity index,
density by linear measurement,
particle size distribution by wet sieving, sedimentation by hydrometer,
undrained strength on single 100 mm diameter specimens in triaxial compression without the measurement of pore pressure,
and
one-dimensional consolidation tests.

S1.19.3 Specifications for tests not covered by BS 1377 and options under BS 1377 (Clauses 14.2.1 and 14.4)

Not required.

S1.19.4 UKAS accreditation to be adopted (Clause 14.3)

UKAS accreditation required.

S1.19.5 Rock testing requirements (Clause 14.5)

Not required.

S1.19.6 (Test Suites A–D) Chemical testing for aggressive ground/groundwater for concrete (Clause 14.6)

Only Suite A (Greenfield site – pyrite absent) is required. The test methods which the Contractor can offer are to be detailed in Schedule S1.19.6 Suite A below.

Test Suites B, C and D are not required and have been deleted.

S1.19.7 Laboratory testing on site (Clause 14.7)

Not required.

S1.19.8 Special laboratory testing (Clause 14.8)

Not required.

Further particular Contract restrictions/relaxations shall be entered below, using sequential numbers to those above

None.

CHEMICAL TESTS ON POTENTIALLY AGGRESSIVE GROUND/GROUNDWATER

Sample type	Determinand	Recommended test methods	Test method ~~specified~~/offered[1]
SUITE A Greenfield site (pyrite absent)			
Soil	pH in 2.5:1 water/soil extract	BR 279 Electrometric	
		BS 1377 Part 3, Method 9	Required
	SO_4 in 2:1 water/soil extract	BR 279 Gravimetric method, cation exchange or ion chromatography	
		BS 1377 Part 3 Method 5.3 + 5.5	Required
		TRL 447 Test 1	
Groundwater	pH	BR 279 Electrometric	
		BS 1377 Part 3, Method 9	Required
	SO_4	BR 279 Gravimetric method, cation exchange or ion chromatography	
		BS 1377 Part 3 Method 5.4 + 5.5	Required
		Commercial lab in-house procedure – determination of sulphur by ICP-AES[2]	

[1] **Either** ~~Investigation Supervisor to specify method required or~~ Contractor to detail method(s) offered.

[2] ICP-AES: inductively coupled plasma atomic emission spectroscopy.

S1.20 Geoenvironmental laboratory testing (Specification Section 15) Particular restrictions/relaxations

Contract specific restrictions/relaxations, if any, shall be inserted below.

S1.20.1 Investigation Supervisor or Contractor to schedule testing (Clause 15.1)

Investigation Supervisor to schedule testing.

S1.20.2 Accreditation required (Clause 15.2)

Contractor to detail the accreditation which can be offered on a test-by-test basis.

S1.20.3 (Test Suites E–G are overleaf) Chemical testing for contamination (Clause 15.3)

Notwithstanding that the site is expected to be free of contamination, the Contractor shall complete the proforma page 'Suite E – soil samples' to provide for the case of unforeseen contamination being encountered.

Test Suites F and G are not required and have been deleted.

SCHEDULE 1.20.3

CHEMICAL LABORATORY TESTING FOR CONTAMINATION

Nominated Test Laboratory? Contractor to specify proposed laboratory

Required Testing Turnaround Times? 10 days

NB 1. This proforma Schedule MUST be reviewed in the light of site-specific desk study results and amended accordingly to include any additional determinands likely to be required.

2. Limits of detection should reflect the guideline/threshold values against which the test results will be compared.

SUITE E – Soil samples			
Determinand (Procurer to list required determinands)	**Limit of detection** required/offered[1]	**Test method** required/offered[1]	**Accreditation** required/offered[1]
Arsenic			
Boron			
Cadmium			
Chromium (total)			
Copper			
Lead			
Mercury			
Nickel			
Zinc			
pH			
Water soluble sulphate (as SO_4)			
Organic matter			
Total petroleum hydrocarbons			
Speciated polyaromatic hydrocarbons (USEPA 16)			
Phenol			
Cyanide (total)			
Asbestos			

[1] Either Investigation Supervisor to specify the test method (except testing under MCERTs), limit of detection and accreditation required or Contractor to detail what can be offered under each of these categories. See also Specification Note for Guidance 15.3.

S1.20.4 Waste characterisation (Clause 15.4)
Not required.

S1.20.5 (Test Suites H–J) Waste Acceptance Criteria testing (Clause 15.5)
No WAC testing is required and Test Suites H, I and J have been deleted.

S1.20.6 Laboratory testing on site (Clause 15.6)
Not required.

S1.20.7 Special laboratory testing (Clause 15.7)
Not required.

Further particular Contract restrictions/relaxations shall be entered below, using sequential numbers to those above
None.

S1.21 Reporting (Specification Section 16) Particular restrictions/relaxations
Contract specific restrictions/relaxations, if any, shall be inserted below.

S1.21.1 Form of exploratory hole logs (Clauses 16.1 and 16.2.1)
Contractor to submit specimen borehole and trial pit logs with tender for approval by the Investigation Supervisor.

S1.21.2 Information on exploratory hole logs (Clause 16.2.2)
As specified.

S1.21.3 Variations to final digital data supply requirements (Clause 16.5.1)
Data to be in AGS format. Digital data to be in a single file.

S1.21.4 Preliminary digital data (Clause 16.5.3)
Preliminary digital data to be issued to the Investigation Supervisor by email attachment within 3 days of completion of fieldwork.

S1.21.5 Type(s) of report required (Clause 16.6)
Factual part of Geotechnical Investigation Report.

S1.21.6 Electronic report requirements (Clause 16.6.3)
Media to be DVD ROM, maximum file size 5 Mb and photographs to be in JPG format.

S1.21.7 Format and contents of Desk Study Report (Clause 16.7)
Not required.

S1.21.8 Contents of Ground Investigation Report (or specified part thereof) (Clause 16.8)
Factual part of Geotechnical Investigation Report in accordance with Specification Clause 16.8.1.

S1.21.9 Contents of Geotechnical Design Report (or specified part thereof) (Clause 16.9)
Not required.

S1.21.10 Times for supply of electronic information (Clause 16.10.1)
Complete set of digital data shall be submitted with the draft and final factual reports.

S1.21.11 Electronic information transmission media (Clause 16.10.2)

Preliminary information to be transmitted by email. Final information to be provided on DVD ROM.

S1.21.12 Report approval (Clause 16.11)

Within 1 week of the completion of laboratory testing, one hard and one electronic copy of the draft report are to be submitted to the Investigation Supervisor who shall approve the draft report (or instruct on any required revisions) within 1 week following its receipt.

Two hard and one electronic copies of the final report (except the hard copy photographic volume which shall be a single copy) are to be submitted to the Investigation Supervisor within 1 week after draft copy approval.

Further particular Contract restrictions/relaxations shall be entered below, using sequential numbers to those above

None.

Schedule 2: Exploratory holes

Hole number	Type	Scheduled depth (m)	National grid reference		Approximate ground level (mOD)	Remarks
			Easting (m)	Northing (m)		
101	Percussion borehole	7.00	**NB** In an actual investigation it is essential that individual Eastings, Northings and ground levels would be entered here for each hole.			
201	Trial pit	3.50				
202	Trial pit	3.50				
203	Trial pit	3.50				
204	Trial pit	3.50				
205	Trial pit	3.50				
206	Trial pit	3.50				One trial pit to be used for soil infiltration test. Pit location and excavation dimensions to be selected by Investigation Supervisor on completion of first 5 pits

Schedule 3: Investigation Supervisor's facilities

S3.1   Accommodation

Not required.

S3.2   Furnishings

Not required.

S3.3   Services

Not required.

S3.4   Equipment

Not required.

S3.5   Transport

Not required.

S3.6   Personal Protective Equipment for Investigation Supervisor

Not required.

Schedule 4: Specification amendments

The following clauses are amended			
Section number	**Clause number**	**Delete the following**	**Substitute the following**
			No amendments

Schedule 5: Specification additions

The following clauses are added to the Specification		
Section number	**Clause number**	**Clause wording**
		No additions

Annex 1 Bill of Quantities for Ground Investigation

Preamble amendments and additions

The following clauses are amended or added to the Preamble.

None.

Bill of Quantities

The following pages constitute the Bill of Quantities.

Bill of Quantities

Bill A   General items, provisional services and additional items

Number	Item description	Unit	Quantity	Rate	Amount £
A	**General items, provisional services and additional items**				
A1	Offices and stores for the Contractor	sum			
A2	Establish on site all plant, equipment and services for a Green Category site	sum			
A3	Extra over Item A2 for a Yellow Category site	sum	Not required		
A4	Maintain on site all site safety equipment for a Yellow Category site	week	Not required		
A5	Decontamination of equipment during and at end of intrusive investigation for a Yellow Category site	sum	Not required		
A6	Appropriate storage, transport and off-site disposal of contaminated arisings and any PPE equipment, excluding laboratory testing	provisional sum			600.00
A7	Provide professional attendance in accordance with Clause 3.5.2				
A7.1	Provide Technician	p.day			
A7.2	Provide graduate ground engineer	p.day			
A7.3	Provide Experienced Ground Engineer	p.day	2.5		
A7.4	Provide Registered Ground Engineering Professional	p.day			
A7.5	Provide Registered Ground Engineering Specialist	p.day			
A7.6	Provide Registered Ground Engineering Advisor	p.day			
A8	Establish the location and elevation of the ground at each exploratory hole	sum			
A9	Preparation of Health and Safety documentation and Safety Risk Assessment	sum			
A10	Facilities for the Investigation Supervisor	sum	Not required		
A11	Vehicle(s) for the Investigation Supervisor	v.wk	Not required		
A12	Fuel for vehicle for the Investigation Supervisor	provisional sum	Not required		
A13	Investigation Supervisor's telephone and facsimile charges	provisional sum	Not required		
A14	Deliver selected cores and samples to the specified address	provisional sum	Not required		
A15	Special testing and sampling required by Investigation Supervisor	provisional sum	Not required		
A16	Traffic safety and management	provisional sum	Not required		
A17	One master copy of the Desk Study Report	sum	Not required		
A18	Additional copies of the Desk Study Report	nr	Not required		
A19	One master copy of the Ground Investigation Report (or specified part thereof)	sum			

Number	Item description	Unit	Quantity	Rate	Amount £
A20	Additional copies of the Ground Investigation Report (or specified part thereof)	nr	2		
A21	Electronic copy of Ground Investigation Report (or specified part thereof)	sum			
A22	One master copy of the Geotechnical Design Report (or specified part thereof)	sum	Not required		
A23	Additional copies of the Geotechnical Design Report (or specified part thereof)	nr	Not required		
A24	Electronic copy of Geotechnical Design Report (or specified part thereof)	sum	Not required		
A25	Digital data in AGS transfer format	sum			
A26	Hard-copy photographs	nr	34		
A27	Photographic volume	nr	1		
A28	Long-term storage of geotechnical samples (Appendix B)	provisional sum	Not required		
A29	Long-term storage of geoenvironmental samples (Appendix B)	provisional sum	Not required		
	Contract specific additional bill items None				

Total section A carried to summary _____

Bill of Quantities

Bill B   Percussion boring

Number	Item description	Unit	Quantity	Rate	Amount £
B	**Percussion boring**				
B1	Move boring plant and equipment to the site of each exploratory hole and set up	nr	1		
B2	Extra over Item BI for setting up on a slope of gradient greater than 20%	nr	Not required		
B3	Break out surface obstruction where present at exploratory borehole	h	Not required		
B4	Advance borehole between existing ground level and 10 m depth	m	7.00		
B5	As Item B4 but between 10 and 20 m depth	m	Not required		
B6	As Item B4 but between 20 and 30 m depth	m	Not required		
B7	As Item B4 but between 30 and 40 m depth	m	Not required		
B8	As Item B4 but between 40 and 50 m depth	m	Not required		
B9	Advance borehole through hard stratum or obstruction	h	3.00		
B10	Provide aquifer protection measures at a single aquiclude/aquifer boundary or cross-contamination control measures at a single soil boundary in a borehole	nr	Not required		
B11	Backfill borehole with cement/bentonite grout or bentonite pellets	m	7.00		
B12	Standing time for borehole plant, equipment and crew	h	1.00		
	Dynamic sampling		Not required		
	Contract specific additional bill items				
	None				

Total section B carried to summary _____

Bill of Quantities

Bill C   Rotary drilling

Number	Item description	Unit	Quantity	Rate	Amount £
C	**Rotary drilling**		Not required		

Bill of Quantities

Bill D   Pitting and trenching

Number	Item description	Unit	Quantity	Rate	Amount £
D	**Pitting and trenching**				
	Inspection pits				
D1	Excavate inspection pit by hand to 1.2 m depth	nr	1		
D2	Extra over Item Dl for breaking out surface obstructions	h	Not required		
	Trial pits and trenches				
D3	Move equipment to the site of each trial pit or trench of not greater than 4.5 m depth	nr	6		
D4	Extra over Item D3 for setting up on a slope of gradient greater than 20%	nr	Not required		
D5	Extra over Item D3 for trial pit or trench between 4.5 and 6 m depth	nr	Not required		
D6	Excavate trial pit between existing ground level and 3.0 m depth	m	18.00		
D7	As Item D6 but between 3.0 and 4.5 m depth	m	3.00		
D8	As Item D6 but between 4.5 and 6 m depth	m	Not required		
D9	Excavate trial trench between existing ground level and 3.0 m depth	m^3	Not required		
D10	As Item D9 between 3.0 and 4.5 in depth	m^3	Not required		
D11	As Item D9 between 4.5 and 6 m depth	m^3	Not required		
D12	Extra over Items D6 to D11 inclusive for breaking out hard material or surface obstructions	h	Not required		
D13	Standing time for excavation plant, equipment and crew for machine-dug trial pit or trench	h	2.00		
	Observation pits and trenches		Not required		
	Daily provision of pitting crew and equipment		Not required		
	General				
D37	Bring pump to the position of each exploratory pit or trench	nr	Not required		
D38	Pump water from pit or trench	h	Not required		
D39	Extra over Item D38 for temporary storage, treatment and disposal of contaminated water	Provisional sum	Not required		
D40	Leave open observation pit or trench	m^2/day	Not required		
D41	Leave open trial pit or trench	m^2/day	4.00		
	Contract specific additional bill items				
	None				

Total section D carried to summary _____

Bill of Quantities

Bill E   Sampling and monitoring during intrusive investigation

Number	Item description	Unit	Quantity	Rate	Amount £
E	**Sampling and monitoring during intrusive investigation**				
	Samples for geotechnical purposes				
E1	Small disturbed sample	nr	29		
E2	Bulk disturbed sample	nr	20		
E3	Large bulk disturbed sample	nr	Not required		
E4.1	Open-tube sample using thick-walled (OS-TK/W) sampler	nr	Not required		
E4.2	Open-tube sample using thin-walled (OS-T/W) sampler	nr	2		
E5	Piston sample	nr	Not required		
E6	Groundwater sample	nr	1		
E7	Ground gas sample	nr	Not required		
E8	Cut, prepare and protect core sub-sample	nr	Not required		
	Continuous or semi-continuous sampling		Not required		
	Containers for contamination assessment and WAC testing		Not required		
	Contract specific additional bill items				
	None				

Total section E carried to summary _____

Bill of Quantities

Bill F   Probing and cone penetration testing

Number	Item description	Unit	Quantity	Rate	Amount £
F	Probing and cone penetration testing		Not required		

Bill of Quantities

Bill G   Geophysical testing

Number	Item description	Unit	Quantity	Rate	Amount £
G	Geophysical testing		Not required		

Bill of Quantities

Bill H   In situ testing

Number	Item description	Unit	Quantity	Rate	Amount £
H	**In situ testing**				
H1	Standard penetration test in borehole	nr	6		
H2	Standard penetration test in rotary drillhole	nr	Not required		
H3	In situ density testing		Not required		
H3.1	Small pouring cylinder method	nr	Not required		
H3.2	Large pouring cylinder method	nr	Not required		
H3.3	Water replacement method	nr	Not required		
H3.4	Core cutter method	nr	Not required		
H3.5	Nuclear method	day	Not required		
H4	California Bearing Ratio test	nr	Not required		
H5	Vane shear strength test in borehole	nr	Not required		
H6	Penetration vane test, penetration from ground level	nr	Not required		
H7	Hand penetrometer test (set of 3 readings)	nr	Not required		
H8	Hand vane test (set of 3 readings)	nr	Not required		
	Other tests		Not required		
	Permeability testing		Not required		
	Self-boring pressuremeter		Not required		
	High-pressure dilatometer		Not required		
	Driven or push-in pressuremeter		Not required		
	Menard pressuremeter		Not required		
	Soil infiltration test				
H81	Provide equipment and carry out set of 3 infiltration tests at selected location up to 1 day, including hire of excavation equipment	nr	1		
H82	Extra over item H81 for additional days	day	1		

Number	Item description	Unit	Quantity	Rate	Amount £
H83	Calculation of infiltration rate for each tested location Miscellaneous site testing	nr	1 Not required		
	Contract specific additional bill items None				

Total section H carried to summary _____

Bill of Quantities

Bill I   Instrumentation

Number	Item description	Unit	Quantity	Rate	Amount £
I	**Instrumentation**		Not required		

Bill of Quantities

Bill J   Installation monitoring and sampling

Number	Item description	Unit	Quantity	Rate	Amount £
J	**Installation monitoring and sampling** (during fieldwork period)		Not required		
	Installation monitoring and sampling (post fieldwork period)		Not required		

Bill of Quantities

Bill K   Geotechnical laboratory testing

Number	Item description	Unit	Quantity	Rate	Amount £
K	**Geotechnical laboratory testing**				
K1	Classification	nr			
K1.1	Moisture content	nr	6		
K1.2	Liquid limit, plastic limit and plasticity index	nr	6		
K1.3	Volumetric shrinkage	nr	Not required		
K1.4	Linear shrinkage	nr	Not required		
K1.5	Density by linear measurement	nr	2		
K1.6	Density by immersion in water or water displacement	nr	Not required		
K1.7	Dry density and saturation moisture content for chalk	nr	Not required		

Number	Item description	Unit	Quantity	Rate	Amount £
K1.8	Particle density by gas jar or pyknometer	nr	Not required		
K1.9	Particle size distribution by wet sieving	nr	2		
K1.10	Particle size distribution by dry sieving	nr	Not required		
K1.11	Sedimentation by pipette	nr	Not required		
K1.12	Sedimentation by hydrometer	nr	2		
K2	Chemical and electrochemical		Not required		
K3	Compaction related		Not required		
K4	Compressibility, permeability, durability	nr			
K4.1	One-dimensional consolidation properties, test period 5 days	nr	2		
K4.2	Extra over Item K4.1 for test period in excess of 5 days	day	6		
K4.3	Measurements of swelling pressure, test period 2 days	nr	Not required		
K4.4	Measurement of swelling, test period 2 days	nr	Not required		
K4.5	Measurement of settlement on saturation, test period 1 day	nr	Not required		
K4.6	Extra over Items K4.3 to K4.5 for test period in excess of 2 or 1 day(s)	day	Not required		
K4.7	Permeability by constant head method	nr	Not required		
K4.8	Dispersibility by pinhole method	nr	Not required		
K4.9	Dispersibility by crumb method	nr	Not required		
K4.10	Dispersibility by dispersion method	nr	Not required		
K4.11	Frost heave of soil	nr	Not required		
K5	Consolidation and permeability in hydraulic cells		Not required		
K6	Shear strength (total stress)				
K6.1	Shear strength by the laboratory vane method (set of 3)	nr	Not required		
K6.2	Shear strength by hand vane (set of 3)	nr	Not required		
K6.3	Shear strength by hand penetrometer (set of 3)	nr	Not required		
K6.4	Shear strength of a set of three 60 mm × 60 mm square specimens by direct shear, test duration not exceeding 1 day per specimen	nr	Not required		
K6.5	Extra over Item K6.4 for test durations in excess of 1 day per specimen	sp.day	Not required		
K6.6	Shear strength of a single 300 mm × 300 mm square specimen by direct shear, test duration not exceeding 1 day	nr	Not required		

Number	Item description	Unit	Quantity	Rate	Amount £
K6.7	Extra over Item K6.6 for test durations in excess of 1 day	day	Not required		
K6.8	Residual shear strength of a set of three 60 mm × 60 mm square specimens by direct shear, test duration not exceeding 4 days per specimen	nr	Not required		
K6.9	Extra over Item K6.8 for test durations in excess of 4 days per specimen	sp.day	Not required		
K6.10	Residual shear strength of a 300 mm square specimen by direct shear, test duration not exceeding 4 days	nr	Not required		
K6.11	Extra over Item K6.10 for test duration in excess of 4 days	day	Not required		
K6.12	Residual shear strength using the small ring shear apparatus at three normal pressures, test duration not exceeding 4 days	nr	Not required		
K6.13	Extra over Item K6.12 for test duration in excess of 4 days	day	Not required		
K6.14	Unconfined compressive strength of 38 mm diameter specimen	nr	Not required		
K6.15	Undrained shear strength of a set of three 38 mm diameter specimens in triaxial compression without the measurement of pore pressure	nr	Not required		
K6.16	Undrained strength of a single 100 mm diameter specimen in triaxial compression without the measurement of pore pressure	nr	2		
K6.17	Undrained shear strength of single 100 mm diameter specimen in triaxial compression with multistage loading and without measurement of pore pressure	nr	Not required		
K7	Shear strength (effective stress)		Not required		
K8	Rock testing		Not required		
	Ground/groundwater aggressivity				
K9.1	Suite A (Greenfield site – pyrite absent Schedule 1.19.6)	nr	4		
K9.2	Suite B (Greenfield site – pyrite present Schedule 1.19.6)	nr	Not required		
K9.3	Suite C (Brownfield site – pyrite absent Schedule 1.19.6)	nr	Not required		
K9.4	Suite D (Brownfield site – pyrite present Schedule 1.19.6)	nr	Not required		
	Contract specific additional bill items None				

Total section K carried to summary _____

Bill of Quantities

Bill L   Geoenvironmental laboratory testing

Number	Item description	Unit	Quantity	Rate	Amount £
L	**Geoenvironmental laboratory testing**				
	Contamination testing				
L1.1	Suite E (Soil samples Schedule S1.20.3)	nr	Rate only		
L1.2	Suite F (Water samples Schedule S1.20.3)	nr	Not required		
L1.3	Suite G (Gas samples Schedule S1.20.3)	nr	Not required		
	Waste acceptance criteria testing		Not required		
	Contract specific additional bill items				
	None				

Total section L carried to summary _____

Summary of Bill of Quantities

	£
A. General items, provisional services and additional items	
B. Percussion boring	
C. Rotary drilling	Not required
D. Pitting and trenching	
E. Sampling during intrusive investigation	
F. Probing and cone penetration testing	Not required
G. Geophysical testing	Not required
H. In situ testing	
I. Instrumentation	Not required
J. Installation monitoring and sampling	Not required
K. Geotechnical laboratory testing	
L. Geoenvironmental laboratory testing	
Total tender	

Appendix A. Rates for Ground Practitioners and other Personnel

NOT REQUIRED

Appendix B. Long-term sample storage

NOT REQUIRED

Example B

Particulars of the example

The hypothetical site is assumed to be occupied by former railway sidings, constructed in the 1890s and abandoned in the late 1960s. The desk study findings are assumed to have revealed the following.

- The sidings were used as a load-out area for locally excavated clay being transported by rail to a remote off-site brickworks. Steam locomotives were used over most of the life of the sidings, being replaced latterly by diesel locomotives. Two asbestos-roofed railway workers' huts (now demolished) were present close to the site entrance; these were believed to be provided with water and domestic voltage electricity services (feeding from the nearby Railway Lane) which were disconnected on abandonment. No other known services were present on the site.
- Likely potential contaminants comprise metals/metaloids from ash deposits, asbestos from the roofs of the railway workers' huts, timber sleeper preservatives, chlorinated aliphatics from cleaning solvents and fuel and lubricating oils and greases. Herbicides were used to control weed growth until abandonment of the facility but, due to their rate of decay, are not now expected to pose a contamination threat.
- A former clay excavation area, about 200 m to the east of the site, has been used as a landfill since 1985 but was designed on containment principles and records indicate no contamination problems which are likely to affect the railway sidings site.
- Previous site investigations nearby, combined with published geological data, indicate the expected natural downward succession to be 1–3 m thickness of probably firm clay (Brickearth), 3–4 m of medium dense to dense glacial gravel, 2 m of probably stiff clay (weathered mudstones which could be pyrite rich) overlying a major aquifer of Coal Measures sandstone. The aquifer is thought to be at least 40 m thick. The walk-over reconnaissance indicates the railway ballast to be up to about 1 m thick.

In this example of the use of the Schedules and Bill of Quantities, it has been assumed that the site is to be re-developed for two-storey housing with the railway ballast being taken off site to suitable disposal. The desk study results indicate that the houses could be supported either on shallow strip foundations in the brickearth/top of the gravel or short piles founding in the gravel. As a result, the required maximum depth of investigation is not more than 2 m into the mudstone. This differs from Example C where, because of the different proposed development, investigation holes are required to penetrate into the underlying major aquifer and aquifer protection measures are deemed to be required.

The main contamination concerns relate to the shallow strata and the risks to construction workers, the housing residents and any groundwater in the gravels. In the laboratory contamination testing of water and ground gas samples, both the test method and required accreditation have been specified. For soil samples MCERTS accredition has been specified as far as possible; in those cases it has to be left to the Contractor to detail the test methods for which that accreditation is held. Consideration also needs to be given to disposal of the railway ballast and, in respect of the WAC testing, MCERTS accreditation is generally specified; again, it is for the Contractor to detail what test methods can be offered with accreditation. The limits of detection are also specified.

The investigation methods are to comprise percussion borings, dynamic (windowless) sampling, dynamic probing and trial pitting. It is required that the relevant plant and equipment are decontaminated on completion of each exploratory hole. However, instead of using the lump sum Item A5 (Decontamination of equipment during and at the end of intrusive investigation for a Yellow Category site) the Bill Preambles have been amended using Preamble Item 23 to include these costs within the rates for moving plant and equipment between exploratory hole locations.

It is also assumed that the Investigation Supervisor will be appointed by the Developer. For this example, the Contractor is required to estimate in the tender the grades of staff and the person days to be spent both in site operations and reporting. This approach offers the opportunity for the Investigation Supervisor to compare the various tendering Contractors' assessments of technical staff input (Professional Attendance and Provision of Ground Practitioners and Other Personnel). Recovery by the Contractor for the actual staff utilised will subsequently be for agreement between the Contractor and the Investigation Supervisor as the work progresses.

Although the Contractor is only required to compile the factual report part of the Ground Investigation Report, Appendix A (Rates for Ground Practitioners and Other Personnel is to be completed) to cover the possibility of being instructed to provide further technical input. Appendix B (Long-term sample storage) is not required.

Schedule 1: Information and site-specific requirements

S1.1   Name of Contract
Redevelopment of Old Railway Sidings, near Anytown, Someshire.

S1.2   Investigation Supervisor
A N Other of XYZ Associates, Site Investigation House, Anytown AB1 2CD, Someshire.

The Conditions of Contract shall be the NEC3 Engineering and Construction Contract (2005), Option B and Option W1.

All duties and powers vested in the Project Manager, except those which cannot be delegated, shall be delegated to the Investigation Supervisor.

The Project Manager for the Contract shall be the Finance Director of New Developments Ltd, Development House, Anytown AB1 2CD, Someshire.

S1.3   Description of site
The site comprises approximately x hectares of disused railway sidings centred at approximate National Grid reference AB 100 200.

A desk study has been carried out by XYZ Associates and a copy of that report is appended to the documents. The following comprises a summary of the desk study findings.

The site is bounded to the north by Railway Lane and to the east, south and west by farmland. The site is approximately level but is located in an area sloping gently westwards.

Access to the site is via the padlocked double gates on Railway Lane. Keys are available from the Investigation Supervisor.

Prior to the construction of the sidings in about 1890, the site comprised farmland. The sidings were used as a loading area for clay excavated from an area 200 m to the east which was then transported by rail to a former small brickworks about 4 km north of Anytown. The sidings became disused in 1960. Shortly thereafter, the rail lines were removed for salvage and the former railway workers' huts close to Railway Lane were demolished, with the demolition rubble being removed from site. The use of herbicides to control weed growth ceased about the time of abandonment.

The former clay excavation area (200 m to the east) has been used as a landfill from 1985 but was designed on a containment basis.

There is a small housing estate immediately on the north side of Railway Lane.

There are two wells about 400 m to the west of the site abstracting water from a major aquifer underlying the site.

The classification of the whole of the site is Yellow.

S1.4   Main works proposed and purpose of this contract
This main ground investigation is in connection with a proposed two-storey housing development. Soakaway drainage is proposed for surface run-off water.

There is no detailed layout available for the proposed housing, but it is expected that it will comprise a central access road (off Railway Lane) running north/south with houses on either side.

It is proposed that the railway ballast will be removed from site during the development.

S1.5 Scope of investigation

The aim of the investigation is to provide assessments of the ground conditions for foundations including its aggressiveness to below-ground concrete, the type and severity of ground/groundwater contamination and the condition of the railway ballast in respect of off-site disposal.

The intrusive fieldwork will comprise inspection pits, dynamic probing combined with dynamic (windowless) sampling, percussion borings with thin-walled open-tube samples, disturbed samples and SPTs and trial pits.

Standpipe piezometers and gas monitoring standpipes as combined installations are to be installed in the boreholes. Three variable head permeability tests in standpipe piezometers and two soil infiltration tests are to be carried out.

Geotechnical laboratory testing is required for the purposes of foundation design. Chemical laboratory testing is required for aggressiveness to concrete, contamination assessment and WAC testing in respect of the material to be taken off site. The laboratory testing will be scheduled by the Investigation Supervisor.

Only the factual part of the Ground Investigation Report is to be provided by the Contractor.

The following Schedules are not required for this investigation:

S1.10 (Rotary drilling)
S1.14 (Geophysical testing)

The associated Bills C and G are also not required.

S1.6 Geology and ground conditions

The following general assessment of the geology of the site and ground conditions has been inferred from available information. No assurance is given to its accuracy.

The downward succession is expected to comprise up to about 1 m thickness of railway ballast, 1–3 m thickness of probably firm clay (Brickearth), 3–4 m of glacial gravel, 3–4 m of probably very stiff potentially pyrite-rich clay (weathered mudstone) overlying a major aquifer of Coal Measures sandstone. The aquifer is thought to be at least 40 m thick.

The railway ballast, underlying natural soils and groundwater may be contaminated by metals/metalloids, asbestos, fuel and lubricating oil/grease and cleaning solvents.

S1.7 Schedule of drawing(s) and documents

A site plan (Drg No. 100 Rev 0 in AutoCAD format), included in the documentation, shows the extent of the site, the layout of the former sidings (including railway workers' huts, now demolished), the adjacent topographical features, setting-out points, land ownership details and the positions of the exploratory holes. No access routes are prescribed but the Contractor is required to comply with the Specification Clause 3.15.1 in respect of causing least damage.

The desk study report is included in the documentation.

No service drawings have been found but it is believed that there were electricity and water supplies to the railway workers' huts. Enquiries to the utility companies have indicated no other known services within the site boundaries.

Previous ground investigations in connection with the landfill site and the housing immediately to the north of Railway Lane are available for inspection at the Investigation Supervisor's offices.

S1.8 General requirements (Specification Section 3) Particular restrictions/relaxations

Contract specific restrictions/relaxations, if any, shall be inserted below.

S1.8.1 Quality management system (Clause 3.3)

Quality management to BS EN ISO 9001, BS EN ISO 14001 and BS OHSAS 18001 required.

S1.8.2 Professional Attendance (Clause 3.5.2)

The Contractor shall provide Professional Attendance to perform those tasks detailed in Specification Note for Guidance 3.5.2 which are relevant to this investigation.

The Contractor shall detail in his tender the number, names and experience details of the proposed staff and the times which each member of staff is expected to spend. Bill of Quantities Item A7 shall be used to detail the Contractor's expected Professional Attendance.

S1.8.3 Provision of ground practitioners and other personnel (Clauses 3.6.1 and 3.6.2)

The Contractor is to prepare the specified factual part of the Ground Investigation Report. The Contractor's expected staff times for report compilation, preparation and checking are to be included in Bill of Quantities Item A7.

No Other Personnel (see Specification Clause 3.6.2) are to be provided by the Contractor. The Contractor is, however, required to complete the table of rates included in Appendix A.

S1.8.4 Hazardous ground, land affected by contamination and notifiable and invasive weeds (Clauses 3.7.1 and 3.22)

Land affected by contamination as detailed above under 'Description of site' and 'Geology and ground conditions'.

There are no known notifiable or invasive weeds.

S1.8.5 Additional information on services not shown on Contract drawings (Clause 3.7.2)

Suspected electricity and water services as detailed above under 'Schedule of drawing(s) and documents'.

S1.8.6 Known/suspected mine workings, mineral extractions, etc. (Clause 3.7.3)

None.

S1.8.7 Protected species (Clause 3.7.4)

None.

S1.8.8 Archaeological remains (Clause 3.7.5)

None.

S1.8.9 Security of site (Clause 3.11)

Except for access to and from the site, the gates on Railway Lane shall be kept locked at all times. The site perimeter fence shall not be breached without the written permission of the Investigation Supervisor.

S1.8.10 Traffic management measures (Clause 3.12)

Not required.

S1.8.11 Restricted working hours (Clause 3.13)

Fieldwork hours to be restricted to 0800 to 1800 hours (Monday to Friday inclusive). No weekend working permitted.

S1.8.12 Trainee site operatives (Clause 3.14.1)

Not permitted.

S1.8.13 Contamination avoidance and/or aquifer protection measures required (Clauses 3.15.2 and 3.15.3)

Percussion boring, dynamic probing and sampling and trial pitting plant and equipment to be decontaminated on completion of each exploratory hole and on completion of the site works.

Trial pit arisings to be temporarily stockpiled on boards underlain by plastic sheeting to prevent contamination of the railway ballast.

S1.8.14 Maximum period for boring, pitting or trenching through hard material, hard stratum or obstruction (Clauses 2.8, 4.3 and 6.4)

2 hours at which time the instructions of the Investigation Supervisor shall be obtained.

S1.8.15 Reinstatement requirements (Clause 3.16)

Arisings to be stored on site in locked covered skips until laboratory test results allow the appropriate off-site disposal to be determined.

Trial pits to be backfilled with arisings placed in reverse order to excavation.

S1.8.16 Hygiene facilities required (Clauses 2.20 and 3.16.1)

Extra over statutory requirements, personnel washing and changing facilities and a bunded vehicle wheel wash to be provided at site entrance.

S1.8.17 Unavoidable damage to be reinstated by Contractor (Clause 3.16.1)

Not applicable.

S1.8.18 Accuracy of exploratory hole locations (Clauses 3.19 and 3.20)

As specified.

S1.8.19 Photography requirements (Clause 3.25)

Sufficient photographs to show the condition of the whole of the site prior to the start of investigation works and an analogous set of photographs on completion of the investigation.

Digital photographs to be submitted by email to the Investigation Supervisor within one working day of the photographs being taken.

Further particular Contract restrictions/relaxations shall be entered below, using sequential numbers to those above

None.

S1.9 Percussion boring (Specification Section 4) Particular restrictions/relaxations

Contract specific restrictions/relaxations, if any, shall be inserted below.

S1.9.1 Permitted methods and restrictions (Clauses 4.1 to 4.4)

No borehole to penetrate more than 2 m into the weathered mudstone.

Restrictions as detailed in Schedule S1.8.13; see also Schedule S1.11.1.

S1.9.2 Backfilling (Clause 4.5)

Bentonite pellets

S1.9.3 Dynamic sampling (Clause 4.6)

Windowless sampling required.

Holes to be backfilled with bentonite pellets with particular care being taken to prevent arching within the hole.

Further particular Contract restrictions/relaxations shall be entered below, using sequential numbers to those above

None.

S1.10 Rotary drilling (Specification Section 5) Particular restrictions/relaxations

Not required.

S1.11 Pitting and trenching (Specification Section 6) Particular restrictions/relaxations

Contract specific restrictions/relaxations, if any, shall be inserted below.

S1.11.1 Indirect detection of buried services and inspection pits (Clauses 3.8.3 and 6.1)

All exploratory hole locations are to be CAT scanned.

Inspection pits are required at all borehole locations: percussion boreholes, dynamically (windowless) sampled holes and probe holes.

S1.11.2 Restrictions on plant or pitting/trenching methods (Clauses 6.2 and 6.3)

All 2 and 3 m deep trial pits to be completed prior to excavating any 4 m deep trial pits.

Excavation of trial pits is to comply with recommended method of excavation described in Specification Note for Guidance 6.2.

All pits to be backfilled on day of excavation unless required to be kept open for a second day in connection with soil infiltration tests. If a trial pit needs to be left open overnight, a rigid reflective two-rail barrier is to be erected around the pit during the overnight period.

S1.11.3 Entry of personnel (Clause 6.5)

Not permitted.

S1.11.4 Alternative pit and trench dimensions (Clause 6.7)

As specified.

S1.11.5 Abstracted groundwater from land affected by contamination (Clause 6.9.2)

On-site measures for collection and temporary storage (prior to the availability of laboratory test results to determine appropriate disposal) to be agreed with Investigation Supervisor.

S1.11.6 Backfilling (Clause 6.10)

As specified in Schedules S1.8.13 and S1.8.15 above, with compaction of the arisings using excavation plant bucket.

S1.11.7 Photographic requirements (Clause 6.12)

As specified.

S1.11.8 Artificial lighting (Clause 6.12.2)

Required if natural daylight is insufficient to give clear views of all strata exposed in the pits.

S1.11.9 Provision of pitting equipment and crew for Investigation Supervisor's use (Clause 6.13)

Not required.

Further particular Contract restrictions/relaxations shall be entered below, using sequential numbers to those above

None.

S1.12 Sampling and monitoring during intrusive investigation (Specification Section 7) Particular restrictions/relaxations

Contract specific restrictions/relaxations, if any, shall be inserted below.

S1.12.1 Address for delivery of selected geotechnical samples (Clause 7.6.1)

Not required.

S1.12.2 Retention and disposal of geotechnical samples (Clause 7.6.2)

As specified.

S1.12.3 Frequency of sampling for geotechnical purposes (Clauses 7.6.3–7.6.11)

Small disturbed samples at 0.3 m depth intervals in inspection pits.

In percussion boreholes:

A. Open-tube, small disturbed and bulk samples as specified in Clause 7.6.4

B. No large bulks required

C. Groundwater samples as specified

In pits: as specified.

S1.12.4 Open-tube and piston sample diameters (Clause 7.6.5)

100 mm diameter samples to be taken using thin-wall sampler (OS-T/W).

S1.12.5 Retention of cutting shoe samples (Clause 7.6.5)

As specified.

S1.12.6 Delft and Mostap sampling (Clause 7.6.12)
Not required.

S1.12.7 Groundwater level measurements during exploratory hole construction (Clause 7.7)
As specified.

S1.12.8 Special geotechnical sampling (Clause 7.8)
Not required.

S1.12.9 Address for delivery of selected samples (Clause 7.9.2)
Not required.

S1.12.10 Retention and disposal of contamination/WAC samples (Clause 7.9.3)
As specified.

S1.12.11 Frequency of sampling (Clause 7.9.4)
Minimum sampling in each trial pit is to comprise soil samples at 0.5 m depth intervals in railway ballast and Brickearth plus 1 No sample of groundwater where encountered. Additional samples may be required where evidence of contamination is observed.

Minimum sampling in the windowless sampling holes is to comprise samples at 0.5 m depth intervals down to the base of the Brickearth. This will require samples to be recovered from the inspection pits at the windowless sampling locations.

S1.12.12 Sampling method (Clause 7.9.5)
Sampling to be under the supervision of an environmental scientist, geoenvironmental engineer or geochemist meeting the requirements of Clause 2.3 item (c).

S1.12.13 Headspace testing (Clause 7.9.8)
Required – details to be agreed on site with Investigation Supervisor.

Further particular Contract restrictions/relaxations shall be entered below, using sequential numbers to those above
None.

S1.13 Probing and cone penetration testing (Specification Section 8) Particular restrictions/relaxations
Contract specific restrictions/relaxations, if any, shall be inserted below.

S1.13.1 Type(s) and reporting of dynamic probing (Clauses 8.1.1 and 8.1.2)
DPH capacity equipment required.

Reporting to accord with BS EN ISO 22476-2.7.

S1.13.2 Capacity and equipment requirements for cone penetration testing (Clause 8.2.1)
Not required.

S1.13.3 Reporting of cone penetration testing parameters (Clause 8.2.4)
Not required.

S1.13.4 Seismic cone equipment requirements (Clause 8.3.1)
Not required.

S1.13.5 Interpretation of seismic cone tests (Clause 8.3.4)
Not required.

S1.13.6 Other cone or specialist probes (Clause 8.4)
Not required.

Further particular Contract restrictions/relaxations shall be entered below, using sequential numbers to those above

None.

S1.14 Geophysical testing (Specification Section 9) Particular restrictions/relaxations
Not required.

S1.15 In situ testing (Specification Section 10) Particular restrictions/relaxations
Contract specific restrictions/relaxations, if any, shall be inserted below.

S1.15.1 Tests in accordance with British Standards (Clause 10.3)
SPTs in percussion boreholes at depth intervals specified in Specification Clause 7.6.4.

S1.15.2 Hand penetrometer and hand vane for shear strength (Clause 10.4.1)
Not required.

S1.15.3 Self-boring pressuremeter and high-pressure dilatometer testing and reporting (Clause 10.5.1)
Not required.

S1.15.4 Driven or push-in pressuremeter testing and reporting requirements (Clause 10.5.2)
Not required.

S1.15.5 Menard pressuremeter tests (Clause 10.5.3)
Not required.

S1.15.6 Soil infiltration test (Clause 10.6)
Two infiltration tests to be carried out in pits excavated to top of gravel horizon below the Brickearth and nominally 0.5 m wide by 2.0 m long, with actual dimensions measured on site. Infiltration test locations to be determined by the Investigation Supervisor following completion of the 2 and 3 m deep trial pits; see also Schedule S1.11.2.

S1.15.7 Special in situ testing and reporting requirements (Clause 10.7)
Not required

S1.15.8 Interface probes (Clause 10.8)
Required for percussion boreholes and/or windowless sampling holes to be selected on site by the Investigation Supervisor.

S1.15.9 Contamination screening tests (Clause 10.9)
Required with use to be directed by Investigation Supervisor.

S1.15.10 Metal detection (Clause 10.10)
Not required.

Further particular Contract restrictions/relaxations shall be entered below, using sequential numbers to those above

None.

S1.16 Instrumentation (Specification Section 11) Particular restrictions/relaxations

Contract specific restrictions/relaxations, if any, shall be inserted below.

S1.16.1 Protective covers for installations (Clause 11.2)

Lockable steel covers to be set in a concrete surround and raised nominally 200 mm above ground level.

S1.16.2 Protective fencing (Clause 11.3)

Not required but the location of each instrumented exploratory hole is to be marked with a secure 1 m high wooden post clearly marked with the exploratory hole number.

S1.16.3 Standpipe and standpipe piezometer installations (Clauses 11.4.1 and 11.4.2)

See Schedule S1.16.6 for general principles.

Installations to be based on 50 mm diameter uPVC tubing with installation details (filter lengths, depths, etc.) to be agreed on site with the Investigation Supervisor.

S1.16.4 Other piezometer installations (Clause 11.4.3)

Not required.

S1.16.5 Development of standpipes and standpipe piezometers (Clause 11.4.5)

All standpipe piezometers to be developed using an MP1 pump.

S1.16.6 Ground gas standpipes (Clause 11.5)

Ground gas standpipes penetrating into gravel stratum required in percussion boreholes as generally described in Schedule 2. These installations also to be used for groundwater level monitoring.

S1.16.7 Inclinometer installations (Clause 11.6)

Not required.

S1.16.8 Slip indicators (Clause 11.7)

Not required.

S1.16.9 Extensometers and settlement gauges (Clause 11.8)

Not required.

S1.16.10 Settlement monuments (Clause 11.9)

Not required.

S1.16.11 Removal of installations (Clause 11.10)

No installations to be removed.

S1.16.12 Other instrumentation (Clause 11.11)

Not required.

Further particular Contract restrictions/relaxations shall be entered below, using sequential numbers to those above

None.

S1.17 Installation monitoring and sampling (Specification Section 12) Particular restrictions/relaxations

Contract specific restrictions/relaxations, if any, shall be inserted below.

S1.17.1 Groundwater level readings in installations (Clause 12.2)

Groundwater level readings to be taken weekly in combined groundwater/soil gas standpipes during fieldwork period.

Readings also to be taken during return visits to site at 2 monthly intervals for 12 months following the end of fieldwork. The frequency of return visits to site may be adjusted if major variations in groundwater level readings occur.

S1.17.2 Groundwater sampling from installations (Clause 12.3.1)

Single sample required from each standpipe piezometer and each combined groundwater/soil gas standpipe during fieldwork period.

Further samples may be required, as directed by the Investigation Supervisor, during return visits to site.

S1.17.3 Purging/micro-purging (Clause 12.3.2)

Purging of all installations where groundwater sampling is required to continue until conductivity, pH, temperature, dissolved oxygen and Redox potential have stabilised.

S1.17.4 Ground gas monitoring (Clause 12.4)

Monitoring required weekly in combined groundwater/soil gas standpipes during fieldwork period.

Readings also to be taken during return visits to site at 2 monthly intervals for 12 months following the end of fieldwork.

S1.17.5 Sampling from ground gas installations (Clause 12.5)

Samples to be taken during fieldwork period and/or during return visits to site, as directed by the Investigation Supervisor.

S1.17.6 Other monitoring (Clause 12.8)

Not required.

S1.17.7 Sampling and testing of surface water bodies (Clause 12.9)

Not required

Further particular Contract restrictions/relaxations shall be entered below, using sequential numbers to those above

None.

S1.18 Daily records (Specification Section 13) Particular restrictions/relaxations

Contract specific restrictions/relaxations, if any, shall be inserted below.

S1.18.1 Information for daily records (Clause 13.1)

Contractor to submit a proforma or example record for approval by the Investigation Supervisor.

S1.18.2 Special in situ tests and instrumentation records (Clause 13.4)

Instrument installation records shall clearly include the hole diameter, installation casing and perforated screen diameter and installed depths, material descriptions and installed depths of the filter(s) and seal(s) and cover arrangements.

> Further particular Contract restrictions/relaxations shall be entered below, using sequential numbers to those above

None.

S1.19 Geotechnical laboratory testing (Specification Section 14) Particular restrictions/relaxations

Contract specific restrictions/relaxations, if any, shall be inserted below.

S1.19.1 Investigation Supervisor or Contractor to schedule testing (Clause 14.1.1)

Investigation Supervisor to schedule testing based on the daily records.

S1.19.2 Tests required (Clause 14.1.2)

Natural moisture content, Atterberg Limits, undrained shear strength without pore pressure measurement, particle size distribution and one-dimensional consolidation oedometers.

S1.19.3 Specifications for tests not covered by BS 1377 and options under BS 1377 (Clauses 14.2.1 and 14.4)

Not required.

S1.19.4 UKAS accreditation to be adopted (Clause 14.3)

All testing to be UKAS accredited.

S1.19.5 Rock testing requirements (Clause 14.5)

Not required.

S1.19.6 (Test Suites A–D) Chemical testing for aggressive ground/ groundwater for concrete (Clause 14.6)

Test Suite C (Brownfield pyrite absent) and Test Suite D (Brownfield pyrite present) testing required; see Schedules presented in the following pages.

Tests Suites A and B are not required and have been deleted.

S1.19.7 Laboratory testing on site (Clause 14.7)

Not required.

S1.19.8 Special laboratory testing (Clause 14.8)

Not required.

> Further particular Contract restrictions/relaxations shall be entered below, using sequential numbers to those above

None.

SCHEDULE 1.19.6 (Derived from BRE Special Digest SD1)

CHEMICAL TESTS ON POTENTIALLY AGGRESSIVE GROUND/GROUNDWATER

SUITE C Brownfield site (pyrite absent)			
Sample type	**Determinand**	**Recommended test methods**	**Test method specified/~~offered~~**[1]
Soil	pH in 2.5:1 water/soil extract	BR 279 Electrometric	
		BS 1377 Part 3, Method 9	✓
	SO$_4$ in 2:1 water/soil extract	BR 279 Gravimetric method, cation exchange or ion chromatography	
		BS 1377 Part 3 Method 5.3 + 5.5	
		TRL 447 Test 1	✓
	Mg (only required if water soluble SO$_4$ >3000 mg/l)	BR 279 AAS[2] method	
		Commercial lab in-house procedure – variant of BR 279 using ICP-AES[3]	✓ Lab to determine whether test required
	NO$_3$ in 2:1 water/soil extract (only required if pH <5.5)	BR 279	✓ Lab to determine whether test required
	Cl in 2:1 water/soil extract (only required if pH <5.5)	BR279	
		BS1377 Part 3, Method 7.2	✓ Lab to determine whether test required
Groundwater	pH	BR 279 Electrometric	
		BS 1377 Part 3, Method 9	✓
	SO$_4$	BR 279 Gravimetric method, cation exchange or ion chromatography	
		BS 1377 Part 3 Method 5.4 + 5.5	
		Commercial lab in-house procedure – determination of sulphur by ICP-AES[3]	✓
	Mg (only required if water soluble SO$_4$ ⩾3000 mg/l)	BR 279 AAS[2] method	
		Commercial lab in-house procedure – Mg in solution by ICP-AES[3]	✓ Lab to determine whether test required
	NO$_3$ (only required if pH <5.5)	BR 279	✓ Lab to determine whether test required
	Cl (only required if pH <5.5)	BR 279	
		BS 1377 Part 3, Method 7.2	✓ Lab to determine whether test required

[1] **Either** Investigation Supervisor to specify method required ~~or Contractor to indicate method(s) offered~~.
[2] AAS: atomic absorption spectrometry.
[3] ICP-AES: inductively coupled plasma atomic emission spectroscopy.

SCHEDULE S1.19.6 (Derived from BRE Special Digest SD1)

CHEMICAL TESTS ON POTENTIALLY AGGRESSIVE GROUND/GROUNDWATER

SUITE D Brownfield site (pyrite present)			
Sample type	Determinand	Recommended test methods	Test method specified/~~offered~~[1]
Soil	pH in 2.5:1 water/soil extract	BR 279 Electrometric	
		BS 1377 Part 3, Method 9	✓
	SO_4 in 2:1 water/ soil extract	BR 279 Gravimetric method, cation exchange or ion chromatography	
		BS 1377 Part 3 Method 5.3 + 5.5	
		TRL 447 Test 1	✓
	Acid soluble SO_4	BR 279 Gravimetric method	
		BS 1377 Part 3, Method 5.2 + 5.5	
		TRL 447 Test 2	✓
	Total sulphur	BR 279 Ignition in oxygen	
		TRL 447 Test 4A	
		TRL 447 Test 4B	✓
	Mg (only required if water soluble SO_4 >3000 mg/l)	BR 279 AAS[2] method	
		Commercial lab in-house procedure – variant of BR 279 using ICP-AES[3]	✓ Lab to determine whether test required
	NO_3 in 2:1 water/soil extract (only required if pH <5.5)	BR 279	✓ Lab to determine whether test required
	Cl in 2:1 water/soil extract (only required if pH <5.5)	BR 279	
		BS 1377 Part 3, Method 7.2	✓ Lab to determine whether test required
Groundwater	pH	BR 279 Electrometric	
		BS 1377 Part 3, Method 9	✓
	SO_4	BR 279 Gravimetric method, cation exchange or ion chromatography	
		BS 1377 Part 3 Method 5.4 + 5.5	
		Commercial lab in-house procedure – determination of sulphur by ICP-AES[3]	✓
	Mg (only required if water soluble SO_4 ≥3000 mg/l)	BR 279 AAS[2] method	
		Commercial lab in-house procedure – Mg in solution by ICP-AES[3]	✓ Lab to determine whether test required
	NO_3 (only required if pH <5.5)	BR 279	✓ Lab to determine whether test required
	Cl (only required if pH <5.5)	BR 279	
		BS 1377 Part 3, Method 7.2	✓ Lab to determine whether test required

[1] **Either** Investigation Supervisor to specify method required ~~or Contractor to indicate method(s) offered.~~

[2] AAS: atomic absorption spectrometry.

[3] ICP-AES: inductively coupled plasma atomic emission spectroscopy.

S1.20 Geoenvironmental laboratory testing (Specification Section 15) Particular restrictions/relaxations

Contract specific restrictions/relaxations, if any, shall be inserted below.

S1.20.1 Investigation Supervisor or Contractor to schedule testing (Clause 15.1)

Investigation Supervisor.

S1.20.2 Accreditation required (Clause 15.2)

MCERTS where available, otherwise UKAS.

S1.20.3 (Test Suites E–G are overleaf) Chemical testing for contamination (Clause 15.3)

Test Suites E and F testing required. Test Suite G testing may be required dependent upon results of on-site ground gas monitoring.

For Test Suite E: Contractor to detail what test methods can be offered to comply with the accreditation requirements.

SCHEDULE 1.20.3

CHEMICAL LABORATORY TESTING FOR CONTAMINATION

Nominated Test Laboratory ? None specified

Required Testing Turnaround Times ? 10 days unless test procedure requires extended time

NB

1. This proforma Schedule MUST be reviewed in the light of site-specific desk study results and amended accordingly to include any additional determinands likely to be required.

2. Limits of detection should reflect the guideline/threshold values against which the test results will be compared.

SUITE E – Soil samples			
Determinand (Procurer to list required determinands)	**Limit of detection required/~~offered~~**[1] (mg/kg unless stated otherwise)	**Test method required/offered**[1]	**Accreditation required/~~offered~~**[1]
Arsenic	0.1		MCERTS
Boron (water soluble)	0.5		MCERTS
Cadmium	0.1		MCERTS
Chromium (total)	0.5		MCERTS
Copper	0.5		MCERTS
Lead	0.5		MCERTS
Mercury	0.1		MCERTS
Nickel	0.5		MCERTS
Zinc	3		MCERTS
pH	Not applicable		MCERTS
Water soluble sulphate (as SO_4)	0.3 mg/l		MCERTS
Organic matter	0.1%	Dichromate oxidation/ colorimetric determination	UKAS
Total petroleum hydrocarbons	10		MCERTS
Speciated polyaromatic hydrocarbons (USEPA 16)	0.08		MCERTS
~~Phenol~~			
Cyanide (total)	1		MCERTS
Asbestos	0.001%	Wet sieve/gravimetry/ microscopy and dispersion staining	UKAS
Additional determinands			
Vanadium	2		MCERTS
VOC	0.005 to 0.025		MCERTS
SVOC	0.2 to 10		MCERTSs

[1] ~~Either Investigation Supervisor to specify the test method (except testing under MCERTs), limit of detection and accreditation required~~ **or** Contractor to detail what can be offered under each of these categories. See also Specification Note for Guidance 15.3.

CHEMICAL LABORATORY TESTING FOR CONTAMINATION

Nominated Test Laboratory ? None specified

Required Testing Turnaround Times ? 10 days unless test procedure requires extended time

NB

1. This proforma Schedule MUST be reviewed in the light of site-specific desk study results and amended accordingly to include any additional determinands likely to be required.

2. Limits of detection should reflect the guideline/threshold values against which the test results will be compared.

SUITE F – Water samples			
Determinand (Procurer to list required determinands)	**Limit of detection** required/~~offered~~[1] (mg/kg)	**Test method** required/~~offered~~[1]	**Accreditation** required/~~offered~~[1]
Arsenic	0.001	ICPMS	
Boron	0.05	ICPOES	
Cadmium	0.0001	ICPMS	
Chromium (total)	0.001	ICPMS	
Copper	0.001	ICPMS	
Lead	0.001	ICPMS	
Mercury	0.0001	ICPMS	
Nickel	0.001	ICPMS	
Zinc	0.001	ICPMS	
pH	Not applicable	BS 1377	
Sulphate (as SO_4)	0.06	ICPOES	
Total petroleum hydrocarbons	0.01	GCFID with carbon banding	UKAS
Speciated polyaromatic hydrocarbons (USEPA 16)	Variably 0.005–0.05	GCMS 15 priority pollutants	
~~Phenol~~			
Cyanide (total)	0.1	Acid distillation/ion chromatography	
Additional determinands			
Vanadium	0.001	ICPMS	
VOC	0.001 to 0.005		
SVOC	0.002 to 0.1		

[1] ~~Either~~ Investigation Supervisor to specify the test method, limit of detection and accreditation required ~~or Contractor to detail what can be offered under each of these categories. See also Specification Note for Guidance 15.3.~~

SCHEDULE 1.20.3

CHEMICAL LABORATORY TESTING FOR CONTAMINATION

Nominated Test Laboratory ? None specified

Required Testing Turnaround Times ? 10 days unless test procedure requires extended time

NB

1. This proforma Schedule MUST be reviewed in the light of site-specific desk study results and amended accordingly to include any additional determinands likely to be required.

2. Limits of detection should reflect the guideline/threshold values against which the test results will be compared.

SUITE G – Ground gas samples			
Determinand (Procurer to list required determinands)	**Limit of detection** required/~~offered~~[1] (% unless otherwise stated)	**Test method** required/~~offered~~[1]	**Accreditation** required/~~offered~~[1]
Oxygen	0.05	Paramagnetic analysis	UKAS
Nitrogen	1	Gas chromatography with katharometer	
Carbon dioxide	0.02	Infrared absorption	
Carbon monoxide	0.001	Infrared absorption	
Hydrogen	5 ppm	Gas chromatography with katharometer	
Hydrogen sulphide	1 ppm	Gas chromatography with FPD	
Methane	0.02	Infrared absorption	
~~Ethane~~	Not required	Not required	Not required
~~Propane~~	Not required	Not required	Not required
~~Butane~~	Not required	Not required	Not required
~~Iso-butane~~	Not required	Not required	Not required

[1] ~~Either~~ Investigation Supervisor to specify the test method, limit of detection and accreditation required ~~or Contractor to detail what can be offered under each of these categories. See also Specification Note for Guidance 15.3.~~

S1.20.4 Waste characterisation (Clause 15.4)

Contractor to carry out assessment.

S1.20.5 (Test Suites H–J are overleaf) Waste Acceptance Criteria testing (Clause 15.5)

Test Suites I and J testing required. The Contractor is to detail what test methods can be offered to comply with the accreditation requirements.

Tests Suite H is not required and has been deleted.

S1.20.6 Laboratory testing on site (Clause 15.6)

Not required.

S1.20.7 Special laboratory testing (Clause 15.7)

Not required.

Further particular Contract restrictions/relaxations shall be entered below, using sequential numbers to those above

None.

SCHEDULE 1.20.5

CHEMICAL TESTING FOR WASTE ACCEPTANCE CRITERIA TESTING (from STWAPs 2003)

SUITE I – Stable non-reactive hazardous waste in non-hazardous landfill			
Determinand	**Limit of detection required/~~offered~~[1]**	**Test method required/offered[1]**	**Accreditation required/~~offered~~[1]**
Soil analyses			
Total organic carbon			MCERTS
pH			MCERTS
Leachate analyses			
Arsenic			MCERTS
Barium			MCERTS
Cadmium			MCERTS
Chromium (total)			MCERTS
Copper			MCERTS
Mercury			MCERTS
Molybdenum	Equal to or better than WAC limits		MCERTS
Nickel			MCERTS
Lead			MCERTS
Antimony			MCERTS
Selenium			MCERTS
Zinc			MCERTS
Chloride			MCERTS
Fluoride			MCERTS
Sulphate (as SO_4)			MCERTS
Total dissolved solids		BS 2690 Part 121	UKAS
Phenol Index			MCERTS
Dissolved organic carbon			MCERTS

[1] ~~Either Investigation Supervisor to specify the test method, limit of detection and accreditation required or~~ Contractor to detail what can be offered under each of these categories. See also Specification Note for Guidance 15.5.

SCHEDULE 1.20.5

CHEMICAL TESTING FOR WASTE ACCEPTANCE CRITERIA TESTING (from STWAPs 2003)

SUITE J – Hazardous waste landfill			
Determinand	**Limit of detection required/~~offered~~[1]**	**Test method required/offered[1]**	**Accreditation required/~~offered~~[1]**
Soil analyses			
Total organic carbon			MCERTs
Loss on ignition			MCERTs
Leachate analyses			
Arsenic			MCERTs
Barium			MCERTs
Cadmium			MCERTs
Chromium (total)			MCERTs
Copper			MCERTs
Mercury			MCERTs
Molybdenum	Equal to or better than WAC limits		MCERTs
Nickel			MCERTs
Lead			MCERTs
Antimony			MCERTs
Selenium			MCERTs
Zinc			MCERTs
Chloride			MCERTs
Fluoride			MCERTs
Sulphate (as SO_4)			MCERTs
Total dissolved solids		BS 2690 Part 121	UKAS
Phenol Index			MCERTs
Dissolved organic carbon			MCERTs

[1] ~~Either Investigation Supervisor to specify the test method, limit of detection and accreditation required or~~ Contractor to detail what can be offered under each of these categories. See also Specification Note for Guidance 15.5.

S1.21 Reporting (Specification Section 16) Particular restrictions/relaxations

Contract specific restrictions/relaxations, if any, shall be inserted below.

S1.21.1 Form of exploratory hole logs (Clauses 16.1 and 16.2.1)

Contractor to submit a proforma or example record for approval by the Investigation Supervisor.

S1.21.2 Information on exploratory hole logs (Clause 16.2.2)

As specified.

S1.21.3 Variations to final digital data supply requirements (Clause 16.5.1)

Data to be in AGS format. Digital data to be in a single file.

Contractor to detail the highest AGS edition which can be offered.

No additional groups, fields or codes required.

S1.21.4 Preliminary digital data (Clause 16.5.3)

Final digital data only required.

S1.21.5 Type(s) of report required (Clause 16.6)

Factual part of Ground Investigation Report including all information required by Cl 16.8.1.

S1.21.6 Electronic report requirements (Clause 16.6.3)

Media to be DVD ROM, maximum file size to be 5 Mb and photographs to be in JPG format.

S1.21.7 Format and contents of Desk Study Report (Clauses 16.7)

Not required.

S1.21.8 Contents of Ground Investigation Report (or specified part thereof) (Clause 16.8)

As specified in Schedule S1.21.5 but data obtained during return visits to site shall be the subject of a supplementary report.

S1.21.9 Contents of Geotechnical Design Report (or specified part thereof) (Clause 16.9)

Not required.

S1.21.10 Times for supply of electronic information (Clause 16.10.1)

Complete set of digital data to be supplied with draft and approved final copies of the report.

S1.21.11 Electronic information transmission media (Clause 16.10.2)

DVD ROM.

S1.21.12 Report approval (Clause 16.11)

One hard and one electronic copy of the draft factual part of the Ground Investigation Report required for submission to the Investigation Supervisor 6 weeks after the completion of fieldwork.

Investigation Supervisor's comments on the draft Ground Investigation Report and associated digital data to be issued within 2 weeks from receipt of the draft and one hard and one electronic copy of the approved report submitted by the Contractor within a further 2 weeks.

The supplementary report containing post-fieldwork monitoring data to be submitted as one hard and one electronic copy within 2 weeks of the final return visit.

Further particular Contract restrictions/relaxations shall be entered below, using sequential numbers to those above

None.

Schedule 2: Exploratory holes

Hole number	Type	Scheduled depth (m)	National grid reference		Approximate ground level (mOD)	Remarks Including in situ testing and installations
			Easting (m)	Northing (m)		
						1. Exploratory holes generally spread across the site in a regular grid pattern, except where stated below.
1	Percussion borehole	7	**NB** In an actual investigation individual Eastings, Northings and ground levels would be entered here for each hole			
2	Percussion borehole	7				2. Three trial pits targeted close to the location of the former railway workers' huts to provide samples for contamination testing, particularly in respect of asbestos and chlorinated aliphatics (cleaning solvents).
3	Percussion borehole	8				
4	Percussion borehole	8				
5	Percussion borehole	8				
						3. All percussion boreholes with thin-walled tube samples at 0.75 m depth intervals in the Brickearth to provide samples for undrained strength and consolidation laboratory testing in connection with possible shallow strip foundations. Small disturbed samples primarily for soil description.
101	Dynamic (windowless) sample	2	In an actual investigation individual Eastings, Northings and ground levels would be entered here for each hole			
102	Dynamic (windowless) sample	2				
103	Dynamic (windowless) sample	3				
104	Dynamic (windowless) sample	4				
105	Dynamic (windowless) sample	4				
						4. All percussion boreholes with SPTs at 0.75 m depth intervals in the gravel to determine its relative density in connection with possible short piles founding in the gravel stratum.
201	Trial pit	2	In an actual investigation individual Eastings, Northings and ground levels would be entered here for each hole			
202	Trial pit	2				
203	Trial pit	2				5. All dynamic probes to penetrate as far as possible into the gravel stratum to supplement the SPT data in the percussion boreholes.
204	Trial pit	2				
205	Trial pit	2				
206	Trial pit	3				
207	Trial pit	3				6. Two of the scheduled dynamic probes to be selected by the Investigation Supervisor are to be located immediately adjacent to percussion boreholes to facilitate correlation between the SPT values and the dynamic probe results.
208	Trial pit	3				
209	Trial pit	3				
210	Trial pit	3				
211	Trial pit	4				
212	Trial pit	4				
213	Trial pit	4				
214	Trial pit	4				
215	Trial pit	4				

Hole number	Type	Scheduled depth (m)	National grid reference		Approximate ground level (mOD)	Remarks Including in situ testing and installations
			Easting (m)	Northing (m)		
301	Dynamic probe	5	In an actual investigation individual Eastings, Northings and ground levels would be entered here for each hole			7. Dynamic (windowless) sampling holes to give fuller coverage of the site in respect of the made ground (ballast) and Brickearth, together with the depth to the top of the gravel stratum.
302	Dynamic probe	5				
303	Dynamic probe	5				
304	Dynamic probe	6				8. Samples from trial pits and selected sub-samples from dynamic (windowless) sampling to be used for contamination testing.
305	Dynamic probe	6				
306	Dynamic probe	6				
307	Dynamic probe	6				9. Combined groundwater/ ground gas monitoring standpipes to be installed in each percussion borehole to enable checks for the presence of ground gas and groundwater sampling from and groundwater level monitoring in the gravel stratum.
308	Dynamic probe	7				
309	Dynamic probe	7				
310	Dynamic probe	7				10. Soil infiltration tests to be carried out in two of the 4 m deep trial pits, the actual pits to be selected on site by the Investigation Supervisor.

Schedule 3: Investigation Supervisor's facilities

S3.1   Accommodation

Not required.

S3.2   Furnishings

Not required.

S3.3   Services

Not required.

S3.4   Equipment

Not required.

S3.5   Transport

Not required.

S3.6   Personal Protective Equipment for Investigation Supervisor

Not required.

Schedule 4: Specification amendments

The following clauses are amended			
Section number	**Clause number**	**Delete the following**	**Substitute the following**
			No amendments

Schedule 5: Specification additions

The following clauses are added to the Specification		
Section number	**Clause number**	**Clause wording**
		No additions

Annex 1 Bill of Quantities for Ground Investigation

Preamble amendments and additions

The following clauses are amended or added to the Preamble.

23

Rates for moving percussion boring, dynamic (windowless) sampling, dynamic probing and trial pitting plant and equipment between exploratory hole locations shall include for the costs of their decontamination on completing each hole.

Bill of Quantities

The following pages constitute the Bill of Quantities.

Bill of Quantities

Bill A   General items, provisional services and additional items

Number	Item description	Unit	Quantity	Rate	Amount £
A	**General items, provisional services and additional items**				
A1	Offices and stores for the Contractor	sum			
A2	Establish on site all plant, equipment and services for a Green Category site	sum			
A3	Extra over Item A2 for a Yellow Category site	sum			
A4	Maintain on site all site safety equipment for a Yellow Category site	week			
A5	Decontamination of equipment during and at end of intrusive investigation for a Yellow Category site	sum	Not required		
A6	Appropriate storage, transport and off-site disposal of contaminated arisings and any PPE equipment, excluding laboratory testing	provisional sum			2000.00
A7	Provide professional attendance in accordance with Clause 3.5.2				
A7.1	Provide Technician	p.day			
A7.2	Provide graduate ground engineer	p.day			
A7.3	Provide Experienced ground engineer	p.day			
A7.4	Provide Registered Ground Engineering Professional	p.day			
A7.5	Provide Registered Ground Engineering Specialist	p.day			
A7.6	Provide Registered Ground Engineering Advisor	p.day			
A8	Establish the location and elevation of the ground at each exploratory hole	sum			
A9	Preparation of Health and Safety documentation and Safety Risk Assessment.	sum			
A10	Facilities for the Investigation Supervisor	sum	Not required		
A11	Vehicle(s) for the Investigation Supervisor	v.wk	Not required		
A12	Fuel for vehicle for the Investigation Supervisor	provisional sum	Not required		
A13	Investigation Supervisor's telephone and facsimile charges	provisional sum	Not required		
A14	Deliver selected cores and samples to the specified address	provisional sum	Not required		
A15	Special testing and sampling required by Investigation Supervisor	provisional sum	Not required		
A16	Traffic safety and management	provisional sum	Not required		
A17	One master copy of the Desk Study Report	sum	Not required		
A18	Additional copies of the Desk Study Report	nr	Not required		
A19	One master copy of the Ground Investigation Report (or specified part thereof)	sum			
A20	Additional copies of the Ground Investigation Report (or specified part thereof)	nr	1		

Number	Item description	Unit	Quantity	Rate	Amount £
A21	Electronic copy of Ground Investigation Report (or specified part thereof)	sum	1		
A22	One master copy of the Geotechnical Design Report (or specified part thereof)	sum	Not required		
A23	Additional copies of the Geotechnical Design Report (or specified part thereof)	nr	Not required		
A24	Electronic copy of Geotechnical Design Report (or specified part thereof)	sum	Not required		
A25	Digital data in AGS transfer format	sum			
A26	Hard copy photographs	nr	30		
A27	Photographic volume	nr	1		
A28	Long-term storage of geotechnical samples (Appendix B)	provisional sum	Not required		
A29	Long-term storage of geoenvironmental samples (Appendix B)	provisional sum	Not required		
	Contract specific additional bill items				
	None				

Total section A carried to summary _____

Bill of Quantities

Bill B   Percussion boring

Number	Item description	Unit	Quantity	Rate	Amount £
B	**Percussion boring**				
B1	Move boring plant and equipment to the site of each exploratory hole and set up	nr	5		
B2	Extra over Item BI for setting up on a slope of gradient greater than 20%	nr	Not required		
B3	Break out surface obstruction where present at exploratory borehole	h	Not required		
B4	Advance borehole between existing ground level and 10 m depth	m	38		
B5	As Item B4 but between 10 and 20 m depth	m	Not required		
B6	As Item B4 but between 20 and 30 m depth	m	Not required		
B7	As Item B4 but between 30 and 40 m depth	m	Not required		
B8	As Item B4 but between 40 and 50 m depth	m	Not required		
B9	Advance borehole through hard stratum or obstruction	h	5		
B10	Provide aquifer protection measures at a single aquiclude/aquifer boundary or cross-contamination control measures at a single soil boundary in a borehole	nr	Not required		
B11	Backfill borehole with cement/bentonite grout or bentonite pellets	m	Not required		
B12	Standing time for borehole plant, equipment and crew	h	3		
	Dynamic sampling				
B13	Move dynamic sampling equipment to the site of each exploratory hole and set up	nr	5		
B14	Extra over Item BI3 for setting up on a slope of gradient greater than 20%	nr	Not required		
B15	Advance dynamic sample hole between existing ground level and 5 m depth	m	15		
B16	As Item B15 but between 5 and 10 m depth	m	Not required		
B17	As Item B15 but between 10 and 15 m depth	m	Not required		
B18	Standing time for dynamic sampling equipment and crew	hr	Not required		
B19	Provision of dynamic sampling equipment and crew for sampling as directed by the Investigation Supervisor; maximum depth 15 m	day	Not required		
B20	Backfill dynamic sampling hole with cement/bentonite grout or bentonite pellets	m	15		
	Contract specific additional bill items				
	None				

Total section B carried to summary _____

241

Bill of Quantities

Bill C   Rotary drilling

Number	Item description	Unit	Quantity	Rate	Amount £
C	**Rotary drilling**		Not required		

Bill of Quantities

Bill D   Pitting and trenching

Number	Item description	Unit	Quantity	Rate	Amount £
D	**Pitting and trenching**				
	Inspection pits				
D1	Excavate inspection pit by hand to 1.2 m depth	nr	20		
D2	Extra over Item D1 for breaking out surface obstructions	h	Not required		
	Trial pits and trenches				
D3	Move equipment to the site of each trial pit or trench of not greater than 4.5 m depth	nr	15		
D4	Extra over Item D3 for setting up on a slope of gradient greater than 20%	nr	Not required		
D5	Extra over Item D3 for trial pit or trench between 4.5 and 6 m depth	nr	Not required		
D6	Excavate trial pit between existing ground level and 3.0 m depth	m	40		
D7	As Item D6 but between 3.0 and 4.5 m depth	m	5		
D8	As Item D6 but between 4.5 and 6 m depth	m	Not required		
D9	Excavate trial trench between existing ground level and 3.0 m depth	m³	Not required		
D10	As Item D9 between 3.0 and 4.5 in depth	m³	Not required		
D11	As Item D9 between 4.5 and 6 m depth	m³	Not required		
D12	Extra over Items D6–D11 inclusive for breaking out hard material or surface obstructions	h	Not required		
D13	Standing time for excavation plant, equipment and crew for machine-dug trial pit or trench	h	3		
	Observation pits and trenches		Not required		
	Daily provision of pitting crew and equipment		Not required		
	General				
D37	Bring pump to the position of each exploratory pit or trench	nr	7		
D38	Pump water from pit or trench	h	4		
D39	Extra over Item D38 for temporary storage, treatment and disposal of contaminated water	Provisional sum			750.00

Number	Item description	Unit	Quantity	Rate	Amount £
D40	Leave open observation pit or trench	m²/day	Not required		
D41	Leave open trial pit or trench	m²/day	Not required		
	Contract specific additional bill items				
	None				

Total section D carried to summary _____

Bill of Quantities

Bill E   Sampling and monitoring during intrusive investigation

Number	Item description	Unit	Quantity	Rate	Amount £
E	**Sampling and monitoring during intrusive investigation**				
	Samples for geotechnical purposes				
E1	Small disturbed sample	nr	60		
E2	Bulk disturbed sample	nr	50		
E3	Large bulk disturbed sample	nr	Not required		
E4.1	Open-tube sample using thick-walled (OS-TK/W) sampler	nr	Not required		
E4.2	Open-tube sample using thin-walled UT100 (OS-T/W) sampler		20		
E5	Piston sample	nr	Not required		
E6	Groundwater sample	nr	15		
E7	Ground gas sample	nr	5		
E8	Cut, prepare and protect core sub-sample	nr	Not required		
	Continuous or semi-continuous sampling		Not required		
	Containers for contamination assessment and WAC testing				
E14.1	Provision of containers and collection of samples for contamination Suite E (S1.20.3)	nr	100		
E14.2	Provision of containers and collection of samples for contamination Suite F (S1.20.3)	nr	10		
E14.3	Provision of containers and collection of samples for contamination Suite G (S1.20.3)	nr	3		
E15.1	Provision of containers and collection of samples for WAC Suite H (S1.20.5)	nr	Not required		
E15.2	Provision of containers and collection of samples for WAC Suite I (S1.20.5)	nr	8		
E15.3	Provision of containers and collection of samples for WAC Suite J (S1.20.5)	nr	8		
	Contract specific additional bill items				
	None				

Total section E carried to summary _____

Bill of Quantities

Bill F   Probing and cone penetration testing

Number	Item description	Unit	Quantity	Rate	Amount £
F	**Probing and cone penetration testing**				
	Dynamic probing				
F1	Bring dynamic probe equipment to the site of each test location	nr	10		
F2	Extra over Item F1 for setting up on a slope of gradient greater than 20%	nr	Not required		
F3	Carry out dynamic probe test from existing ground level to 5 m depth	m	50		
F4	As Item F3 but between 5 and 10 m depth	m	10		
F5	As Item F3 but between 10 and 15 m depth	m	Not required		
F6	Standing time for dynamic probe test equipment and crew	h	2		
F7	Provision of dynamic probing equipment and crew for probing as directed by the Investigation Supervisor maximum depth 15 m	day	Not required		
	Cone penetration testing		Not required		
	Contract specific additional bill items				
	None				

Total section F carried to summary _____

Bill of Quantities

Bill G   Geophysical testing

Number	Item description	Unit	Quantity	Rate	Amount £
G	**Geophysical testing**		Not required		

Bill of Quantities

Bill H   In situ testing

Number	Item description	Unit	Quantity	Rate	Amount £
H	**In situ testing**				
H1	Standard penetration test in borehole	nr	17		
H2	Standard penetration test in rotary drillhole	nr	Not required		
H3	In situ density testing		Not required		
H3.1	Small pouring cylinder method	nr	Not required		
H3.2	Large pouring cylinder method	nr	Not required		
H3.3	Water replacement method	nr	Not required		
H3.4	Core cutter method	nr	Not required		
H3.5	Nuclear method	day	Not required		
H4	California Bearing Ratio test	nr	Not required		
H5	Vane shear strength test in borehole	nr	Not required		
H6	Penetration vane test, penetration from ground level	nr	Not required		
H7	Hand penetrometer test (set of 3 readings)	nr	Not required		
H8	Hand vane test (set of 3 readings)	nr	Not required		
	Other tests		Not required		
	Permeability testing				
H11	Set up and dismantle variable head permeability test in borehole	nr	Not required		
H12	Set up and dismantle constant head permeability test in borehole	nr	Not required		
H13	Carry out permeability test in borehole	h	Not required		
H14	Set up and dismantle variable head permeability test in standpipe/ standpipe piezometer	nr	3		
H15	Set up and dismantle constant head permeability test in standpipe/ standpipe piezometer	nr	Not required		
H16	Carry out permeability test in standpipe/standpipe piezometer	h	3		
H17	Set up and dismantle variable head permeability test in rotary drillhole	nr	Not required		
H18	Set up and dismantle constant head permeability test in rotary drillhole	nr	Not required		
H19	Carry out permeability test in rotary drillhole	h	Not required		

Number	Item description	Unit	Quantity	Rate	Amount £
H20	Set up and dismantle single packer permeability test	nr	Not required		
H21	Set up and dismantle double packer permeability test	nr	Not required		
H22	Carry out single packer permeability test	h	Not required		
H23	Carry out double packer permeability test	h	Not required		
	Self-boring pressuremeter		Not required		
	High-pressure dilatometer		Not required		
	Driven or push-in pressuremeter		Not required		
	Menard pressuremeter		Not required		
	Soil infiltration test				
H81	Provide equipment and carry out set of 3 infiltration tests at selected location up to 1 day, including hire of excavation equipment	nr	2		
H82	Extra over item H81 for additional days	day	Not required		
H83	Calculation of infiltration rate for each tested location	nr	2		
	Miscellaneous site testing				
H84	Reading of free product level in borehole using an interface probe	nr	10		
H85	Provide contamination screening test kits per sample	nr	2		
H86	Carry out headspace testing by FID/PID	nr	20		
	Contract specific additional bill items				
	None				

Total section H carried to summary _____

Bill of Quantities

Bill I   Instrumentation

Number	Item description	Unit	Quantity	Rate	Amount £
I	**Instrumentation**				
	Standpipes and piezometers				
I1	Backfill exploratory hole with cement/bentonite grout below standpipe or standpipe piezometer	m	10		
I2	Provide and install standpipe (19 mm)	m	Not required		
I3	Provide and install standpipe piezometer (19 mm)	m	Not required		
I4	Provide and install standpipe piezometer (50 mm)	m	Not required		
I5	Provide and install standpipe piezometer (75 mm)	m	Not required		
I6	Provide and install ground gas monitoring standpipe (19 mm)	m	Not required		
I7	Provide and install ground gas monitoring standpipe (50 mm)	m	28		
I8	Provide and install ground gas monitoring standpipe (75 mm)	m	Not required		
I9	Provide and install headworks for ground gas monitoring standpipe, standpipe or standpipe piezometer	nr	5		
I10	Provide and install protective cover (flush)	nr	Not required		
I11	Provide and install protective cover (raised)	nr	5		
I12	Extra over item I10 for heavy-duty cover in highways	nr	Not required		
I13	Supply and erect protective fencing around standpipe or piezometer installation	nr	Not required		
I14	Supply and erect 1.5 m high marker post	nr	5		
I15	Standpipe and piezometer development				
I15.1	Supply equipment and personnel to carry out development by surging	nr	Not required		
I15.2	Develop standpipe or piezometer by surging	h	Not required		
I15.3	As Item I15.1 but by airlift pumping	nr	Not required		
I15.4	As Item I15.2 but by airlift pumping	h	Not required		
I15.5	As Item I15.1 but by over pumping	nr	1		
I15.6	As Item I15.2 but by over pumping	h	5		
I15.7	As Item I5.1 but by jetting	nr	Not required		
I15.8	As Item I15.2 but by jetting	h	Not required		

Number	Item description	Unit	Quantity	Rate	Amount £
I15.9	Disposal of development water, not including chemical testing	Provisional sum			350.00
	Inclinometer		Not required		
	Slip indicators		Not required		
	Contract specific additional bill items				
	None				

Total section I carried to summary _____

Bill of Quantities

Bill J   Installation monitoring and sampling

Number	Item description	Unit	Quantity	Rate	Amount £
J	**Installation monitoring and sampling** (during fieldwork period)				
J1	Reading of water level in standpipe or standpipe piezometer during fieldwork period	nr	10		
J2	Ground gas measurement in gas monitoring standpipe during fieldwork period	nr	10		
J3	Set of inclinometer readings (as defined in Specification Clause 11.6.6 or Schedule S1.16.7) per installation during fieldwork period and report results	nr	Not required		
J4	Check for ground slippage in slip indicator installation during fieldwork period	nr	Not required		
J5	Water sample from standpipe or standpipe piezometer during fieldwork period, including purging or micro-purging up to 3.0 hours	nr	5		
J6	Extra over Item J5 for purging or micro-purging in excess of 3.0 hours	h	1.5		
J7	Ground gas sample from gas monitoring standpipe during fieldwork period	nr	3		
J8	Reading of free product level in standpipe using an interface probe during fieldwork period	nr	2		
	Installation monitoring and sampling (post-fieldwork period)				
J9	Return visit to site following completion of fieldwork to take readings in, or recover samples from, installations	nr	6		
J10	Extra over item J9 for reading of water level in standpipe or standpipe piezometer during return visit	nr	30		
J11	Extra over item J9 for ground gas measurement in ground gas monitoring standpipe during return visit	nr	30		
J12	Extra over item J9 for set of inclinometer readings (as defined in Specification Clause 11.6.6 or Schedule S1.16.7) per installation during return visit and report results	nr	Not required		
J13	Extra over item J9 to check for ground slippage in slip indicator installation during return visit to site	nr	Not required		
J14	Extra over item J9 for water sample from standpipe or standpipe piezometer during return visit to site, including purging or micro-purging up to 3.0 hours	nr	15		
J15	Extra over Item J14 for purging or micro-purging in excess of 3.0 hours	h	2		
J16	Extra over item J9 for ground gas sample from gas monitoring standpipe during return visit to site	nr	8		

Number	Item description	Unit	Quantity	Rate	Amount £
J17	Extra over item J9 for reading of free product level in standpipe using an interface probe during return visit to site Surface water body sampling and testing	nr	8 Not required		
	Contract specific additional bill items None				

Total section J carried to summary _____

Bill of Quantities

Bill K Geotechnical laboratory testing

Number	Item description	Unit	Quantity	Rate	Amount £
K	**Geotechnical laboratory testing**				
K1	Classification	nr			
K1.1	Moisture content	nr	10		
K1.2	Liquid limit, plastic limit and plasticity index	nr	25		
K1.3	Volumetric shrinkage	nr	Not required		
K1.4	Linear shrinkage	nr	Not required		
K1.5	Density by linear measurement	nr	Not required		
K1.6	Density by immersion in water or water displacement	nr	Not required		
K1.7	Dry density and saturation moisture content for chalk	nr	Not required		
K1.8	Particle density by gas jar or pyknometer	nr	Not required		
K1.9	Particle size distribution by wet sieving	nr	5		
K1.10	Particle size distribution by dry sieving	nr	Not required		
K1.11	Sedimentation by pipette	nr	Not required		
K1.12	Sedimentation by hydrometer	nr	2		
K2	Chemical and electrochemical		Not required		
K3	Compaction related		Not required		
K4	Compressibility, permeability, durability	nr			
K4.1	One-dimensional consolidation properties, test period 5 days	nr	4		
K4.2	Extra over Item K4.1 for test period in excess of 5 days	day	12		

Number	Item description	Unit	Quantity	Rate	Amount £
K4.3	Measurements of swelling pressure, test period 2 days	nr	Not required		
K4.4	Measurement of swelling, test period 2 days	nr	Not required		
K4.5	Measurement of settlement on saturation, test period 1 day	nr	Not required		
K4.6	Extra over Items K4.3 to K4.5 for test period in excess of 2 or 1 day(s)	day	Not required		
K4.7	Permeability by constant head method	nr	Not required		
K4.8	Dispersibility by pinhole method	nr	Not required		
K4.9	Dispersibility by crumb method	nr	Not required		
K4.10	Dispersibility by dispersion method	nr	Not required		
K4.11	Frost heave of soil	nr	Not required		
K5	Consolidation and permeability in hydraulic cells	nr	Not required		
K6	Shear strength (total stress)				
K6.1	Shear strength by the laboratory vane method (set of 3)	nr	Not required		
K6.2	Shear strength by hand vane (set of 3)	nr	Not required		
K6.3	Shear strength by hand penetrometer (set of 3)	nr	Not required		
K6.4	Shear strength of a set of three 60 mm × 60 mm square specimens by direct shear, test duration not exceeding 1 day per specimen	nr	Not required		
K6.5	Extra over Item K6.4 for test durations in excess of 1 day per specimen	sp.day	Not required		
K6.6	Shear strength of a single 300 mm × 300 mm square specimen by direct shear, test duration not exceeding 1 day	nr	Not required		
K6.7	Extra over Item K6.6 for test durations in excess of 1 day	day	Not required		
K6.8	Residual shear strength of a set of three 60 mm × 60 mm square specimens by direct shear, test duration not exceeding 4 days per specimen	nr	Not required		
K6.9	Extra over Item K6.8 for test durations in excess of 4 days per specimen	sp.day	Not required		
K6.10	Residual shear strength of a 300 mm square specimen by direct shear, test duration not exceeding 4 days	nr	Not required		
K6.11	Extra over Item K6.10 for test duration in excess day of 4 days	day	Not required		
K6.12	Residual shear strength using the small ring shear apparatus at three normal pressures, test duration not exceeding 4 days	nr	Not required		
K6.13	Extra over Item K6.12 for test duration in excess of 4 days	day	Not required		
K6.14	Unconfined compressive strength of 38 mm diameter specimen	nr	Not required		

Number	Item description	Unit	Quantity	Rate	Amount £
K6.15	Undrained shear strength of a set of three 38 mm diameter specimens in triaxial compression without the measurement of pore pressure	nr	Not required		
K6.16	Undrained strength of a single 100 mm diameter specimen in triaxial compression without the measurement of pore pressure	nr	10		
K6.17	Undrained shear strength of single 100 mm diameter specimen in triaxial compression with multistage loading and without measurement of pore pressure	nr	Not required		
K7	Shear strength (effective stress)		Not required		
K8	Rock testing		Not required		
	Ground/groundwater aggressivity				
K9.1	Suite A (Greenfield site – pyrite absent Schedule 1.19.6)	nr	Not required		
K9.2	Suite B (Greenfield site – pyrite present Schedule 1.19.6)	nr	Not required		
K9.3	Suite C (Brownfield site – pyrite absent Schedule 1.19.6)	nr	5		
K9.4	Suite D (Brownfield site – pyrite present Schedule 1.19.6)	nr	3		
	Contract specific additional bill items				
	None				

Total section K carried to summary _____

Bill of Quantities

Bill L   Geoenvironmental laboratory testing

Number	Item description	Unit	Quantity	Rate	Amount £
L	**Geoenvironmental laboratory testing**				
	Contamination testing				
L1.1	Suite E – Soil samples (Schedule S1.20.3)	nr	30		
L1.2	Suite F – Groundwater samples (Schedule S1.20.3)	nr	15		
L1.3	Suite G – Gas samples (Schedule S1.20.3)	nr	8		
	Waste acceptance criteria testing				
L2.1	Suite H (Inert waste landfill Schedule S1.20.5)	nr	Not required		
L2.2	Suite I – Stable non-reactive hazardous waste in non-hazardous waste landfill (Schedule S1.20.5)	nr	6		
L2.3	Suite J – Hazardous waste landfill (Schedule S1.20.5)	nr	6		
	Contract specific additional bill items				
	None				

Total section L carried to summary _____

Summary of Bill of Quantities

	£
A. General items, provisional services and additional items	
B. Percussion boring	
C. Rotary drilling	Not required
D. Pitting and trenching	
E. Sampling during intrusive investigation	
F. Probing and cone penetration testing	
G. Geophysical testing	Not required
H. In situ testing	
I. Instrumentation	
J. Installation monitoring and sampling	
K. Geotechnical laboratory testing	
L. Geoenvironmental laboratory testing	
Total tender	

Appendix A. Rates for Ground Practitioners and other Personnel

Rates shall be entered for the various grades of staff listed, who will be employed by agreement with the Investigation Supervisor to provide advice or assistance during the course of the investigation and/or the preparation of the Ground Investigation Report and/or the Geotechnical Design Report all in accordance with Specification Clauses 3.6.1 and 3.6.2 and Schedule S1.8.3.

These services exclude the contract management, superintendence and technical direction required under the Conditions of Contract and the requirements of Specification Clause 3.5.1 which are to be included in the general rates and prices of the main Bill of Quantities (see Clause 1 of the Preamble to the Bill of Quantities).

Item	Item description	Unit	Rate
1	Technician	h	
2	Graduate ground engineer	h	
3	Experienced ground engineer	h	
4	Registered Ground Engineering Professional	h	
5	Registered Ground Engineering Specialist	h	
6	Registered Ground Engineering Advisor	h	
7	Expenses incurred by staff on site visits or who are resident by agreement with the Investigation Supervisor	day	
8	Fare per kilometre[1] from Contractor's premises and return for Items 1, 2 and 3	km[1]	
9	As above but for Items 4, 5 and 6	km[1]	
10	All other expenses incurred in conjunction with a site visit where a return journey is made on the same day for Items 1, 2 and 3	visit	
11	As above but for Items 4, 5 and 6	visit	
12	All other expenses incurred in connection with visit where an overnight stay is necessary for Items 1, 2 and 3	overnight	
13	As above but for Items 4, 5 and 6	overnight	

[1] Where considered more appropriate, 'mile' may be used.

Estimate of costs under Appendix A to the Bill of Quantities where the provision of the Contractor's staff for work in accordance with Specification Clauses 3.5.2, 3.6.1 and 3.6.2 cannot be adequately specified at tender. **(To be assessed by the Investigation Supervisor)**

£	

Appendix B. Long-term sample storage

NOT REQUIRED

Example C

Particulars of the example

The site is the same as that used for Example B but here the proposed development is different, resulting in changed investigation requirements. Other changes from Example B are made here to illustrate some of the flexibility of the documents. For completeness, the site details are reiterated below.

The hypothetical site is assumed to be occupied by former railway sidings, constructed in the 1890s and abandoned in 1960. The desk study findings are assumed to have revealed the following.

- The sidings were used as a load-out area for locally excavated clay being transported by rail to a remote off-site brickworks. Steam locomotives were used over most of the life of the sidings, being replaced latterly by diesel locomotives. Two asbestos-roofed railway workers' huts (now demolished) were present close to the site entrance; these were provided with water and domestic voltage electricity services (feeding from the nearby Railway Lane) which were disconnected on abandonment. No other services were present on the site.
- Likely potential contaminants comprise metals/metaloids from ash deposits, asbestos from the roofs of the railway workers' huts, timber sleeper preservatives, chlorinated aliphatics from cleaning solvents and fuel and lubricating oils and greases. Herbicides were used to control weed growth until abandonment of the facility but, due to their rate of decay, are not now expected to pose a contamination threat.
- A former clay excavation area, about 200 m to the east of the site, has been used as a landfill since 1985. It was designed on containment principles and records indicate no contamination problems which are likely to affect the railway sidings site.
- Previous site investigations nearby, combined with published geological data, indicate the expected natural downward succession to be 1–3 m thickness of probably firm clay (Brickearth), 3–4 m of medium dense to dense glacial gravel and 2 m of probably stiff clay (weathered mudstones which could be pyrite rich) overlying a major aquifer of Coal Measures sandstone. The aquifer is thought to be at least 40 m thick. The walk-over reconnaissance indicates the railway ballast to be up to about 1 m thick.

In this example of the use of the Schedules and Bill of Quantities an industrial development has been assumed, including heavy machinery which is likely to require deep piled foundations founding in the sandstone aquifer and several deep basements which may found in a potentially pyrite-rich weathered mustone. A considerably greater depth of investigation will be required with some holes penetrating into a major aquifer, necessitating aquifer protection measures. There are also assumed to be a few lightweight ancillary buildings which can be expected to be shallow founded.

In contrast to Example B, here it is assumed that no material is to be removed from site. It is therefore not necessary to include any WAC testing. However, it is still necessary to consider the question of contamination of the shallow strata, the main risk being to construction workers. As noted above, deep-piled foundations into the sandstone aquifer are likely to be required and it is appropriate to install two piezometers into the sandstone: one at the upstream end of the site and the other downstream. These will enable water levels in this stratum to be measured but, in addition, allow samples to be taken for contamination testing. Comparison of the upstream and downstream results will help to determine whether any on-site contaminants are leaking down into the aquifer. The contamination results will also provide a baseline for subsequently checking that the construction works themselves have not caused contamination of the aquifer.

For this example, limits of detection, test methods and accreditation for the laboratory contamination testing are left for the Contractor to state what can be offered. This should allow more flexibility for the Contractors tendering, although the Employer (or their agent) is not bound to accept any particular offer.

The investigation methods are to comprise percussion borings, rotary core drilling and trial pitting. As in Example B, it is required that the relevant plant and equipment are decontaminated on completion of each exploratory hole. However, here the costs of decontamination are to be paid for by means of the lump sum (Item A5 in the Bill of Quantities) instead of within the rate for moving, as is the case for Example B.

The four holes where rotary drilling is required are billed as 'follow on' from the percussion borings. However, the Contractor is permitted to offer the alternative of drilling a separate hole from ground surface alongside the percussion borehole. The Contractor will have to assess whether this will lead to any cost or time savings.

As in Example B, it is assumed that the Investigation Supervisor will be appointed by the Developer. Here, however, estimates of the required staff grades and person days have been included under Professional Attendance in Bill Item A7 by the Investigation Supervisor. The grades of graduate ground engineer and experienced ground engineer are assumed to be full-time on site with all others presumed to be visiting as required. The Contractor is required to explicitly detail any adjustments that are considered to be necessary to comply with his responsibilities for completing the specified report.

The Contractor is required to compile the full Ground Investigation Report. For the purposes of this example it has been assumed that payment for compiling the report will be based on the rates provided by the Contractor under Appendix A. If the Contractor is subsequently required to assist in the compilation of the Geotechnical Design Report, then rates for this additional work will already be in place.

Schedule 1: Information and site-specific requirements

S1.1   Name of Contract

Redevelopment of Old Railway Sidings, near Anytown, Someshire.

S1.2   Investigation Supervisor

Mr A N Other of XYZ Associates, Site Investigation House, Anytown AB1 2CD, Someshire.

The Conditions of Contract shall be the NEC3 Engineering and Construction Contract (2005), Option B and Option W1.

All duties and powers vested in the Project Manager, except those which cannot be delegated, shall be delegated to the Investigation Supervisor.

The Project Manager for the Contract shall be the Finance Director of New Developments Ltd, Development House, Anytown AB1 2CD, Someshire.

S1.3   Description of site

The site comprises approximately x hectares of disused railway sidings centred at approximate National Grid reference AB 100 200.

A desk study has been carried out by XYZ Associates and a copy of that report is appended to the documents. The following comprises a summary of the desk study findings.

The site is bounded to the north by Railway Lane and to the east, south and west by farmland. The site is approximately level but is located in an area sloping gently westwards.

Access to the site is via the padlocked double gates on Railway Lane. Keys are available from the Investigation Supervisor.

Prior to the construction of the sidings in about 1890 the site comprised farmland. The sidings were used as a loading area for clay excavated from an area 200 m to the east which was then transported by rail to a former small brickworks about 4 km north of Anytown. The sidings became disused in 1960. Shortly thereafter, the rail lines were removed for salvage and the former railway workers' huts close to Railway Lane were demolished with the demolition rubble being removed from site. The use of herbicides to control weed growth ceased about the time of abandonment.

The former clay excavation area (200 m to the east) was used as a landfill from 1985 but it was designed on a containment basis.

There is a small housing estate immediately on the north side of Railway Lane.

There are two wells about 400 m to the west of the site abstracting water from a major aquifer underlying the site.

The classification of the whole of the site is YELLOW.

S1.4   Main works proposed and purpose of this contract

This main ground investigation is in connection with a proposed industrial development which will include heavy machinery likely to require deep-piled foundations into the sandstone aquifer and deep basements likely to be found in weathered mudstone. It is intended that the site will be connected to the public sewer system.

It is not expected that any materials will be disposed of off site during the construction; excavation arisings are to be incorporated in landscaping bunds.

There is no detailed layout available for the proposed construction.

S1.5 Scope of investigation

The aim of the investigation is to provide assessments of the ground conditions for foundations, including its aggressiveness to below-ground concrete and the type and severity of ground/groundwater contamination.

The fieldwork will comprise inspection pits, percussion borings with driven tube samples, disturbed samples and SPTs, rotary core drilling in the sandstone bedrock with SPTs at 3 m depth intervals and trial pits. Standpipe piezometers and gas monitoring standpipes as combined installations are to be installed in the shallow strata (Brickearth and gravel) as specified, or as directed by the Investigation Supervisor if the as-found ground/groundwater conditions vary from those expected. In addition, two piezometers are to be installed in the sandstone aquifer. One piezometer is to be installed at the upstream edge and the other at the downstream edge of the site. These are to check on the expectation that any contamination on the site is not penetrating into the major aquifer and to provide baseline data for future reference during the construction phase.

Geotechnical laboratory testing is required for the purposes of foundation design. Chemical laboratory testing is required for aggressiveness to concrete and contamination assessment. The laboratory testing will be scheduled by the Investigation Supervisor in consultation with the Contractor.

The Contractor is to provide a full Ground Investigation Report in accordance with the requirements of Eurocode 7.

The following Schedules are not required for this investigation:

S1.13 (Probing and cone penetration testing)

S1.14 (Geophysical testing)

The associated Bills F and G are also not required.

S1.6 Geology and ground conditions

The following general assessment of the geology of the site and ground conditions has been inferred from available information. No assurance is given to its accuracy.

The downward succession is expected to comprise up to about 1 m thickness of railway ballast, 1–3 m thickness of probably firm clay (Brickearth), 3–4 m of glacial gravel and 3–4 m of probably very stiff potentially pyrite-rich clay (weathered mudstone) overlying a major aquifer of Coal Measures sandstone. The aquifer is thought to be at least 40 m thick.

The railway ballast, underlying natural soils and groundwater may be contaminated by metals/metalloids, asbestos, fuel and lubricating oil/grease and cleaning solvents.

S1.7 Schedule of drawing(s) and documents

A site plan (Drg No. 100 Rev 0 in AutoCAD format) included in the documentation shows the extent of the site, the layout of the former sidings (including railway workers' huts, now demolished), the adjacent topographical features, setting-out points, land ownership details and the positions of the exploratory holes. No access routes are prescribed but the Contractor is required to comply with the Specification Clause 3.15.1 in respect of causing least damage.

The Desk Study Report is included in the documentation.

No service drawings have been found but it is believed that there were electricity and water supplies to the railway workers' huts. Enquiries to the utility companies have indicated no other known services within the site boundaries.

Previous ground investigations in connection with the landfill site and the housing immediately to the north of Railway Lane are available for inspection at the Investigation Supervisor's offices.

S1.8 General requirements (Specification Section 3) Particular restrictions/relaxations

Contract specific restrictions/relaxations, if any, shall be inserted below.

S1.8.1 Quality management system (Clause 3.3)

Quality management to BS EN ISO 9001, BS EN ISO 14001 and BS OHSAS 18001 required.

S1.8.2 Professional Attendance (Clause 3.5.2)

The Contractor shall provide Professional Attendance to perform those tasks detailed in Specification Note for Guidance 3.5.2 which are relevant to this investigation.

The Contractor shall detail in their tender the number, names and experience details of his proposed staff and the times which each member of staff is expected to spend. Bill of Quantities Item A7 shall be used to detail the Contractor's expected Professional Attendance.

The Contractor shall note the inclusion of staff grades and person days suggested by the Investigation Supervisor in Bill Item A7. The grades of graduate ground engineer and experienced ground engineer are assumed to be full time on site with all others presumed to be visiting as required. The Contractor shall explicitly detail any adjustments required in staff and person days necessary for the provision of data to accord with their responsibilities for completing the specified report.

S1.8.3 Provision of ground practitioners and other personnel (Clauses 3.6.1 and 3.6.2)

The Contractor is to prepare a full Ground Investigation Report in accordance with the requirements of Eurocode 7. The Contractor's expected staff times for report compilation, preparation and checking are to be charged for based on the rates to be entered in Appendix A. The Contractor is required to complete the table of rates included in Appendix A.

No other personnel (see Specification Cl 3.6.2) are to be provided by the Contractor.

S1.8.4 Hazardous ground, land affected by contamination and notifiable and invasive weeds (Clauses 3.7.1 and 3.22)

Land affected by contamination as detailed above under 'Description of site' and 'Geology and ground conditions'.

There are no known notifiable or invasive weeds.

S1.8.5 Additional information on services not shown on Contract drawings (Clause 3.7.2)

Suspected electricity and water services as detailed above under 'Schedule of drawings and documents'.

S1.8.6 Known/suspected mine workings, mineral extractions, etc. (Clause 3.7.3)

None.

S1.8.7 Protected species (Clause 3.7.4)

None.

S1.8.8 Archaeological remains (Clause 3.7.5)

None.

S1.8.9 Security of site (Clause 3.11)

Except for access to and from the site, the gates on Railway Lane shall be kept locked at all times. The site perimeter fence shall not be breached without the written permission of the Investigation Supervisor.

S1.8.10 Traffic management measures (Clause 3.12)

Not required.

S1.8.11 Restricted working hours (Clause 3.13)

Fieldwork hours to be restricted to 0800 to 1700 hours (Monday to Friday inclusive). No weekend working permitted.

S1.8.12 Trainee site operatives (Clause 3.14.1)

Not permitted.

S1.8.13 Contamination avoidance and/or aquifer protection measures required (Clauses 3.15.2 and 3.15.3)

Percussion boring, rotary drilling and trial pitting plant and equipment to be decontaminated on completion of each exploratory hole and on completion of the site works.

Aquifer protection measures (based on two nested casings and a bentonite seal) are required for the rotary drillholes at the mudstone/sandstone boundary. The Contractor should note the minimum specified core diameter when selecting the commencement diameter of the percussion boreholes.

Trial pit arisings are to be temporarily stockpiled on boards underlain by plastic sheeting to prevent contamination of the railway ballast.

S1.8.14 Maximum period for boring, pitting or trenching through hard material, hard stratum or obstruction (Clauses 2.8, 4.3 and 6.4)

As specified.

For percussion boreholes 4–7 that are to be extended by rotary core drilling, the Contractor is to inform the Investigation Supervisor immediately upon encountering bedrock.

S1.8.15 Reinstatement requirements (Clause 3.16)

Arisings to be stored on site in locked covered skips until laboratory test results allow the appropriate off-site disposal to be determined.

Trial pits to be backfilled with arisings placed in reverse order to excavation.

S1.8.16 Hygiene facilities required (Clauses 2.20 and 3.16.1)

Extra over any statutory requirements, personnel washing and changing facilities and a bunded vehicle wheel wash to be provided at site entrance.

S1.8.17 Unavoidable damage to be reinstated by Contractor (Clause 3.16.1)

Not required.

S1.8.18 Accuracy of exploratory hole locations (Clauses 3.19 and 3.20)

As specified.

S1.8.19 Photography requirements (Clause 3.25)

Sufficient photographs to show the condition of the whole of the site prior to the start of investigation works and an analogous set of photographs on completion of the investigation.

Digital photographs to be submitted by email to the Investigation Supervisor within 1 working day of the photographs being taken.

Further particular Contract restrictions/relaxations shall be entered below, using sequential numbers to those above

None.

S1.9 Percussion boring (Specification Section 4) Particular restrictions/relaxations

Contract specific restrictions/relaxations, if any, shall be inserted below.

S1.9.1 Permitted methods and restrictions (Clauses 4. 1 to 4.4)

Restrictions as detailed in Schedule S1.8.13.

See also Schedule S1.11.1.

S1.9.2 Backfilling (Clause 4.5)

Cement bentonite grout as directed by the Investigation Supervisor on site.

S1.9.3 Dynamic sampling (Clause 4.6)

Not required.

Further particular Contract restrictions/relaxations shall be entered below, using sequential numbers to those above

None.

S1.10 Rotary drilling (Specification Section 5) Particular restrictions/relaxations

Contract specific restrictions/relaxations, if any, shall be inserted below.

S1.10.1 Augering requirements and restrictions (Clauses 5.1)

Not required.

S1.10.2 Particular rotary drilling techniques (Clause 5.2)

Percussion boreholes 4–7 are to be extended by rotary drilling to investigate the condition of sandstone bedrock for deep-piled foundations. The Contractor will be permitted to drill a separate hole from ground level alongside the percussion borehole as an alternative to extending the original hole.

Continuous core is to be obtained using 'P'-size double-tube barrel(s), utilising core liner unless the specified requirements for core recovery can be met without its use.

SPTs are required at nominally 3 m depth intervals within the cored depth range, usually at the end of core runs. Allowance will be made by the Investigation Supervisor for the detrimental effects this will have on core recovery.

S1.10.3 Drilling fluid type and collection (Clause 5.3)
Air mist.

S1.10.4 Rotary core drilling coring equipment and core diameter (Clauses 5.4.1 and 5.4.2)
See Schedule S1.10.2.

S1.10.5 Core logging (Clause 5.4.6)
Core logging on site not required.

The Investigation Supervisor will attend the logging of selected cores.

S1.10.6 Core sub-samples for laboratory testing (Clause 5.4.7)
Sub-samples are required for laboratory testing and are to be taken after core preparation and during core logging. Subject to the condition of the core, sub-samples are to be taken at nominally 3 m depth intervals.

S1.10.7 Address for delivery of selected cores (Clauses 5.4.8 and 5.4.9)
Not required.

S1.10.8 Rotary open-hole drilling general requirements (Clause 5.5.1)
Not required.

S1.10.9 Rotary open-hole drilling for locating mineral seams, mine workings, etc. (Clause 5.5.2)
Not required.

S1.10.10 Open-hole resonance (sonic) drilling (Clause 5.6.1)
Not required.

S1.10.11 Resonance (sonic) drilling with sampling or continuous coring (Clause 5.6.2)
Not required.

S1.10.12 Backfilling (Clause 5.7)
As specified with cement/bentonite grout.

S1.10.13 Core photographic requirements (Clause 5.8)
As specified, except that prior to photography labelling of the core is to be added to show where it has or may have been affected by SPTs. All subspecimen locations are to be identified by spacers with clear labelling of the depth range and sub-sample number.

Further particular Contract restrictions/relaxations shall be entered below, using sequential numbers to those above
None.

S1.11 Pitting and trenching (Specification Section 6) Particular restrictions/relaxations
Contract specific restrictions/relaxations, if any, shall be inserted below.

S1.11.1 Indirect detection of buried services and inspection pits (Clauses 3.8.3 and 6.1)

All exploratory hole locations are to be CAT scanned.

Inspection pits are required at all percussion borehole locations and all rotary drillhole locations if drilled from the ground surface as an alternative to 'follow on' drilling.

S1.11.2 Restrictions on plant or pitting/trenching methods (Clauses 6.2 and 6.3)

Excavation of trial pits is to comply with recommended method of excavation described in Specification Note for Guidance 6.2.

All pits are to be backfilled on day of excavation.

S1.11.3 Entry of personnel (Clause 6.5)

Not permitted.

S1.11.4 Alternative pit and trench dimensions (Clause 6.7)

As specified.

S1.11.5 Abstracted groundwater from land affected by contamination (Clause 6.9.2)

On-site measures for collection and temporary storage (prior to the availability of laboratory test results to determine appropriate disposal) to be agreed with Investigation Supervisor.

S1.11.6 Backfilling (Clause 6.10)

As specified in Schedules S1.8.13 and S1.8.15 above with compaction of the arisings using excavation plant bucket.

S1.11.7 Photographic requirements (Clause 6.12)

As specified.

S1.11.8 Artificial lighting (Clause 6.12.2)

Required if natural daylight is insufficient to give clear views of all strata exposed in the pits.

S1.11.9 Provision of pitting equipment and crew for Investigation Supervisor's use (Clause 6.13)

Not required.

Further particular Contract restrictions/relaxations shall be entered below, using sequential numbers to those above

None.

S1.12 Sampling during intrusive investigation (Specification Section 7) Particular restrictions/ relaxations

Contract specific restrictions/relaxations, if any, shall be inserted below.

S1.12.1 Address for delivery of selected geotechnical samples (Clause 7.6.1)

Not required.

S1.12.2 Retention and disposal of geotechnical samples (Clause 7.6.2)

As specified.

S1.12.3 Frequency of sampling for geotechnical purposes (Clauses 7.6.3–7.6.11)

Small disturbed samples at 0.3 m depth intervals in inspection pits.

In percussion boreholes:

A. Open-tube, small disturbed and bulk samples and SPTs in granular soil as specified in Clause 7.6.4

B. No large bulk samples required

C. Groundwater samples as specified

In pits: as specified

In rotary drillholes: See Schedule S1.10.2.

S1.12.4 Open-tube and piston sample diameters (Clause 7.6.5)

100 mm diameter samples to be taken using thin-wall sampler (OS-T/W).

S1.12.5 Retention of cutting shoe samples (Clause 7.6.5)

As specified.

S1.12.6 Delft and Mostap sampling (Clause 7.6.12)

Not required.

S1.12.7 Groundwater level measurements during exploratory hole construction (Clause 7.7)

As specified.

S1.12.8 Special geotechnical sampling (Clause 7.8)

Not required.

S1.12.9 Address for delivery of selected samples (Clause 7.9.2)

Not required.

S1.12.10 Retention and disposal of contamination/WAC samples (Clause 7.9.3)

As specified.

S1.12.11 Frequency of sampling (Clause 7.9.4)

Minimum sampling in each trial pit is to comprise soil samples at 0.5 m depth intervals in railway ballast and Brickearth plus 1 No sample of groundwater where encountered. Additional samples may be required where evidence of contamination is observed.

S1.12.12 Sampling method (Clause 7.9.5)

Sampling to be under the supervision of an environmental scientist, geoenvironmental engineer, or geochemist meeting the requirements of Clause 2.3 item (c).

S1.12.13 Headspace testing (Clause 7.9.8)

Required; details to be agreed on site with Investigation Supervisor.

Further particular Contract restrictions/relaxations shall be entered below, using sequential numbers to those above

None.

S1.13 Probing and cone penetration testing (Specification Section 8) Particular restrictions/relaxations

Not required.

S1.14 Geophysical testing (Specification Section 9) Particular restrictions/relaxations

Not required.

S1.15 In situ testing (Specification Section 10) Particular restrictions/relaxations

Contract specific restrictions/relaxations, if any, shall be inserted below.

S1.15.1 Tests in accordance with British Standards (Clause 10.3)

SPTs in cable percussion boreholes at depth intervals specified in Specification Clause 7.6.4. SPTs in rotary drilled boreholes at nominally 3 m depth intervals with the maximum blow count extended to 100 blows.

S1.15.2 Hand penetrometer and hand vane for shear strength (Clause 10.4.1)

Not required.

S1.15.3 Self-boring pressuremeter and high-pressure dilatometer testing and reporting (Clause 10.5.1)

Not required.

S1.15.4 Driven or push-in pressuremeter testing and reporting requirements (Clause 10.5.2)

Not required.

S1.15.5 Menard pressuremeter tests (Clause 10.5.3)

Not required.

S1.15.6 Soil infiltration test (Clause 10.6)

Not required.

S1.15.7 Special in situ testing and reporting requirements (Clause 10.7)

Not required

S1.15.8 Interface probes (Clause 10.8)

Required for cable percussion and/or rotary drilled boreholes to be selected on site by the Investigation Supervisor.

S1.15.9 Contamination screening tests (Clause 10.9)

Required with use to be directed by Investigation Supervisor.

S1.15.10 Metal detection (Clause 10.10)

Not required.

Further particular Contract restrictions/relaxations shall be entered below, using sequential numbers to those above

None.

S1.16 Instrumentation (Specification Section 11) Particular restrictions/relaxations

Contract specific restrictions/relaxations, if any, shall be inserted below.

S1.16.1 Protective covers for installations (Clause 11.2)

Lockable steel covers to be set in a concrete surround and raised nominally 200 mm above ground level.

S1.16.2 Protective fencing (Clause 11.3)

Not required but the location of each instrumented exploratory hole is to be marked with a secure 1 m high wooden post clearly marked with the exploratory hole number.

S1.16.3 Standpipe and standpipe piezometer installations (Clauses 11.4.1 and 11.4.2)

Standpipe piezometer installations to be based on 50 mm diameter uPVC tubing in sandstone aquifer required. Actual installation depths of response zones and seals to be determined on site by the Investigation Supervisor. These installations to be used for groundwater level monitoring and sampling.

See also Schedule S1.16.6.

S1.16.4 Other piezometer installations (Clause 11.4.3)

Not required.

S1.16.5 Development of standpipes and standpipe piezometers (Clause 11.4.5)

All standpipe piezometers to be developed using an MP1 pump.

S1.16.6 Ground gas standpipes (Clause 11.5)

Ground gas standpipes penetrating into gravel stratum required in cable percussion boreholes as generally described in Schedule 2. These installations also to be used for groundwater level monitoring and sampling.

S1.16.7 Inclinometer installations (Clause 11.6)

Not required.

S1.16.8 Slip indicators (Clause 11.7)

Not required.

S1.16.9 Extensometers and settlement gauges (Clause 11.8)

Not required.

S1.16.10 Settlement monuments (Clause 11.9)

Not required.

S1.16.11 Removal of installations (Clause 11.10)

No installations to be removed.

S1.16.12 Other instrumentation (Clause 11.11)

Not required.

Further particular Contract restrictions/relaxations shall be entered below, using sequential numbers to those above

None.

S1.17 Installation monitoring and sampling (Specification Section 12) Particular restrictions/relaxations

Contract specific restrictions/relaxations, if any, shall be inserted below.

S1.17.1 Groundwater level readings in installations (Clause 12.2)

Groundwater level readings to be taken weekly in all standpipe piezometers and all combined groundwater/ground gas standpipes during fieldwork period.

Readings also to be taken in both types of installation during return visits to site at 2 monthly intervals for 12 months following the end of fieldwork. The frequency of return visits to site may be adjusted if major variations in groundwater level readings occur.

S1.17.2 Groundwater sampling from installations (Clause 12.3.1)
Single sample required from each standpipe piezometer and each combined groundwater/ground gas standpipe during fieldwork period.

Further samples may be required, as directed by the Investigation Supervisor, during return visits to site.

S1.17.3 Purging/micro-purging (Clause 12.3.2)
Purging of all installations where groundwater sampling is required to continue until conductivity, pH, temperature, dissolved oxygen and Redox potential have stabilised.

S1.17.4 Ground gas monitoring (Clause 12.4)
Monitoring required weekly in combined groundwater/ground gas standpipes during fieldwork period.

Readings also to be taken during return visits to site at 2 monthly intervals for 12 months following the end of fieldwork.

S1.17.5 Sampling from ground gas installations (Clause 12.5)
Samples to be taken during fieldwork period and/or during return visits to site, as directed by the Investigation Supervisor dependent upon ground gas monitoring results.

S1.17.6 Other monitoring (Clause 12.8)
Not required.

S1.17.7 Sampling and testing of surface water bodies (Clause 12.9)
Not required

> **Further particular Contract restrictions/relaxations shall be entered below, using sequential numbers to those above**

None.

S1.18 Daily records (Specification Section 13) Particular restrictions/relaxations
Contract specific restrictions/relaxations, if any, shall be inserted below.

S1.18.1 Information for daily records (Clause 13.1)
Contractor to submit a proforma or example record for approval by the Investigation Supervisor.

S1.18.2 Special in situ tests and instrumentation records (Clause 13.4)
Instrument installation records shall clearly include the hole diameter, installation casing and perforated screen diameter and installed depths, material descriptions and installed depths of the filter(s) and seal(s) and cover arrangements

> **Further particular Contract restrictions/relaxations shall be entered below, using sequential numbers to those above**

None.

S1.19 Geotechnical laboratory testing (Specification Section 14) Particular restrictions/relaxations

Contract specific restrictions/relaxations, if any, shall be inserted below.

S1.19.1 Investigation Supervisor or Contractor to schedule testing (Clause 14.1.1)

The Investigation Supervisor, in conjunction with the Contractor, will schedule the testing on the basis of the daily records.

S1.19.2 Tests required (Clause 14.1.2)

Natural moisture content, Atterberg Limits, undrained shear strength without pore pressure measurement, particle size distribution and one-dimensional consolidation oedometers.

S1.19.3 Specifications for tests not covered by BS 1377 and options under BS 1377 (Clauses 14.2.1 and 14.4)

Not required.

S1.19.4 UKAS accreditation to be adopted (Clause 14.3)

All testing to be UKAS accredited.

S1.19.5 Rock testing requirements (Clause 14.5)

Natural moisture content, unconfined compressive strength, indirect tensile strength, point load strength (axial and diametral) and Cerchar abrasivity tests on selected rotary drilling core sub-samples.

Natural moisture content and point load strength index tests on suitable irregular fragments of core between core sub-samples.

S1.19.6 (Test Suites A–D are overleaf) Chemical testing for aggressive ground/groundwater for concrete (Clause 14.6)

Suite C (Brownfield pyrite absent) and Suite D (Brownfield pyrite present) testing required; see Schedule presented in the following pages. The Contractor is to detail test methods which can be offered.

Tests Suites A and B are not required and have been deleted.

S1.19.7 Laboratory testing on site (Clause 14.7)

Not required.

S1.19.8 Special laboratory testing (Clause 14.8)

Cerchar abrasivity tests on selected core sub-samples. Test procedure as described in ISRM.

Further particular Contract restrictions/relaxations shall be entered below, using sequential numbers to those above

None.

SCHEDULE 1.19.6 (Derived from BRE Special Digest SD1)

CHEMICAL TESTS ON POTENTIALLY AGGRESSIVE GROUND/GROUNDWATER

SUITE C Brownfield site (pyrite absent)			
Sample type	Determinand	Recommended test methods	Test method ~~specified~~/offered[1]
Soil	pH in 2.5:1 water/soil extract	BR 279 Electrometric	
		BS 1377 Part 3, Method 9	
	SO$_4$ in 2:1 water/soil extract	BR 279 Gravimetric method, cation exchange or ion chromatography	
		BS 1377 Part 3 Method 5.3 + 5.5	
		TRL 447 Test 1	
	Mg (only required if water soluble SO$_4$ >3000 mg/l)	BR 279 AAS[2] method	
		Commercial lab in-house procedure – variant of BR 279 using ISP-AES[3]	
	NO$_3$ in 2:1 water/soil extract (only required if pH <5.5)	BR 279	
	Cl in 2:1 water/soil extract (only required if pH <5.5)	BR 279	
		BS 1377 Part 3, Method 7.2	
Groundwater	pH	BR 279 Electrometric	
		BS 1377 Part 3, Method 9	
	SO$_4$	BR 279 Gravimetric method, cation exchange or ion chromatography	
		BS 1377 Part 3 Method 5.4 + 5.5	
		Commercial lab in-house procedure – determination of sulphur by ICP-AES[3]	
	Mg (only required if water soluble SO$_4$ $\geqslant$3000 mg/l)	BR 279 AAS[2] method	
		Commercial lab in-house procedure – Mg in solution by ICP-AES[3]	
	NO$_3$ (only required if pH <5.5)	BR 279	
	Cl (only required if pH <5.5)	BR 279	
		BS 1377 Part 3, Method 7.2	

[1] ~~Either Investigation Supervisor to specify method required or~~ Contractor to indicate method(s) offered.
[2] AAS: atomic absorption spectrometry.
[3] ICP-AES: inductively coupled plasma atomic emission spectroscopy.

SCHEDULE S1.19.6 (Derived from BRE Special Digest SD1)

CHEMICAL TESTS ON POTENTIALLY AGGRESSIVE GROUND/GROUNDWATER

SUITE D Brownfield site (pyrite present)			
Sample type	**Determinand**	**Recommended test methods**	**Test method ~~specified~~/offered[1]**
Soil	pH in 2.5:1 water/soil extract	BR 279 Electrometric	
		BS 1377 Part 3, Method 9	
	SO_4 in 2:1 water/soil extract	BR 279 Gravimetric method, cation exchange or ion chromatography	
		BS 1377 Part 3 Method 5.3 + 5.5	
		TRL 447 Test 1	
	Acid soluble SO_4	BR 279 Gravimetric method	
		BS 1377 Part 3, Method 5.2 + 5.5	
		TRL 447 Test 2	
	Total sulphur	BR 279 Ignition in oxygen	
		TRL 447 Test 4A	
		TRL 447 Test 4B	
	Mg (only required if water soluble SO_4 >3000 mg/l)	BR 279 AAS[2] method	
		Commercial lab in-house procedure – variant of BR 279 using ICP-AES[3]	
	NO_3 in 2:1 water/soil extract (only required if pH <5.5)	BR 279	
	Cl in 2:1 water/soil extract (only required if pH <5.5)	BR 279	
		BS 1377 Part 3, Method 7.2	
Groundwater	pH	BR 279 Electrometric	
		BS 1377 Part 3, Method 9	
	SO_4	BR 279 Gravimetric method, cation exchange or ion chromatography	
		BS 1377 Part 3 Method 5.4 + 5.5	
		Commercial lab in-house procedure – determination of sulphur by ICP-AES[3]	
	Mg (only required if water soluble SO_4 ⩾3000 mg/l)	BR 279 AAS[2] method	
		Commercial lab in-house procedure – Mg in solution by ICP-AES[3]	
	NO_3 (only required if pH <5.5)	BR 279	
	Cl (only required if pH <5.5)	BR 279	
		BS 1377 Part 3, Method 7.2	

[1] ~~Either Investigation Supervisor to specify method required or~~ Contractor to indicate method(s) offered.
[2] AAS: atomic absorption spectrometry.
[3] ICP-AES: inductively coupled plasma atomic emission spectroscopy.

S1.20 Chemical laboratory testing (Specification Section 15) Particular restrictions/relaxations

Contract specific restrictions/relaxations, if any, shall be inserted below.

S1.20.1 Investigation Supervisor or Contractor to schedule testing (Clause 15.1)

The Investigation Supervisor, in conjunction with the Contractor, will schedule the testing on the basis of the daily records.

S1.20.2 Accreditation required (Clause 15.2)

MCERTS where available, otherwise UKAS.

S1.20.3 (Test Suites E–G are overleaf) Chemical testing for contamination (Clause 15.3)

Test Suites E and F required. Test Suite G may be required dependent upon results of on-site ground gas monitoring.

Contractor to detail limits of detection, test methods and accreditation which can be offered for each individual determinand. Contractor to also detail laboratory to be used for the testing and the testing turnaround times.

SCHEDULE 1.20.3

CHEMICAL LABORATORY TESTING FOR CONTAMINATION

Nominated Test Laboratory ? <u>Contractor to specify proposed laboratory</u>

Required Testing Turnaround Times ? <u>10 days</u>

NB

1. This proforma Schedule MUST be reviewed in the light of site-specific desk study results and amended accordingly to include any additional determinands likely to be required.

2. Limits of detection should reflect the guideline/threshold values against which the test results will be compared.

SUITE E – Soil samples			
Determinand (Procurer to list required determinands)	**Limit of detection** ~~required~~/offered[1]	**Test method** ~~required~~/offered[1]	**Accreditation** ~~required~~/offered[1]
Arsenic			
Boron (water soluble)			
Cadmium			
Chromium (total)			
Copper			
Lead			
Mercury			
Nickel			
Zinc			
pH			
Water soluble sulphate (as SO_4)			
Organic matter			
Total petroleum hydrocarbons			
Speciated polyaromatic hydrocarbons (USEPA 16)			
~~Phenol~~			
Cyanide (total)			
Asbestos			
Additional determinands			
Vanadium			
VOC			
SVOC			

[1] ~~Either Investigation Supervisor to specify the test method (except testing under MCERTs), limit of detection and accreditation required or~~ Contractor to detail what can be offered under each of these categories. ~~See also Specification Note for Guidance 15.3.~~

SCHEDULE 1.20.3

CHEMICAL LABORATORY TESTING FOR CONTAMINATION

Nominated Test Laboratory ? Contractor to specify proposed laboratory

Required Testing Turnaround Times ? 10 days

NB

1. This proforma Schedule MUST be reviewed in the light of site-specific desk study results and amended accordingly to include any additional determinands likely to be required.

2. Limits of detection should reflect the guideline/threshold values against which the test results will be compared.

SUITE F – Water samples			
Determinand (Procurer to list required determinands)	**Limit of detection** ~~required~~/offered[1]	**Test method** ~~required~~/offered[1]	**Accreditation** ~~required~~/offered[1]
Arsenic			
Boron			
Cadmium			
Chromium (total)			
Copper			
Lead			
Mercury			
Nickel			
Zinc			
pH			
Sulphate (as SO$_4$)			
Total petroleum hydrocarbons			
Speciated polyaromatic hydrocarbons (USEPA 16)			
~~Phenol~~			
Cyanide (total)			
Additional determinands			
Vanadium			
VOC			
SVOC			

[1] ~~Either Investigation Supervisor to specify the test method, limit of detection and accreditation required or~~ Contractor to detail what can be offered under each of these categories. ~~See also Specification Note for Guidance 15.3.~~

SCHEDULE 1.20.3

CHEMICAL LABORATORY TESTING FOR CONTAMINATION

Nominated Test Laboratory ? Contractor to specify proposed laboratory

Required Testing Turnaround Times ? 10 days

NB

1. This proforma Schedule MUST **be reviewed in the light of site-specific desk study results and amended accordingly to include any additional determinands likely to be required.**

2. Limits of detection should reflect the guideline/threshold values against which the test results will be compared.

SUITE G – Ground gas samples			
Determinand **(Procurer to list required determinands)**	**Limit of detection** ~~required~~/offered[1]	**Test method** ~~required~~/offered[1]	**Accreditation** ~~required~~/offered[1]
Oxygen			
Nitrogen			
Carbon dioxide			
Carbon monoxide			
Hydrogen			
Hydrogen sulphide			
Methane			
~~Ethane~~	Not required	Not required	Not required
~~Propane~~	Not required	Not required	Not required
~~Butane~~	Not required	Not required	Not required
~~Iso-butane~~	Not required	Not required	Not required

[1] ~~Either Investigation Supervisor to specify the test method, limit of detection and accreditation required or~~ Contractor to detail what can be offered under each of these categories. ~~See also Specification Note for Guidance 15.3.~~

S1.20.4 Waste characterisation (Clause 15.4)

Not required.

S1.20.5 (Test Suites H–J are presented in the following pages) Waste Acceptance Criteria testing (Clause 15.5)

Not required; Test Suites H–J inclusive have been deleted.

S1.20.6 Laboratory testing on site (Clause 15.6)

Not required.

S1.20.7 Special laboratory testing (Clause 15.7)

Not required.

Further particular Contract restrictions/relaxations shall be entered below, using sequential numbers to those above

None.

S1.21 Reporting (Specification Section 16) Particular restrictions/relaxations

Contract specific restrictions/relaxations, if any, shall be inserted below.

S1.21.1 Form of exploratory hole logs (Clauses 16.1 and 16.2.1)

Contractor to submit a proforma or example record for approval by the Investigation Supervisor.

S1.21.2 Information on exploratory hole logs (Clause 16.2.2)

As specified.

S1.21.3 Variations to final digital data supply requirements (Clause 16.5.1)

Data to be in AGS format. Digital data to be in a single file.

Contractor to detail the highest AGS edition which can be offered.

No additional groups, fields or codes required.

S1.21.4 Preliminary digital data (Clause 16.5.3)

Final digital data only required.

S1.21.5 Type(s) of report required (Clause 16.6)

Full Ground Investigation Report.

S1.21.6 Electronic file requirements (Clause 16.6.3

Media to be DVD ROM, maximum file size to be 5 Mb and photographs to be in JPG format.

S1.21.7 Format and contents of Desk Study Report (Clauses 16.7)

Not required.

S1.21.8 Contents of Ground Investigation Report (or specified part thereof) (Clause 16.8)

As specified in Schedule S1.21.5 but data obtained during return visits to site shall be the subject of a supplementary report.

S1.21.9 Contents of Geotechnical Design Report (or specified part thereof) (Clause 16.9)

Not required.

S1.21.10 Times for supply of electronic information (Clause 16.10.1)

Complete set of digital data to be supplied with draft and approved final copies of the report.

S1.21.11 Electronic information transmission media (Clause 16.10.2)

DVD ROM.

S1.21.12 Report approval (Clause 16.11)

One hard and one electronic copy of the draft Ground Investigation Report required for submission 4 weeks after the completion of laboratory testing.

Investigation Supervisor's comments on the draft Ground Investigation Report and associated digital data to be issued within 2 weeks from receipt of the draft and one hard and one electronic copy of an approved final report to be submitted by the Contractor within a further 2 weeks.

The supplementary report containing post fieldwork monitoring data to be submitted as one hard and one electronic copy within 2 weeks of the final return visit to site.

Further particular Contract restrictions/relaxations shall be entered below, using sequential numbers to those above

None.

Schedule 2: Exploratory holes

Hole number	Type	Scheduled depth (m)	National grid reference		Approximate ground level (mOD)	Remarks Including in situ testing and installations
			Easting (m)	Northing (m)		
1	Percussion borehole	7				1. Exploratory holes generally spread across the site in a regular grid pattern, except where stated below.
2	Percussion borehole	7				
3	Percussion borehole	7	In an actual investigation individual Eastings, Northings and ground levels would be entered here for each hole			2. Three trial pits targeted close to the location of the former railway workers' huts to provide samples for contamination testing, particularly in respect of asbestos and chlorinated aliphatics (cleaning solvents).
4	Percussion borehole	8				
5	Percussion borehole	9				
6	Percussion borehole	9				
7	Percussion borehole	9				
						3. Percussion boreholes with piston tube samples at 1.0 m depth intervals in the Brickearth to provide samples for limited undrained strength and consolidation laboratory testing in connection with possible shallow foundations for ancillary structures. Also driven small disturbed samples, primarily for soil description.
4/104	Rotary cored extension to BH4	20				
5/105	Rotary cored extension to BH5	20	In an actual investigation individual Eastings, Northings and ground levels would be entered here for each hole			
6/106	Rotary cored extension to BH6	20				
7/107	Rotary cored extension to BH7	20				4. Percussion boreholes with SPTs at 1.0 m depth intervals in the gravel to determine its relative density.
201	Trial pit	2	In an actual investigation individual Eastings, Northings and ground levels would be entered here for each hole			5. Percussion boreholes (4–7) to be extended by rotary drilling to investigate the condition of sandstone bedrock for deep-piled foundations. Continuous coring with SPTs at nominally 3 m depth intervals.
202	Trial pit	2				
203	Trial pit	2				
204	Trial pit	2				
205	Trial pit	2				
206	Trial pit	3				6. Samples from trial pits to be used for contamination testing.
207	Trial pit	3				7. Combined groundwater/ ground gas monitoring standpipes to be installed in percussion boreholes 1–4 to enable checks for the presence of ground gas and groundwater sampling and level monitoring in the gravel stratum.
208	Trial pit	3				
209	Trial pit	3				
210	Trial pit	3				
211	Trial pit	4				
212	Trial pit	4				
213	Trial pit	4				8. Two standpipe piezometers to be installed in the sandstone to check on contamination in the major aquifer.
214	Trial pit	4				
215	Trial pit	4				

Schedule 3: Investigation Supervisor's facilities

S3.1 Accommodation

Not required.

S3.2 Furnishings

Not required.

S3.3 Services

Not required.

S3.4 Equipment

Not required.

S3.5 Transport

Not required.

S3.6 Personal Protective Equipment for Investigation Supervisor

Not required.

Schedule 4: Specification amendments

The following clauses are amended			
Section number	**Clause number**	**Delete the following**	**Substitute the following**
			No amendments

Schedule 5: Specification additions

The following clauses are added to the Specification		
Section number	**Clause number**	**Clause wording**
		No additions

Schedule 5: Specification additions

Annex 1 Bill of Quantities for Ground Investigation

Preamble amendments and additions
The following clauses are amended or added to the Preamble.

None.

Bill of Quantities
The following pages constitute the Bill of Quantities.

Bill of Quantities

Bill A   General items, provisional services and additional items

Number	Item description	Unit	Quantity	Rate	Amount £
A	**General items and provisional sums**				
A1	Offices and stores for the Contractor	sum			
A2	Establish on site all plant, equipment and services for a Green Category site	sum			
A3	Extra over Item A2 for a Yellow Category site	sum	Not required		
A4	Maintain on site all site safety equipment for a Yellow Category site	week	Not required		
A5	Decontamination of equipment during and at end of intrusive investigation for a Yellow Category site	sum			
A6	Appropriate storage, transport and off-site disposal of contaminated arisings and any PPE equipment, excluding laboratory testing	provisional sum			2500.00
A7	Provide professional attendance in accordance with Clause 3.5.2				
A7.1	Provide Technician	p.day			
A7.2	Provide graduate ground engineer	p.day	15		
A7.3	Provide experienced ground engineer	p.day	15		
A7.4	Provide Registered Ground Engineering Professional	p.day	7		
A7.5	Provide Registered Ground Engineering Specialist	p.day	2		
A7.6	Provide Registered Ground Engineering Advisor	p.day	1		
A8	Establish the location and elevation of the ground at each exploratory hole	sum			
A9	Preparation of Health and Safety documentation and Safety Risk Assessment.	sum			
A10	Facilities for the Investigation Supervisor	sum	Not required		
A11	Vehicle(s) for the Investigation Supervisor	v.wk	Not required		
A12	Fuel for vehicle for the Investigation Supervisor	provisional sum	Not required		
A13	Investigation Supervisor's telephone and facsimile charges	provisional sum	Not required		
A14	Deliver selected cores and samples to the specified address	provisional sum	Not required		
A15	Special testing and sampling required by Investigation Supervisor	provisional sum	Not required		
A16	Traffic safety and management	provisional sum	Not required		
A17	One master copy of the Desk Study Report	sum	Not required		
A18	Additional copies of the Desk Study Report	nr	Not required		
A19	One master copy of the Ground Investigation Report (or specified part thereof)	sum			

Number	Item description	Unit	Quantity	Rate	Amount £
A20	Additional copies of the Ground Investigation Report (or specified part thereof)	nr	1		
A21	Electronic copy of Ground Investigation Report (or specified part thereof)	sum	1		
A22	One master copy of the Geotechnical Design Report (or specified part thereof)	sum	Not required		
A23	Additional copies of the Geotechnical Design Report (or specified part thereof)	nr	Not required		
A24	Electronic copy of Geotechnical Design Report (or specified part thereof)	sum	Not required		
A25	Digital data in AGS transfer format	sum			
A26	Hard copy photographs	nr	50		
A27	Photographic volume	nr	1		
A28	Long-term storage of geotechnical samples (Annex B)	provisional sum	Not required		
A29	Long-term storage of geoenvironmental samples (Annex B)	provisional sum	Not required		
	Contract specific additional bill items None				

Total section A carried to summary _____

Bill of Quantities

Bill B   Percussion boring

Number	Item description	Unit	Quantity	Rate	Amount £
B	**Percussion boring**				
B1	Move boring plant and equipment to the site of each exploratory hole and set up	nr	7		
B2	Extra over Item BI for setting up on a slope of gradient greater than 20%	nr	Not required		
B3	Break out surface obstruction where present at exploratory borehole	h	Not required		
B4	Advance borehole between existing ground level and 10 m depth	m	56		
B5	As Item B4 but between 10 and 20 m depth	m	Not required		
B6	As Item B4 but between 20 and 30 m depth	m	Not required		
B7	As Item B4 but between 30 and 40 m depth	m	Not required		
B8	As Item B4 but between 40 and 50 m depth	m	Not required		
B9	Advance borehole through hard stratum or obstruction	h	7		
B10	Provide aquifer protection measures at a single aquiclude/aquifer boundary or cross-contamination control measures at a single soil boundary in a borehole	nr	4		
B11	Backfill borehole with cement/bentonite grout or bentonite pellets	m	Not required		
B12	Standing time for borehole plant, equipment and crew	h	5		
	Dynamic sampling		Not required		
	Contract specific additional bill items				
	None				

Total section B carried to summary _____

Bill of Quantities

Bill C   Rotary drilling

Number	Item description	Unit	Quantity	Rate	Amount £
C	**Rotary drilling**				
	Hand augering		Not required		
	Continuous flight and hollow-stem flight augering		Not required		
	Rotary drilling with and without core recovery				
C15	Move rotary drilling plant and equipment to the site of each exploratory drillhole and set up	nr	4		
C16	Extra over Item C15 for setting up on a slope of gradient greater than 20%	nr	Not required		
C17	Extra over Item C15 for setting up drilling plant for inclined drillhole	nr	Not required		
C18	Break out surface obstructions where present at exploratory drillhole	h	Not required		
C19	Standing time for rotary drilling plant, equipment and crew	h	3		
C20	Provide aquifer protection measures at a single aquiclude/aquifer boundary in a drillhole	nr	Not required		
	Drilling without cores		Not required		
	Drilling to obtain cores				
C34	Rotary drill in materials other than hard strata to obtain cores of the specified diameter between existing ground level and 10 m depth	m	Not required		
C35	As Item C34 but between 10 and 20 m depth	m	Not required		
C36	As Item C34 but between 20 and 30 m depth	m	Not required		
C37	As Item C34 but between 30 and 40 m depth	m	Not required		
C38	As Item C34 but between 40 and 50 m depth	m	Not required		
C39	Extra over Items C34–C38 for use of semi-rigid core liner	m	Not required		
C40	Extra over Items C34–C38 for coring inclined rotary drillhole	m	Not required		
C41	Rotary drill in hard strata to obtain cores of the specified diameter between existing ground level and 10 m depth	m	5		
C42	As Item C41 but between 10 and 20 m depth	m	40		
C43	As Item C41 but between 20 and 30 m depth	m	Not required		
C44	As Item C41 but between 30 and 40 m depth	m	Not required		
C45	As Item C41 but between 40 and 50 m depth	m	Not required		
C46	Extra over items C41–C45 for use of semi-rigid liner	m	Not required		

Number	Item description	Unit	Quantity	Rate	Amount £
C47	Extra over items C41–C45 for coring inclined rotary drillhole	m	Not required		
C48	Backfill rotary drillhole with cement/bentonite grout or bentonite pellets	m	20		
C49	Core box to be retained by client	nr	Not required		
	Rotary percussive drilling		Not required		
	Resonance (sonic) drilling		Not required		
	Sonic drilling without cores		Not required		
	Sonic drilling to obtain cores		Not required		
	Contract specific additional bill items				
	None				

Total section C carried to summary _____

Bill of Quantities

Bill D   Pitting and trenching

Number	Item description	Unit	Quantity	Rate	Amount £
D	**Pitting and trenching**				
	Inspection pits				
D1	Excavate inspection pit by hand to 1.2 m depth	nr	7		
D2	Extra over Item D1 for breaking out surface obstructions	h	Not required		
	Trial pits and trenches				
D3	Move equipment to the site of each trial pit or trench of not greater than 4.5 m depth	nr	15		
D4	Extra over Item D3 for setting up on a slope of gradient greater than 20%	nr	Not required		
D5	Extra over Item D3 for trial pit or trench between 4.5 and 6 m depth	nr	Not required		
D6	Excavate trial pit between existing ground level and 3.0 m depth	m	40		
D7	As Item D6 but between 3.0 and 4.5 m depth	m	5		
D8	As Item D6 but between 4.5 and 6 m depth	m	Not required		
D9	Excavate trial trench between existing ground level and 3.0m depth	m^3	Not required		
D10	As Item D9 between 3.0 and 4.5 in depth	m^3	Not required		
D11	As Item D9 between 4.5 and 6 m depth	m^3	Not required		
D12	Extra over Items D6–D11 inclusive for breaking out hard material or surface obstructions	h	Not required		
D13	Standing time for excavation plant, equipment and crew for machine dug trial pit or trench	h	3		
	Observation pits and trenches		Not required		
	Daily provision of pitting crew and equipment		Not required		
	General				
D37	Bring pump to the position of each exploratory pit or trench	nr	7		
D38	Pump water from pit or trench	h	4		
D39	Extra over Item D38 for temporary storage, treatment and disposal of contaminated water	Provisional sum			750.00
D40	Leave open observation pit or trench	m^2/day	Not required		
D41	Leave open trial pit or trench	m^2/day	Not required		
	Contract specific additional bill items				
	None				

Total section D carried to summary _____

Bill of Quantities

Bill E   Sampling and monitoring during intrusive investigation

Number	Item description	Unit	Quantity	Rate	Amount £
E	**Sampling and monitoring during intrusive investigation**				
	Samples for geotechnical purposes				
E1	Small disturbed sample	nr	55		
E2	Bulk disturbed sample	nr	12		
E3	Large bulk disturbed sample	nr	Not required		
E4.1	Open-tube sample using thick-walled (OS-TK/W) sampler	nr	Not required		
E4.2	Open-tube sample using thin-walled UT100 (OS-T/W) sampler	nr	10		
E5	Piston sample	nr	8		
E6	Groundwater sample	nr	7		
E7	Ground gas sample	nr	Not required		
E8	Cut, prepare and protect core sub-sample	nr	12		
	Continuous or semi-continuous sampling		Not required		
	Containers for contamination assessment				
E14.1	Provision of containers and collection of samples for contamination Suite E (S1.20.3)	nr	25		
E14.2	Provision of containers and collection of samples for contamination Suite F (S1.20.3)	nr	10		
E14.3	Provision of containers and collection of samples for contamination Suite G (S1.20.3)	nr	3		
E15.1	Provision of containers and collection of samples for WAC Suite H (S1.20.5)	nr	Not required		
E15.2	Provision of containers and collection of samples for WAC Suite I (S1.20.5)	nr	Not required		
E15.3	Provision of containers and collection of samples for WAC Suite J (S1.20.5)	nr	Not required		
	Contract specific additional bill items				
	None				

Total section E carried to summary _____

Bill of Quantities

Bill F   Probing and cone penetration testing

Number	Item description	Unit	Quantity	Rate	Amount £
F	Probing and cone penetration testing		Not required		

Bill of Quantities

Bill G   Geophysical testing

Number	Item description	Unit	Quantity	Rate	Amount £
G	Geophysical testing		Not required		

Bill of Quantities

Bill H   In situ testing

Number	Item description	Unit	Quantity	Rate	Amount £
H	**In situ testing**				
H1	Standard penetration test in borehole	nr	20		
H2	Standard penetration test in rotary drillhole	nr	10		
H3	In situ density testing				
H3.1	Small pouring cylinder method	nr	Not required		
H3.2	Large pouring cylinder method	nr	Not required		
H3.3	Water replacement method	nr	Not required		
H3.4	Core cutter method	nr	Not required		
H3.5	Nuclear method	day	Not required		
H4	California Bearing Ratio test	nr	Not required		
H5	Vane shear strength test in borehole	nr	Not required		
H6	Penetration vane test, penetration from ground level	nr	Not required		
H7	Hand penetrometer test (set of 3 readings)	nr	Not required		
H8	Hand vane test (set of 3 readings)	nr	Not required		
	Other tests		Not required		
	Permeability testing		Not required		
	Self-boring pressuremeter		Not required		
	High-pressure dilatometer		Not required		
	Driven or push-in pressuremeter		Not required		
	Menard pressuremeter		Not required		
	Soil infiltration test		Not required		

Number	Item description	Unit	Quantity	Rate	Amount £
	Miscellaneous site testing				
H84	Reading of free product level in borehole using an interface probe	nr	10		
H85	Provide contamination screening test kits per sample	nr	10		
H86	Carry out headspace testing by FID/PID	nr	4		
	Contract specific additional bill items				
	None				

Total section H carried to summary _____

Bill of Quantities

Bill I   Instrumentation

Number	Item description	Unit	Quantity	Rate	Amount £
I	**Instrumentation**				
	Standpipes and piezometers				
I1	Backfill exploratory hole with cement/bentonite grout below standpipe or standpipe piezometer	m	12		
I2	Provide and install standpipe (19 mm)	m	Not required		
I3	Provide and install standpipe piezometer (19 mm)	m	Not required		
I4	Provide and install standpipe piezometer (50 mm)	m	40		
I5	Provide and install standpipe piezometer (75 mm)	m	Not required		
I6	Provide and install ground gas monitoring standpipe (19 mm)	m	Not required		
I7	Provide and install ground gas monitoring standpipe (50 mm)	m	29		
I8	Provide and install ground gas monitoring standpipe (75 mm)	m	Not required		
I9	Provide and install headworks for ground gas monitoring standpipe, standpipe or standpipe piezometer	nr	6		
I10	Provide and install protective cover (flush)	nr	6		
I11	Provide and install protective cover (raised)	nr	Not required		
I12	Extra over item I10 for heavy duty cover in highways	nr	Not required		
I13	Supply and erect protective fencing around standpipe or piezometer installation	nr	Not required		
I14	Supply and erect 1.5 m high marker post	nr	Not required		

Number	Item description	Unit	Quantity	Rate	Amount £
I15	Standpipe and piezometer development				
I15.1	Supply equipment and personnel to carry out development by surging	nr	Not required		
I15.2	Develop standpipe or piezometer by surging	h	Not required		
I15.3	As Item I15.1 but by airlift pumping	nr	6		
I15.4	As Item I15.2 but by airlift pumping	h	12		
I15.5	As Item I15.1 but by over pumping	nr	Not required		
I15.6	As Item I15.2 but by over pumping	h	Not required		
I15.7	As Item I5.1 but by jetting	nr	Not required		
I15.8	As Item I15.2 but by jetting	h	Not required		
I15.9	Disposal of development water, not including chemical testing Provisional sum			475.00	
	Inclinometer		Not required		
	Slip indicators		Not required		
	Contract specific additional bill items None				

Total section I carried to summary _____

Bill of Quantities

Bill J   Installation monitoring and sampling

Number	Item description	Unit	Quantity	Rate	Amount £
J	**Installation monitoring and sampling** (during fieldwork period)				
J1	Reading of water level in standpipe or standpipe piezometer during fieldwork period	nr	12		
J2	Ground gas measurement in gas monitoring standpipe during fieldwork period	nr	8		
J3	Set of inclinometer readings (as defined in Specification Clause 11.6.6 or Schedule S1.16.7) per installation during fieldwork period and report results	nr	Not required		
J4	Check for ground slippage in slip indicator installation during fieldwork period	nr	Not required		
J5	Water sample from standpipe or standpipe piezometer during fieldwork period, including purging or micro-purging up to 3.0 hours	nr	6		
J6	Extra over Item J5 for purging or micro-purging in excess of 3.0 hours	h	3		
J7	Ground gas sample from gas monitoring standpipe during fieldwork period	nr	4		
J8	Reading of free product level in standpipe using an interface probe during fieldwork period	nr	4		
	Installation monitoring and sampling (post fieldwork period)				
J9	Return visit to site following completion of fieldwork to take readings in, or recover samples from, installations	nr	6		
J10	Extra over item J9 for reading of water level in standpipe or standpipe piezometer during return visit	nr	30		
J11	Extra over item J9 for ground gas measurement in ground gas monitoring standpipe during return visit	nr	30		
J12	Extra over item J9 for set of inclinometer readings (as defined in Specification Clause 11.6.6 or Schedule S1.16.7) per installation during return visit and report results	nr	Not required		
J13	Extra over item J9 to check for ground slippage in slip indicator installation during return visit to site	nr	Not required		
J14	Extra over item J9 for water sample from standpipe or standpipe piezometer during return visit to site, including purging or micro-purging up to 3.0 hours	nr	8		
J15	Extra over Item J14 for purging or micro-purging in excess of 3.0 hours	h	2		
J16	Extra over item J9 for ground gas sample from gas monitoring standpipe during return visit to site	nr	4		
J17	Extra over item J9 for reading of free product level in standpipe using an interface probe during return visit to site	nr	Not required		
	Surface water body sampling and testing		Not required		
	Contract specific additional bill items None				

Total section J carried to summary _____

Bill of Quantities

Bill K   Geotechnical laboratory testing

Number	Item description	Unit	Quantity	Rate	Amount £
K	**Geotechnical laboratory testing**				
K1	Classification				
K1.1	Moisture content	nr	20		
K1.2	Liquid limit, plastic limit and plasticity index	nr	30		
K1.3	Volumetric shrinkage	nr	Not required		
K1.4	Linear shrinkage	nr	Not required		
K1.5	Density by linear measurement	nr	Not required		
K1.6	Density by immersion in water or water displacement	nr	Not required		
K1.7	Dry density and saturation moisture content for chalk	nr	Not required		
K1.8	Particle density by gas jar or pyknometer	nr	Not required		
K1.9	Particle size distribution by wet sieving	nr	3		
K1.10	Particle size distribution by dry sieving	nr	Not required		
K1.11	Sedimentation by pipette	nr	Not required		
K1.12	Sedimentation by hydrometer	nr	1		
K2	Chemical and electrochemical		Not required		
K3	Compaction related		Not required		
K4	Compressibility, permeability, durability				
K4.1	One-dimensional consolidation properties, test period 5 days	nr	3		
K4.2	Extra over Item K4.1 for test period in excess of 5 days	day	9		
K4.3	Measurements of swelling pressure, test period 2 days	nr	Not required		
K4.4	Measurement of swelling, test period 2 days	nr	Not required		
K4.5	Measurement of settlement on saturation, test period 1 day	nr	Not required		
K4.6	Extra over Items K4.3 to K4.5 for test period in excess of 2 or 1 day(s)	day	Not required		
K4.7	Permeability by constant head method	nr	Not required		
K4.8	Dispersibility by pinhole method	nr	Not required		
K4.9	Dispersibility by crumb method	nr	Not required		
K4.10	Dispersibility by dispersion method	nr	Not required		
K4.11	Frost heave of soil	nr	Not required		

Number	Item description	Unit	Quantity	Rate	Amount £
K5	Consolidation and permeability in hydraulic cells		Not required		
K6	Shear strength (total stress)				
K6.1	Shear strength by the laboratory vane method (set of 3)	nr	Not required		
K6.2	Shear strength by hand vane (set of 3)	nr	Not required		
K6.3	Shear strength by hand penetrometer (set of 3)	nr	Not required		
K6.4	Shear strength of a set of three 60 mm × 60 mm square specimens by direct shear, test duration not exceeding 1 day per specimen	nr	Not required		
K6.5	Extra over Item K6.4 for test durations in excess of 1 day per specimen	sp.day	Not required		
K6.6	Shear strength of a single 300 mm × 300 mm square specimen by direct shear, test duration not exceeding 1 day	nr	Not required		
K6.7	Extra over Item K6.6 for test durations in excess of 1 day	day	Not required		
K6.8	Residual shear strength of a set of three 60 mm × 60 mm square specimens by direct shear, test duration not exceeding 4 days per specimen	nr	Not required		
K6.9	Extra over Item K6.8 for test durations in excess of 4 days per specimen	sp.day	Not required		
K6.10	Residual shear strength of a 300 mm square specimen by direct shear, test duration not exceeding 4 days	nr	Not required		
K6.11	Extra over Item K6.10 for test duration in excess day of 4 days	day	Not required		
K6.12	Residual shear strength using the small ring shear apparatus at three normal pressures, test duration not exceeding 4 days	nr	Not required		
K6.13	Extra over Item K6.12 for test duration in excess of 4 days	day	Not required		
K6.14	Unconfined compressive strength of 38 mm diameter specimen	nr	Not required		
K6.15	Undrained shear strength of a set of three 38 mm diameter specimens in triaxial compression without the measurement of pore pressure	nr	Not required		
K6.16	Undrained strength of a single 100 mm diameter specimen in triaxial compression without the measurement of pore pressure	nr	14		
K6.17	Undrained shear strength of single 100 mm diameter specimen in triaxial compression with multistage loading and without measurement of pore pressure	nr	Not required		
K7	Shear strength (effective stress)		Not required		
K8	Rock testing				
K8.1	Natural water content of rock sample	nr	6		
K8.2	Porosity/density using saturation and calliper techniques	nr	Not required		
K8.3	Porosity/density using saturation and buoyancy	nr	Not required		
K8.4	Slake durability index	nr	Not required		

Number	Item description	Unit	Quantity	Rate	Amount £
K8.5	Soundness by magnesium sulphate	nr	Not required		
K8.6	Magnesium sulphate test	nr	Not required		
K8.7	Shore scleroscope	nr	Not required		
K8.8	Schmidt rebound hardness	nr	Not required		
K8.9	Resistance to fragmentation	nr	Not required		
K8.10	Aggregate abrasion value	nr	Not required		
K8.11	Polished stone value	nr	Not required		
K8.12	Aggregate frost heave	nr	Not required		
K8.13	Resistance to freezing and thawing	nr	Not required		
K8.14	Uniaxial compressive strength	nr	6		
K8.15	Deformability in uniaxial compression	nr	Not required		
K8.16	Indirect tensile strength by Brazilian test	nr	6		
K8.17	Undrained triaxial compression without measurements of porewater pressure	nr	Not required		
K8.18	Undrained triaxial compression with measurement of porewater pressure	nr	Not required		
K8.19	Direct shear strength of a single specimen	nr	Not required		
K8.20	Swelling pressure test	nr	Not required		
K8.21	Measurement of point load strength index of rock specimen (set of ten individual determinations)	nr	Not required		
K8.22	Single measurement of point load strength on irregular rock lump or core sample (either axial or diametral test)	nr	20		
	Ground/groundwater aggressivity				
K9.1	Suite A (Greenfield site – pyrite absent Schedule 1.19.6)	nr	Not required		
K9.2	Suite B (Greenfield site – pyrite present Schedule 1.19.6)	nr	Not required		
K9.3	Suite C (Brownfield site – pyrite absent Schedule 1.19.6)	nr	5		
K9.4	Suite D (Brownfield site – pyrite present Schedule 1.19.6)	nr	5		
	Contract specific additional bill items None				

Total section K carried to summary _____

Bill of Quantities

Bill L   Geoenvironmental laboratory testing

Number	Item description	Unit	Quantity	Rate	Amount £
L	**Geoenvironmental laboratory testing**				
	Contamination testing				
L1.1	Suite E – Soil samples (Schedule S1.20.3)	nr	10		
L1.2	Suite F – Groundwater samples (Schedule S1.20.3)	nr	10		
L1.3	Suite G – Gas samples (Schedule S1.20.3)	nr	3		
	Waste acceptance criteria testing		Not required		
	Contract specific additional bill items				
	None				

Total section L carried to summary _____

Summary of Bill of Quantities

	£
A. General items, provisional services and additional items	
B. Percussion boring	
C. Rotary drilling	
D. Pitting and trenching	
E. Sampling during intrusive investigation	
F. Probing and cone penetration testing	Not required
G. Geophysical testing	Not required
H. In situ testing	
I. Instrumentation	
J. Installation monitoring and sampling	
K. Geotechnical laboratory testing	
L. Geoenvironmental laboratory testing	
Total tender	

Appendix A. Rates for Ground Practitioners and other Personnel

Rates shall be entered for the various grades of staff listed, who will be employed by agreement with the Investigation Supervisor to provide advice or assistance during the course of the investigation and/or the preparation of the Ground Investigation Report and/or the Geotechnical Design Report, all in accordance with Specification Clauses 3.6.1 and 3.6.2 and Schedule S1.8.3.

These services exclude the contract management, superintendence and technical direction required under the Conditions of Contract and the requirements of Specification Clause 3.5.1 which are to be included in the general rates and prices of the main Bill of Quantities (see Clause 1 of the Preamble to the Bill of Quantities).

Item	Item description	Unit	Rate
1	Technician	h	
2	Graduate ground engineer	h	
3	Experienced ground engineer	h	
4	Registered Ground Engineering Professional	h	
5	Registered Ground Engineering Specialist	h	
6	Registered Ground Engineering Advisor	h	
7	Expenses incurred by staff on site visits or who are resident by agreement with the Investigation Supervisor	day	
8	Fare per kilometre[1] from Contractor's premises and return for Items 1, 2 and 3	km[1]	
9	As above but for Items 4, 5 and 6	km[1]	
10	All other expenses incurred in conjunction with a site visit where a return journey is made on the same day for Items 1, 2 and 3	visit	
11	As above but for Items 4, 5 and 6	visit	
12	All other expenses incurred in connection with visit where an overnight stay is necessary for Items 1, 2 and 3	overnight	
13	As above but for Items 4, 5 and 6	overnight	

[1] Where considered more appropriate, 'mile' may be used.

Estimate of costs under Appendix A to the Bill of Quantities where the provision of the Contractor's staff for work in accordance with Specification Clauses 3.5.2, 3.6.1 and 3.6.2 cannot be adequately specified at tender. **(To be assessed by the Investigation Supervisor)**

£

Appendix B. Long-term sample storage

NOT REQUIRED

UK Specification for Ground Investigation
ISBN: 978-0-7277-3506-5

ICE Publishing: All rights reserved
doi: 10.1680/UKSGI.35065.307

Feedback

Feedback is important and it is recognised that the Specification and accompanying documentation will benefit from being updating in the future.

Users are invited to email recommendations for revision to the Site Investigation Steering Group: please email the following details to **sisg@icepublishing.com**

Name:

Organisation:

Address:

Email:

Date:

Recommendations for revision:

Title: UK Specification for Ground Investigation Second edition

Page No.:

Section:
(e.g. Specification, Schedules, Bills of Quantities, Notes for Guidance)

Clause/Schedule/Bill No.:

Description of problem:

Suggested amendment: